THE JOHN 1:1 FACTOR

AN IN-DEPTH STUDY INTO THE FIRST CHAPTER OF JOHN

MICHAEL W. NEUHAUS

CONTENTS

"The Hebrew language is the best language of all...

If I were younger I would want to learn this language, because no one can really understand the Scriptures without it. For although the New Testament is written in Greek, it is full of Hebraisms and Hebrew expressions. It has therefore been aptly said that the Hebrews drink from the spring, the Greeks from the stream that flows from it, and the Latins from a downstream pool."

Martin Luther

ACKNOWLEDGMENTS

I would like to thank my bride who has pushed me to continue this project. Giving her time to help edit and exhibiting patience in the whole process. Truth be told, she is the reason this project was completed as she has shown me countless times how to have commitment and the fortitude in so many things of life. She is a blessing in my life, and it is a privilege and an honor to be a part of hers. The sacrifice she has made in all of this time such as research, editing, and just being there to listen to my ideas. She is my confidant and my sustainer; praise Yahweh that I can be the man I am for her.

I would also like to thank my brother Danny Reid. His countless hours of editing, reviewing, and sharing of ideas has made this journey a grand one. From kicking the ball back and forth on simple foundational faith items to complex theological statements, Pastor Danny has been integral to this work. A man of character and of sound biblical principles, he has been an asset as a brother, friend, and mentor.

I would also like to thank Jeff Benner. As I do not know him personally, he has become a mentor for me. Mr. Benner has spent a vast amount of time in Hebraic studies and the language thereof. His work in word studies, etymology, and cultural aspects of the Hebrew language is unequivocally ordained by Yahweh. I truly thank his family for their great sacrifice of time that they have made for the advancement of the Kingdom of Yahweh.

All of editors that have given their time to edit, review, and assist in articulation is amazing to me. The outpouring of love and devotion to this project is truly humbling. Thank you so much for all of your help.

Thanks to all of the Scholars of Biblical and Hebraic studies. If it were not for you, we would still be stuck in 17th century understandings of the Word. Your sacrifice of time and your dedication to the truth is unparalleled.

A special thanks to Rev. Ralph Crawford and his wife Tammie for their encouragement and belief in me to see this project to its finality. Your friendship through these years has proved invaluable. Through editing, reviews, and encouragement the devotion to this project will always be in my heart.

THESIS

The topic of this book will argue and define who is the author of the book of John, who is the Logos, who is the Holy Spirit, and was Jesus (Yahshua) truly pre-existent. Taking on the pagan teachings individually that infiltrated the church within the backdrop of John 1:1, utilizing primarily Scripture, as well as secular and non-secular cultural references, histories of religions, and belief systems.

The topic of this book outlined below will bear seven points within the belief system of Christianity.

The sole purpose of this book is to:

- Show that Apostle John did write the gospel of John.
- Explain how the first chapter of John is not stating that the Logos is Jesus (Yahshua).

- Show that Jesus (Yahshua) must fulfill all things to be the Messiah.
- Prove that the Holy Spirit is not its own entity but that it is Yahweh's Spirit and is Holy.
- Disprove that Yahweh and Yahshua are the same person, entity, or divinity.
- Show that Jesus (Yahshua) was not pre-existent.
- Reveal the pagan nature of the trinity and expose the ideology as a heretical teaching.

———

For my Jewish brothers and sisters who have selected this book to read, please understand that I do not subscribe to Hellenistic Judaism that teaches we cannot say the Name of G-d. I love the name and do not view this as a sacrilege but as an honor to know if these days the One Elohim's name and can have that kind of relationship with Him. Please do not be offended as to be offended is a self -inflicted wound.

To my Christian brother and sisters, I am a Peter not a John when it comes to personality type. Please read and study all the way through!

PREFACE

At six years of age, while learning to read in first grade, I gravitated toward the family bible that was isolated yet on public display in the parlor of my grandmother's home. This family bible became my escape from physical, verbal, and sexual abuse. The awe-inspiring stories, flavored with the King James tongue, tantalized my imagination. The idea that there was a just God who used signs and wonders fascinated me. This form of escape became the construct for my self-defense mechanism, thereby satiating the pain.

When I read those fanciful stories of old, they became so magical, so captivating. Walking with Adam and Eve, watching Cain lash out, witnessing Noah's ark become something from nothing, and listening to Noah cry out about the torrent to come. Standing with Abram in the opening of his tent, witnessing his level of excitement when the three angels came down the road. Eavesdropping on the bartering between Abram and Yahweh. Marveling about the asteroid that the planet Jupiter missed catching so that Yahweh could, in his infinite power with complete precision, destroy cities on a plain. I devoured the book over and over, seeing new things every time I read, each chapter providing new information to my young mind.

A couple of years later, I was thrust into in the public-school arena. I use "arena" intentionally, as that's what it felt like going from religious to secular in the blink of an eye. This is when my questioning began as my eyes were opened to the things I observed in the public place. Though I did not question who God was or my faith. Oh no, I went through hell in school, and He guided me completely. He was there with me the whole way. When I arrived in high school. Now there was the second hell: living amongst the attractive degradation of a junior and high public school system. This system, in the seventies and eighties, along with the absence of parental guidance, made the hedonistic pleasures being observed attractive.

The questioning I experienced resulted from the somewhat conflicting display of words on a page. Why did the narrative, in my mind as I understood it, show this Old Testament God as loving and friendly, yet all the sermons were about strictness, sinless, and perfect living? Well, I really didn't think Abram led a perfect life according to the story. So, Gen 26:5 perplexed me, and then King David with all his debauchery was the "man after Yahweh's own heart"? What? The scriptures are not coming out correctly or I am indeed daft!

Life after school became a heavy workload. In and out of marriage throughout my twenties, suddenly, I was nearly thirty years of age. During the tumult of my twenties, I had become interested in Hebrew and learned the consonants and some of the niqqud vowel system. Although, I always had this nagging tug and really loved the language, my second passion was rock 'n roll. All that teenage angst built up and bubbled out until I followed my dream and started a rock band. This caused me to learn more about words. I disliked English and grammar throughout my schooling. I understood nouns, verbs, and prepositions. All that other junk was for the nerds and doctorate degrees out there. I just wanted to sing and create clever lyrics.

Then Yahweh showed up eight years later in a very big way. My world around me shattered, and I lost everything. The man I swore I would not become, I became.

By this point in my life, I had researched many of the denominations, many of the cults within Christianity, and many of the major religions around the world. I had been a Lutheran, Baptist, Pentecostal, non-denominational evangelical. One evening, my close friend and former bandmate came to my house. Now, at this point in our friendship we were not on the best of terms. He had left the band as the bass player, leaving me in a lurch. I say lurch considering we spent the last six years trying to get the band off the ground towards notoriety. I had stayed on the road with his replacement for two more years and finally had enough. I had dismantled the band by now and came home. This old bandmate wanted to see me and had a "word" for me. "Get over here, prophet," I told him. "Share this newfound wisdom you've received."

Upon his arrival he began to share with me awe-so

familiar story. How he knew this particular story he was sharing with me that had happened almost a decade earlier in my life was rather odd. Where did he receive this secret information that I had told no one about? How had the words my friend chose to use come from this wanna be rock-star that tried to take over the world with me? Mind you, this individual previously confessed that he had no belief system whatsoever! No one knew this story beyond one individual who was in Syria at the time, and these two had never met. The message my friend gave me was as though it leapt off a King James Bible page, and I realized how the words could be understood just a little differently. Incredibly, I also perceived my friend's face change, as though there was a superimposed face over his yet transparent, as we conversed during his visit. This man's face morphed as he was speaking to me! Yes, I know this sounds completely off the wall, however, this is when I understood that Yahweh had just spoken to me and revealed that it was Him in two ways. Inside of ten minutes, my life had changed.

This experience inspired me to really look at words and how they are used. How those words can be translated from another language. How the author's intent can be lost going from one culture to another. Or how these words can be manipulated within translation to shore up a denominational powerbase or monetary belief system. Keep in mind, this started out very slowly and took time to generate enough steam to get motivated. As I said before, grammar was not my forte, nor was language or understanding the differences between cultures.

Time passed, and I became, through a series of interesting events, involved in a Hebraic Roots assembly and began to really explore Torah. Wow, now we were talking my language! The deeper I went, the more I discovered how important it was to understand not only the language but the culture as well. As I mentioned previously, in my twenties, I dabbled in some Hebrew, but now this was a buffet table spread before me, stimulating my mind to do something creative, and ironically, this involved my worst subject – English grammar! Hebrew became the dessert section of the buffet I craved. Lo and behold, here I found within the Hebraic Roots movement a whole slew of different interpretations and belief systems. This led me to an interesting conclusion. As I mentioned earlier, I thought I had come to know all of the Christian denominations. I had no idea that there were literally four sects of Christianity, such as Roman Catholic, Orthodox Catholic Church, Protestantism and Hebraic Roots—with a whole lot of denominations within those. I just wanted truth. Not the truth according to Michael! The *actual* truth. Certainly, there is a common thread amongst all four sects in doctrinal beliefs. Believe it or not, when you take a step back and look at this from a seventy-five-thousand-foot view, these similarities will quickly manifest. Suddenly, I recalled what I discovered that night when I received the message from my friend:

How are words being used? How are those words being translated from one language to another language? What is the author's intent? What is the culture of the author? Can these words be manipulated by power, lucre, or a belief system?

How someone reads and understands the text is based on:

The individual's family traditions. The individual's authority in their life. The individual's environment before coming to a knowledge of the Messiah (construct).

I realized these items inform how people form their belief systems and their actions. Because you can only do what you know, and you cannot do what you do not know! How we interpret information in a few seconds and then comprehend that information over the long term is vital to understand how to explain what is being communicated. Words can often be taken in two different ways. After all, that is why we are told, on so many times, to choose our words carefully. Yet, when we do not understand culture, intent, or context, we can derive just about anything out of those words. Couple these realities with an internal political or doctrinal stance, and you can change a civilization. For example, look at the Vatican and the monarchies of Europe. Check out Russia and the Bolsheviks, what Hitler did to Germany, the publication of Strong's Concordance and its effect on Protestantism, or the modern day American evangelical system of salvation.

Because of these, we now have a whole new set of ideologies, or in this case theologies, such as Dispensationalism, Replacement Theology, name it-claim it doctrine, State of Israel, Trinitarianism, Law Abolished, Torah is Law, and on it goes. When this happens, and we do not take the time to really understand what an actual word means and what it impacts, then we allow the bar to be moved. This in turn causes us, as doers of the Word, to abandon our Messiah's instructions and make us culpable to the watering down of Christianity. Polytheism in any form is extremely dangerous and allows, when we express that theology, for the secular world to change our country, diminish our culture, and makes us no different than any other false religion man has ever made up.

My research techniques have developed over the years. My starting point is the plain English text and the initial face value of what that scripture text means to me and our simple application in everyday life. To verify, I utilize Strong's Concordance to find the corresponding Hebrew and Greek meaning of those words. In time, this process led to understanding root words, and the role they play in understanding words and their strict definitions or implied connotations. That is when I learned to look at only the meaning, not the exegesis or eisegesis that Strong's team put into the definition of the word listing entry with the usage of said word in the King James text.

This was crucial because doctrine is not in the Bible. The word of God is in the Bible and man extrapolates doctrine to define denominationally and who or what they perceive to worship. At this point, I take the English understanding of any word in question and compare that word with the original Hebrew word and then compare the results with the different English translations of the original Hebrew or Greek respectively, in the Old and New Testaments. For Hebrew, when I want to confirm the exact structure of the word being used for translation into English, I use the Leningrad Codex, Aleppo, and Masoretic texts. For Greek, I use the Septuagint, Codex Sinaiticus, and Codex Vaticunus. For the Hebrew, Dead Sea scrolls can be checked when applicable. Verifying all usages of the word in question within the selected version is necessary, and utilizing a concordance is also pivotal. The next step is searching for the word or topic in Biblical and secular encyclopedias, as well as dictionaries, to grab a better understanding of what the word means culturally. The last step is to study the Paleo Hebrew and examine how that word correlates as Hebrew.

Hebrew is a concrete, literal language, not abstract, so verify that with the actual letters themselves. Input this all into the text and see how it fits. This will not often dramatically change the meaning of the text, and that is not the purpose of studying. We are not attempting to find fault with scripture or translators, but to find a concrete meaning of the text in an abstract translation.

Is the Word of Yahweh errant? Absolutely not! I do not believe for one second that the Word of Yahweh is errant! Man's translation of text is based on one's own theologies that can alter the meaning of the resulting translation text, causing confusion. This confusion can allow the text to appear to have two different meanings, wreaking havoc on the author's true intent.

The intention of this book is to reveal and discuss the word etymology of pre-incarnate, preexistent, and duality based on John 1:1.

This is one heresy root that infiltrated Christian thought, worship, and doctrine with devastating effects for many centuries.

For the topics mentioned above, subsequent books will follow.

For now, however, we will start focusing on pre-incarnate, pre-existence, and the duality concept.

Let's begin.

JOHN 1:1-18 KJV

1 In the beginning was the Word, and the Word was with God, and the Word was God.

2 The same was in the beginning with God.

3 All things were made by him; and without him was not anything made that was made.

4 In him was life; and the life was the light of men.

5 And the light shineth in darkness; and the darkness comprehended it not.

6 There was a man sent from God, whose name was John.

7 The same came for a witness, to bear witness of the Light, that all men through him might believe.

8 He was not that Light, but was sent to bear witness of that Light.

9 That was the true Light, which lighteth every man that cometh into the world.

10 He was in the world, and the world was made by him, and the world knew him not.

11 He came unto his own, and his own received him not.

12 But as many as received him, to them gave he power to become the sons of God, even to them that believe on his name.

13 Which were born, not of blood, nor of the will of the flesh, nor of the will of man, but of God.

14 And the Word was made flesh, and dwelt among us, (and we beheld his glory, the glory as of the only begotten of the Father,) full of grace and truth.

15 John bare witness of him, and cried, saying, this was he of whom I spake, He that cometh after me is preferred before me: for he was before me.

16 And of his fulness have all we received, and grace for grace.

17 For the law was given by Moses, but grace and truth came by Jesus Christ.

18 No man hath seen God at any time; the only begotten Son, which is in the bosom of the Father, he hath declared him.

JOHN 1:1-18 INTERLINEAR

IN ORIGINal (beginning) WAS THE SAYING (logos) AND THE SAYING (logos) WAS TOWARD THE God AND God WAS THE SAYING (logos)

THIS WAS IN ORIGINal (beginning) TOWARD THE God.

ALL (all things) THRU (through) SAME (him) BECAME (came-to-be) AND apart-from SAME (him) BECAME (came-to-be) NOT-YET (not-yet even) ONE (one-thing) WHICH HAS-BECOME (has-come-to-be).

IN SAME (him) LIFE WAS AND THE LIFE WAS THE LIGHT OF-THE humans.

AND THE LIGHT IN THE DARKness IS-APPEARING AND THE DARKness it NOT DOWN-GOT (grasped)

BECAME (there-came-to-be) human HAVING (been-commissionED) BESIDE God NAME to-him JOHN.

this-one CAME INTO witness (testimony) THAT he-SHOULD-BE-witnessING (he-should-be-testifying) ABOUT concerning THE LIGHT THAT ALL SHOULD-BE-BELIEVING THRU (through) SAME (him).

NOT WAS that-one THE LIGHT but but-he-came THAT he-SHOULD-BE-witnessING (he-should-be-testifying) ABOUT (concerning) THE LIGHT.

it-WAS THE LIGHT THE TRUE WHICH IS-LIGHTenING (is-enlightening) EVERY human COMING INTO THE SYSTEM (world).

IN THE SYSTEM (world) He-WAS AND THE SYSTEM (world) THRU (through) SAME (him) BECAME (came-to-be) AND THE SYSTEM (world) Him NOT KNEW.

INTO THE OWN (own-things) He-CAME AND THE OWN-ones Him NOT BESIDE-GOT (accepted).

as-many-as whoever YET GOT (obtained) Him He-GIVES to-them authority (right) offsprings (children) OF-God TO-BE-BECOMING to-THE BELIEVING ones-believing INTO THE NAME OF-Him.

WHO NOT OUT OF-BLOODS NOT-YET (neither) OUT OF-WILL OF-FLESH NOT-YET (neither) OUT

OF-WILL OF-MAN OUT OF-God WERE-generatED (were-begotten).

AND THE saying (word) FLESH BECAME AND BOOTHS IN (among) US AND WE-gaze THE esteem glory OF-Him esteem glory AS OF-ONLY-generated BESIDE FATHER FULL OF AND TRUTH.

JOHN IS-witnessING (is-testifying) ABOUT (concerning) him AND he-HAS-CRIED sayING this-One WAS WHOM I-said THE-One BEHIND (after) ME COMING IN-TOWARD-PLACE (in-front-of) OF-ME HAS-BECOME (has-come-to-be) BEFORE- OF-ME He-WAS.

AND OUT OF-THE FILLing OF-Him WE ALL GOT (obtained) AND (also) grace INSTEAD OF-grace (for grace).

that THE LAW THRU (through) MOSES WAS-GIVEN THE grace AND THE TRUTH THRU (through) JESUS ANOINTED Christ BECAME.

God NOT-YET-ONE HAS-SEEN THE ONLY-generated (only-begotten) SON THE One-BEING INTO THE BOSOM OF-THE FATHER that-One unfolds (unfolds-him).

CHAPTER 1
PICTURES, LETTERS, AND WORDS
THE JOHN 1:1 FACTOR

As a quick overview, a timeline if you will, the amount of new information being released through archeology concerning the first writings of humans is amazing. The timeline is changing, and with the use of carbon dating, dates are aligning interestingly. With each new discovery, it appears humans began with ideas expressed in the spoken word much earlier than previously believed. While there wasn't much communication with words, pictures were more often drawn. In concrete thought, this makes complete sense when you observed ideas conveyed pictographically.

Many archeologists and linguists agree cuneiform came into use around 4000 - 3000 B.C.E.[1]

However, in Middle Egypt, actual proof of writing with an alphabet has been discovered, circa 1850 B.C.E.[2]

Now, for the first five books of the Bible to have been written by Moses, two things are necessary. The first item needed is an alphabet, due to the sophisticated nature of the biblical text. Secondly, the widely assumed 1050 B.C.E. date for the creation and use of the Hebrew alphabet could not line up. This would have had to occur several centuries earlier, and we now have that proof. (see Fig. 1 & Fig. 2)[3][4] The interesting part of this archeological find is the dating, as it places this fairly close to the time of the Hebrew slaves in Egypt.

In the graphic (Fig. 1) depicts Ancient Hebrew writings also recognized as Paleo Hebrew script or the Semitic alphabet (Table 1).[5] In light of these new findings, it appears this occurred around the time of Joseph between 1850 - 1760 B.C.E. If that is the case, given the new evidence, then we know that Abraham, Isaac, and Jacob were likely writing, communicating, and executing contracts with the written word in the land of Canaan between 2100 – 1850 B.C.E.

However, fascinatingly, the languages of the era were often pictographs or hieroglyphics. Even so, Hebrew Bedouins of that time inscribed the story of creation and their lineage upon their staffs and included their own seal at the end of the staff. In the next graphic (Fig. 2), notice the evolution of the Paleo Hebrew, how the Egyptian culture adopted some of these semitic languages in the region, and then the Hebrew block letter after Babylonian captivity.

Figure 1: A line drawing of some of the world's oldest alphabetic inscriptions from Wadi el-Hol in Egypt's Middle Kingdom (18th Dynasty) around the time of Joseph. - BRUCE ZUCKERMAN IN COLLABORATION WITH LYNN SWARTZ DODD, Pots and Alphabets: Refractions of Relections on Typological Method (MAARAV, A Journal for the Study of the Northwest Semitic Languages and Literature, Vol. 10, p.89) (from Wikimedia commons)

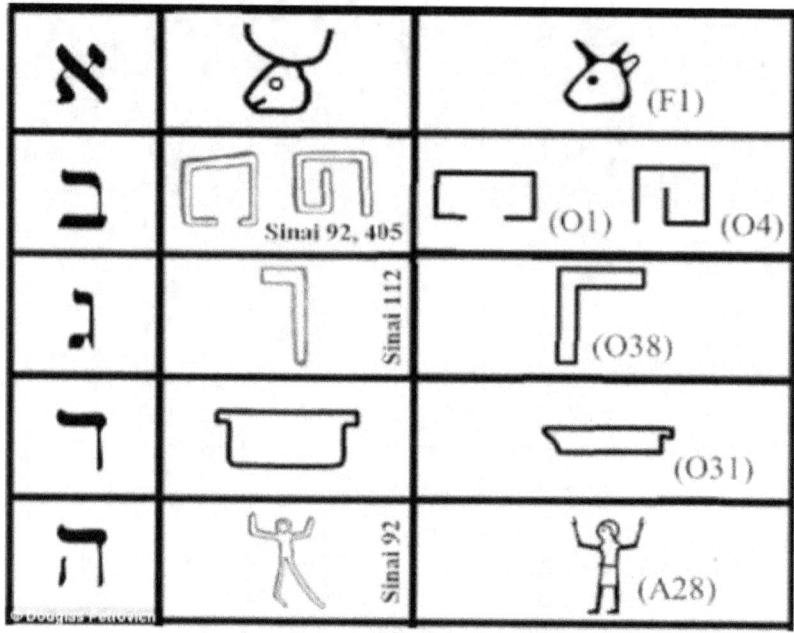

Figure 2: A comparison between the Hebrew block letters that came into use after the Babylonian Captivity (that commenced about 586 BC), the proposed original alphabet of "Proto-Hebrew" and the Egyptian Hieroglyphs that may have been the basis for many of the letters. (From Douglas Petrovich)

Hebrew Block-Letter (Original Letter)	Projected Proto-Hebrew (Original Letter)	Middle-Egyptian Hieroglyphic Exemplar (Sign-List Number)	Original Hebrew Alphabetic Name (NIVEC Number)	Hebrew Consonantals of Middle Kingdom (ca. 1842-1760 BC)	Hebrew Consonantals of New Kingdom (ca. 1560-1307 BC)	Hebrew Consonantals of Iron Age - Canaan (ca. 1150-587 BC)
א		(F1)	*elef*, cattle אלף (477)			
ב		(O1)/(O34)	*bayit*, house בית (1074)			
ג		(O28)	*gāmar*, bend גמר (1566)			
ד		(O31)	*delet*, door דלת (1946)			
ה		(A28)	*hālal*, praise הלל (2146)			
ו		(O30)	*wāw*, pillar-support (2260)			
ז		(D13)	*zǝʿīrāh*, sweat (brows) (2399)			
ח		(O6)/(O26)	*ḥāṣēr*, חצר (2958) *ḥūṭ*, חוט (2562)			
ט		(F35)	*ṭōv*, good טוב (3201)			
י		(D36)/(D47)	*yād*, hand יד (3338)			
כ		(D28)	*kap*, palm כף (4020)			
ל		(S39)	*lāmad*, teach למד (4340)(4913)			
מ		(N35)	*mayim*, water מים (4784)			
נ		(I9)/(I10)	*nāḥāš*, snake נחש (5729)			
ס		(I11)/(K5)	*śēʿār* (8482), שער *sūsāh*, סכה (6244)			
ע		(D4)	*ʿayin*, eye עין (6523)			
פ		(D21)	*peh*, mouth פה (7023)			
צ		(V33)	*ṣārōr*, sack צרור (7655)			
ק		(V25)	*qūr*, spun-fiber קור (7770)			
ר		(D1)	*roʾš*, head ראש (8031)			
ש		(D27)	*šādayim*, breasts שדים (8716)			
ת		(Z42)	*tǝwit*, male goat תיש (9411)			

Table 1: Pictographs and Hieroglyphics of Egyptian and Hebrew alphabets. Benner, Jeff A. Ancient Hebrew Research Center.

Ancient Semitic/Hebrew							Modern Hebrew			Greek		Latin
Early	Middle	Late	Name	Picture	Meaning	Sound	Letter	Name	Sound	Ancient	Modern	
			El	Ox head	Strong, Power, Leader	ah, eh	א	Aleph	[silent]	A	A	A
			Bet	Tent floorplan	Family, House, In	b, bh(v)	ב	Beyt	b, bh(v)	B	B	B
			Gam	Foot	Gather, Walk	g	ג	Gimal	g	Γ	Γ	C G
			Dal	Door	Move, Hang, Entrance	d	ד	Dalet	d	Δ	Δ	D
			Hey	Man with arms raised	Look, Reveal, Breath	h, ah	ה	Hey	h	E	E	E
			Waw	Tent peg	Add, Secure, Hook	w, o, u	ו	Vav	v	F		F
			Zan	Mattock	Food, Cut, Nourish	z	ז	Zayin	z	Z	Z	Z
			Hhet	Tent wall	Wall, Outside, Divide, Half	hh	ח	Chet	hh	H	H	H
			Tet	Basket	Surround, Contain, Mud	t	ט	Tet	t	Θ	Θ	
			Yad	Arm and closed hand	Hand, Work, Throw, Worship	y, ee	י	Yud	y	I	I	I J
			Kaph	Open palm	Bend, Open, Allow, Tame	k, kh	כ	Kaph	k, kh	K	K	K
			Lam	Shepherd Staff	Teach, Yoke, Authority, Bind	l	ל	Lamed	l	Λ	Λ	L
			Mem	Water	Water, Chaos, Mighty, Blood	m	מ	Mem	m	M	M	M
			Nun	Seed	Seed, Continue, Heir, Son	n	נ	Nun	n	N	N	N
			Sin	Thorn	Grab, Hate, Protect	s	ס	Samech	s	Ξ	Ξ	X
			An	Eye	See, Watch, Know, Shade	[silent]	ע	Ayin	[silent]	O	O	O
			Ghah	Rope	Twist, Dark, Wicked	gh						
			Pey	Mouth	Open, Blow, Scatter, Edge	p, ph(f)	פ	Fey	p, ph(f)	Π	Π	P
			Tsad	Trail	Trail, Journey, Chase, Hunt	ts	צ	Tsade	ts	Μ		
			Quph	Sun on the horizon	Condense, Circle, Time	q	ק	Quph	q	Ϙ		Q
			Resh	Head of a man	Head, First, Top, Beginning	r	ר	Resh	r	P	P	R
			Shin	Two front teeth	Sharp, Press, Eat, Two	sh	ש	Shin Sin	sh, s	Σ	Σ	S
			Taw	Crossed sticks	Mark, Sign, Signal, Monument	t	ת	Taw	t	T	T	T

Ancient Hebrew Research Center   www.ancient-hebrew.org

Table 2: Ancient Hebrew to Latin progression of Alphabets in human history. Benner, Jeff A. Ancient Hebrew Research Center.

The Letter Aleph

Table 3: Example of the evolution of the Early Paleo Hebrew letter Aleph to the modern-day letter A and the numeral one. Benner, Jeff A. Ancient Hebrew Research Center.

In these previous graphs above, notice the evolution of the Paleo Hebrew on the left into the Hebrew Aleph-Bet on the right. (Table 3).[6][7] From Joseph to Babylon, the pictograph and middle Hebrew was used. According to the archeological record, it seems the cuneiform was in use in other areas as well.

When Babylon took over the known world, the Hebrew letters were developing into the block letters we see today, tying directly into Aramaic letters and the Aramaic system of writing. Thus, this form became known as Aramaic Hebrew. While both Aramaic and Hebrew are semitic languages and similar in many ways, there are distinct differences.

At this point in history, the Hebrews—or Israelites—were assimilated into the Babylonian culture. Babylonian culture included all the cultures of the Levant, Egypt, Cush, Libya, Turkey, Assyria, and so on, and Aramaic became the new communication standard.

This block form has been in use, albeit evolving, from captivity to present. A language is interconnected to a people's culture, and culture adapts to survive. Being chosen to express Torah to the world, even when exiled by the Almighty, gives direction, purpose, and poise to get Torah accomplished, no matter the penalty box in which you are standing.

Remember, young boys in Israel had to memorize Torah as a part of coming of age. The recitation occurred at their Bar Mitzvah to prove their ability to the community. The schooling of all these students resulted in the cream of the crop, the top students, being given tutelage under a rabbi. Others were not necessarily rejected, but they became carpenters or butchers or fishermen and so on. This continued from Babylon and into the Ashkenazi customs in Europe. These top students learned Aramaic, resulting in a form of Aramaic called Hebrew block letter Aramaic. Again, this system of writing and alphabet came about in Baby-lonian captivity.

As the Greek empire came into power and became the dominant force in the land of Israel, the logical assumption by many members of academia is that these learned Hebrew men decided to write in Greek, as this would have been the language of the day. This thinking helped to propagate the idea that Hebrew became an extinct language. We now know through archeological evidence that these men wrote in their native tongue to spread the word through Israel and to Jews living in the northern Mediterranean areas. Through this period of time, the Paleo or Middle Hebrew, Late Hebrew and Aramaic block was being used. Then the document would have been translated into Greek to spread the news through the Gentile nations. Later in the chapter, I show how this is true because a concrete language can be difficult to express into abstract thought or language.

DID JOHN, SOME GREEK DUDE, OR THE HOLY SPIRIT WRITE THE BOOK OF JOHN?

Most churches today will say the Word of God is perfect as is, and that God chose these men to write down exact words. This appears to be a form of manipulation and indentured servitude or slavery. Why would any man or woman allow themselves to be taken over, to give up free will, or write something someone else wants them to write and perhaps they weren't interested in writing at all?

Let's really think about the implications of our salvation as a part of a belief system which subscribes to a text which was brought about through manipulation or forced coercion!

I am certainly not suggesting that the word of Yahweh is fallible.

I am simply questioning the idea that a manmade dogmatic system of belief which has incorporated a heaping side of paganism and superstition came from the text they allege Yahweh inspired these men to write. It's a questionable premise at best.

The definition of a *scheme* is: (noun) a plan or program of action and a systematic or organized configuration.[8] The definition for *slavery* is: (noun) submission to a dominating influence.[9]

For those of us that have faith in a benevolent God—Yahweh—we believe Yahweh's Holy Spirit is a gentleman, not forcing anyone into the role of indentured servitude or slavery in order to accomplish a scheme by the Creator of the universe. This unwilling compulsion is a preposterous thought, showing the ignorance of someone who is in a faith born of fear or has a complete lack of knowledge and understanding of whom Yahweh is as a perfect father.

Paul willingly put himself in chains to the gospel, the servitude of Yahshua Messiah, not the other way around. When John wrote this first chapter in his gospel, he was not taken over by Yahweh's Holy Spirit to accomplish this task. Yes, it was a task requested by Yahweh to accomplish the goal of describing what Yahweh had given John in knowledge and understanding in light of his newfound faith—much like this book.

My desire is to articulate what Yahweh has shown me, to give this to my brothers and sisters in the Messiah for understanding, knowledge, and yes, correction when applicable. But I have not been forced or coerced under a scheme of Yahweh's. My passion meets the inspiration of Yahweh's Holy Spirit before any voluntary articulation at all.

If Yahweh forced these men to write these books, or these men of their own accord wrote without inspiration, what does this say about salvation? Your salvation and my own? If either situation was true, our salvation would be of no value because it would be based on false pretenses. The idea of faith brought about by the manipulation of someone who is not inspired is a fruitless one, causing believers to walk away from their faith because the idea that man alone wrote Scripture causes too much despair to endure.

Is the Gospel of John a scheme? Yes, however, it's a scheme set in motion by a partnership with man to give the great news. What is this good news? From the beginning, Yahweh has had control in a world of human tragedy, and He is offering a plan of salvation as a father who truly loves you and me. The men who wrote the gospels were excited and about to burst. These disciples just walked away from careers or put their families on hold to walk with this man (Yahshua) who really looked like whom the prophets had spoken.

Remember, these men were most likely rejected from rabbis due to not being the top students in their Torah schooling. These men were rough around the edges while still pretty smart and pretty sharp. After all, they figured out who the Messiah was or at least had a pretty good inkling about him. This young new Rabbi selected them, and John was one of those chosen.

In all of John's letters, we see him as enamored with Yahshua. He discerned something deeper the others did not and was able to express this easily. John has a more passionate writing style compared to the style of Peter or Paul. In his writings, John speaks more of Yahweh's Holy Spirit, revealing the intense and immense love Yahshua has for humankind. This is most likely why he was called "the beloved." Being in the inner circle, John saw and recorded some great insights into the life of Yahshua. Through this man's perspective, we have been given a unique insight into knowing Yahweh through a belief in Yahshua, while giving a different point of view than the other gospels as well.

We can also see how John used words to settle faith issues. However, one cannot be dogmatic when attempting to discern this in the Book of John. That is to say, readers must study out what John was saying. We simply cannot read this gospel like a Sunday newspaper. If we do this, it will lead to a speculation allowing for doctrinal assumptions to be made. These assumptive doctrines can cause conflict with Old Testament writings of the prophets and Torah itself. John's gospel was very straightforward, on point, and never once denied his Torah teaching to put himself or his Messiah in danger of the Sanhedrin. We must understand the Torah and prophets, lest we become complacent and dogmatic, following a religious system instead of a personal relationship with our Messiah. Otherwise, this could cause people to misunderstand the Messiah's teaching thus assuming he is trying to alter Judaism. When one does not know the origins of their faith, these assumptions have devastating and reverberating effects. But that is the point; if you read this at first glance in Hebrew, Greek, or English you can easily see how these Pharisees became enraged at the thought of Yahshua equating himself to Yahweh, something Yahshua and the apostles never once did.

I truly believe John was the author of his own gospel, and in this chapter and the next, we will see this more clearly demonstrated by the words he chose.

The Gospel of John had to be written in Hebrew first and translated for a Greek audience by the same author. The thoughts would not have translated very well from Hebrew to Greek. I say this because of the similarities between John 1:1-2 and Genesis 1:1-3. The verses in John would have been written from a Hebraic mindset to relay the intent and theology of the author.

Remember, Greek is an abstract language, and Hebrew is a concrete language. So, when there is a scene depicting a formless God who is indescribable and not defined by anything near a form, especially not as a human form this can be very difficult. Thus, the description given concretely becomes the idea of our Father's Spirit, Yahweh's Holy Spirit.

He is not an old man with a gray beard and deep discerning look, almost appearing angry.

Wait a minute! I think I recognize that guy. He sounds like Zeus!

Additionally, it was not until the second century B.C.E. that the Jews began to see Yahweh as having form, and this was a major development within Judaism. This coincides with Alexander the Great conquering Jerusalem in 332 B.C.E. and under Persian control, the Holy Land fell into Alexander's control. Within one generation, Judaism had morphed due to the strong Greek abstract influence. A Greek man most likely would have had a hard time translating Hebrew thought into Greek with the precision John used.

Scripturally, it would make sense that Yahweh's Holy Spirit gave inspiration to John. The ability to see clearly and to articulate the foundation of creation and how Yahshua ties into that had to be driven by Yahweh's Holy Spirit. It seems Yahweh's Holy Spirit, being a gentleman, as everyone likes to say, would give the option to write the book or perform a divine task.

So, I would unequivocally declare that John wrote this gospel of his own accord and was inspired by Yahweh's Holy Spirit for layout while given full freedom to express himself. John was created in his mother's womb with a purpose. John's character (shem – a name as in the Hebrew understanding of a name.) is the reason John accepted the task, wrote the Book, and portrayed our Messiah the only way he could.

Yahweh's Holy Spirit gave John the understanding of what exactly happened that first day and how this is understood theologically through Torah. Torah is everlasting, Torah has precedence today, and Torah is the Way, the Truth, and the Life, and all of this, my friends, is Yahshua.

Genesis 26:5, Deuteronomy 10:12-13, Proverbs 6:23, Psalms 1:2, Isaiah 8:20, Acts 24:14, 2 Timothy 3:16, 1 John 3:4, Romans 7:12, Romans 2:13, John 14:6.

WHAT IS THE MEANING OF WORD IN GREEK?

I do not speak Greek. However, I have seen all those Greek letters twisted into complex mathematical equations. Yet some simple research can really go a long way. The question we need to answer is what is the meaning of WORD in Greek?

So, we will begin our deep dive into the Greek word **WORD**.

There are two words that can be used for the word WORD in Greek and those are Logos and Rhema. Often, one or the other of these specific words is chosen based on the context it is to be used in and the abstract ideas it is meant to convey.

I will start with the verse John 1:1, as that is where the questions begin to come up. Many assumptions also begin here, based on doctrinal teachings and traditions. Exploring this will help to focus on and to understand *what* is the word and *who* is the word.[10] [11] [12] [13] [14] [15]

WORD - LOGOS in Greek

LOGOS G3056 – Λόγος – Something said (including thought) by implication, topic (subject of discourse*) also reasoning (the mental faculty) or motive; by extension a computation; specifically, (with the article in John) the Divine Expression (Messiah).

LEGO G3004 – λέγω – Primary verb, properly to lay forth that is figuratively relate in words G2036 and G5346 individual expression or speech respectively G4483 is properly to break silence merely and G2980 means an extended or random harangue*; by implication to mean: - ask, bid, boast, call, describe, give out, name, put forth, say (-ing), shew, speak, tell, utter.

PHEMI G5346 – φημί – Same base as G5457 and G5316. To show or make known one's thoughts that is speak or say – affirm, say.

LALEO G2980 – λαλέω – a prolonged form of otherwise obsolete verb, to talk, that is to utter words – preach, say, speak – talk, tell, utter. **Go to =>G3004**

PHOS G5457 - φῶς – To shine or make manifest especially by rays, luminousness in the widest application. Natural or artificial abstract or concrete, literal or figurative. Fire, light.

PHIANO – G5316 – φαίνω – Prolongation for the base of G5457. To light or shine that is show, (transitive* or intransitive*)(literal* or figurative*): - appear, seen, be seen, shine, think.

WORD - RHEMA in Greek

RHEMA G4487 - ῥῆμα – from G4383 an utterance (individually, collectively or specifically) by implication a matter or topic (especially of command or dispute).

RHEO – G4483 - ῥέω -Certain tenses prolonged from G2036; perhaps akin (or identical) with G4882 (through the idea of pouring forth); to utter that is speak or say: - command, make say, speak (of). **Go to =>G3004**

EPO – G2036 - ἔπω – Primary verb (used only in the definite past tense the other being borrowed extended or random harangue; by implication to mean: - ask, bid, boast, from G2046 G4483 and G5346); speak or say (by word or writing): - answer, bid, bring, word, call, command, grant, say, (on) speak, tell. **Go to =>G3004**

EREO – G2046 - ἐρεῶ - Probably a fuller form of G4483; an alternate for G2036 in certain tenses; to utter, that is to speak or say: - call, say, speak (of), tell.

STRONG'S HEBREW

דבר **dabar, daw-baw'**; noun- from H1696; a word; by implication, a matter (as spoken of) or thing; adverbially, a cause: —act, advice, affair, answer, × any such (thing), because of, book, business, care, case, cause, certain rate, chronicles, commandment, × commune(-ication), concern(-ing), confer, counsel, dearth, decree, deed, × disease, due, duty, effect, eloquent, errand, (evil favoured-) ness, glory, harm, hurt, iniquity, judgment, language, lying, manner, matter, message, (no) thing, oracle, × ought, × parts, pertaining, please, portion, power, promise, provision, purpose, question, rate, reason, report, request, × (as hast) said, sake, saying, sentence, sign, so, some (uncleanness), somewhat to say, song, speech, × spoken, talk, task, that, × there done, thing (concerning), thought, thus, tidings, what(-soever), wherewith, which, word, work.

דבר **dabar, daw-bar'**; verb a primitive root; perhaps properly, to arrange; but used figuratively (of words), to speak; rarely (in a destructive sense) to subdue: —answer, appoint, bid, command, commune, declare, destroy, give, name, promise, pronounce, rehearse, say, speak, be spokesman, subdue, talk, teach, tell, think, use (entreaties), utter, × well, × work.

BROWN DRIVERS BRIGGS

דבר noun, masculine. Speech, word.

Singular – 1. speech, discourse, saying, word as the sum of that which is spoken of men. Word of command. Message, report, tidings. Charge, complaint, decision, sentence.

2. word of God, as a divine communication in the form of commandments, prophecy, and words of to his people, used 394 times.

BIBLICAL USAGE	ANCIENT HEBREW
1. NOUN -speech, word, speaking, thing	2093: (H1697) דבר (DAWBAR) ac: Order co: Word ab ? : An arrangement or placement of something creating order. – order NOUN - MASCULINE — I. Word: An arrangement of words. II. Thing: As something that is arranged. In Hebrew thought words contain substance just as physical objects do. III. Plague: The re-ordering of a population. [freq. 49] |KJV: word, thing, matter, act, chronicle, saying, commandment, pestilence, plague, murrain| {str: 1697, 1698} (Noun feminine first person) — Word: An arrangement of words. [freq. 1] |KJV: word| {str: 1703}
a. speech	
b. saying, utterance	
c. word, words	
d. business, occupation, acts, matter, case something, manner (by extension)	
2. VERB-to speak, declare, converse, command, promise, warn, threaten, sing	
a. (Qal) to speak	
b. (Niphal) to speak with one another, talk	2093: VERB (H1696) דבר — Speak: A careful arrangement of words or commands. [freq. 1488] (VF: Paal, Niphal, Hiphil, Hitpael, Pual, Piel) |KJV: speak, say, talk, promise, tell, commune, pronounce, utter, command| {str: 1696}
c. (Piel) to speak, to promise	
d. (Pual) to be spoken	
e. (Hithpael) to speak	2093: NOUN FEM (H1703) דברה (DABARAH) — Word: An arrangement of words. [freq. 1] |KJV: word| {str: 1703}
f. (Hiphil) to lead away, put to flight	1089) Parent Root דר (DAR) ac: ? co: Circle ab: ?: The pictograph H is a door representing a moving back and forth. The V is the head of a man. Combined these mean "the back-and-forth movement of man". A generation is one revolution of the family line. The Hebraic understanding of order is the continual cyclical process of life and death or renewal and destruction. This root can also have the meanings of circling around of something in a wide area or to cover a large area. (eng: adore - as honor)

Discourse – NOUN – 1: verbal interchange of ideas especially: CONVERSATION, 2a: formal and orderly and usually extended expression of thought on a subject, b: connected speech or writing c: a linguistic unit (such as a conversation or a story) larger than a sentence 3: a mode of organizing knowledge, ideas, or experience that is rooted in language and its concrete contexts (such as history or institutions) critical discourse.[16]

Harangue – NOUN – lengthy and aggressive speech. As a verb – lecture (someone) at length in an aggressive and critical manner.[17]

Transitive – ADJECTIVE 1. Grammar - (of a verb or a sense or use of a verb) able to take a direct object (expressed or implied), e.g., saw in he saw the donkey. 2. logic mathematics - (of a relation) such that, if it applies between successive members of a sequence, it must also apply between any two members taken in order. For instance, if A is larger than B, and B is larger than C, then A is larger than C.[18]

Intransitive – ADJECTIVE 1. (of a verb or a sense or use of a verb) not taking a direct object, e.g., look in look at the sky.[19]

Literal – ADJECTIVE 1. taking words in their usual or most basic sense without metaphor or allegory. "Dreadful in its literal sense, full of dread" 2. (of a translation) representing the exact words of the original text. "a literal translation from the Spanish" 3. (of a person or performance) lacking imagination; prosaic. "his interpretation was rather too literal."[20]

*Figurative – ADJECTIVE 1. departing from a literal use of words; metaphorical. "Gold, in the figurative language of the people, was "the tears wept by the sun." 2. (of an artist or work of art) representing forms that are recognizably derived from life.[21]

Looking at the Word *Logos*, we can clearly see that this is a thought uttered or something said. At the beginning, Yahweh spoke to lay forth this thought. In doing so, He made known His thoughts to His whole host. He uttered those words to convey something, thereby revealing Yahweh's glory or His light and this light could be seen. Within this light, everything could be viewed: you, me, Yahshua, the cross, the fall of man, the wars, Torah, all of it, and this makes it transitive and intransitive, figurative, and literal.

When we look at the word *rhema*, which is not mentioned in the discussed text, we can still see the same thought brought back to the base word *Lego*. *Lego* means to aggressively lay forth. When we study the Hebrew, it becomes clear that the thought expressed was put into order by words. In that light or in that beginning, Yahweh perceived an order of things, and He saw it was good or functional.

This was the word of Yahweh when He spoke. We cannot find anywhere in Scripture where Yahshua created or spoke into creation because Yahshua simply was not there. If we did see that Yahshua created the world, then the New Testament has contradicted the Old Testament and that simply cannot happen! The New Testament is a reiteration of the Old Testament, as Yahweh's word is the same yesterday, today, and forever, Hebrew 13:8 and Malachi 3:6.

These two verses above are truth, not human truth from the mouths or brains of men. But truth that comes from the origination point – Yahweh Himself –thus, satisfying the whole WORD: logos in truth!

There we have it!

How can Yahshua be the *word* in the Book of Revelation yet not be the *word* in Genesis?

Because the *word* from Genesis was a divine thought uttered by a command as a prophetic saving grace, the promise of a future occurrence, specifically to deliver the Torah to the nations through the Israelites who had the law and for recompense when the Torah was inevitably violated.

This was the avenue by which you could be in Yahweh's assembly once again. Blood must pay the price for sin. The Word – Logos – is the promise, and when we understand that the Law, not Torah, was given to show us as sin (Galatians 3:19, Romans 3:30, Romans 16:25), then we will begin to perceive why these things had to take place in the order they did.

Yahshua could not have been the Word – Logos in the beginning—except in thought only, because he had not fulfilled the role of Messiah to be the Word – Logos—yet. The order of events for the Word - Logos to come into flesh must take place as Yahweh's timeline dictates. Moshe (Moses) saw this and expressed it in Deuteronomy18: 15 & 18.

A divine communication in the form of a command-ment: "let there be light". This light was not the sun or moon and stars, as that comes into creation in Genesis 1:14. The biblical usage of the word *word* is used 394 times and is always in context to speech or a thought uttered or written.

In all of these usages in the verb form, all verb forms in the Hebrew follow suit as well. In the Ancient Hebrew, the view of Genesis 1:1-4 and John 1:1-14 is backed up with order, as in an arrangement of words. As a verb, there is a careful arrangement of words or commands. A concept becomes clear, and it is a concept that is not really expressed well from Hebrew to English.

This Word, Logos, is a redeeming promise, as in the future of mankind's continuance, an expression of a future fruit born out of this promise. The thought behind the Logos is that we come to understand that we missed the mark, can recognize this truth, turn around, and come back into the camp of Yahweh. This is the picture of repentance!

That is grace, mercy, and life. Grace is that we even have the ability to turn back and not be discarded in our sin. Mercy in that we have a loving Father who wants us, and we are not destroyed when we make mistakes. Life in that by mercy and grace we can have life, live it to the fullest, and then have everlasting life. This was the promise from day one! This was the thought that Yahweh uttered, commanded, and promised for us, those who choose to accept, his children. This is why I love the ancient Hebrew: it gets to the point.

The parent root *dar* is a circle or order. The Ancient Hebrew takes us to the concrete thought that the door is open for your human reasoning. The implication is that this circle is the Aleph-Tav, the beginning and the end. (Revelation 1:8, Revelation 22:13, Isaiah 44:6).

This thought (Messiah), not in the creation at that point, is the promise – the Word given by the Father and accepted by Yahshua to be that promise. When Yahshua accepted that role, He became the Word made flesh, John 1:14, and that is why Revelation 19:13 says He is the Word of Yahweh. He became the Word Yahweh uttered. This is also why Yahshua is called faithful and true, as He was faithful to the Word of Yahweh, and He was true to the Word of Yahweh. He fulfilled the word and lived the word, Romans 16:25. Torah is the door to the house by human reasoning (דָּבָר H1697 dabar) – Behold I stand at the door, Revelation 3:20.

STRONG'S CONCORDANCE, AMERICA, AND THE EVANGELICAL CHURCH

We can see from above that reading the Bible like a Sunday newspaper will get us nowhere fast. We will see some things on a base level, have a genuine understanding of Yahweh, and we will also pick up a lot of translator thoughts which do not make the Word errant, however this misses a lot of the flavor of the text.

This will give opportunity for misinformation to take hold, and thus, pagan ideas spread, incorporated by a massive church system to fleece a flock, or provide stable governance. We must take the time to study the Word and look at every angle. Finding out the authors' true intent is certainly attainable by spending a little time to truly find out what the original words mean.

Did Strong have malicious intent by inputting into definitions a theological or doctrinal meaning?

No, I believe Strong was given full go-ahead to write his Lexicon by Yahweh's Holy Spirit. Yahweh's Holy Spirit, I believe, inspired him to do all the work and research necessary to create that Lexicon. Strong, most likely, had a passion for studying the Word, as he did have a doctorate in Divinity and was a professor of Exegetical Theology at Drew Theological Seminary. This paved the way to help other people do just that, without all the painstaking work and translation skills needed to accomplish the task.

In this case, we must concern ourselves with Strong's definition of the word *Logos*. At the end of the definition or rendering of the word and after the various approved English versions of that word we have listed *(with the article in John) the Divine Expression (Messiah)*. This was a widely accepted rendering of this word in Christian circles. In no way does the word *Logos* mean that phrase. Furthermore, the article in John 1:1 is not messiah or son, nor is it implied. This unfortunate error came from, I believe, a sign of the times. For example, over a hundred colleagues worked on this index/reference guide of every word used in the King James Version of the Bible. Now we had translators who translated Scripture, and then Strong came along and indexed every word from a translator. Wow!

Exegesis means "to draw the meaning out of." Eisegesis means "to read one's own interpretation into a given text."

Hermeneutics is the science and art of interpreting what an author has written.

There are a couple of issues here. First, Strong's theology got in the way. While trying to be objective, for the most part exegetical, he still input his own theological/doctrinal eisegesis when it came to certain words, to benefit the Methodist or Wesleyan doctrines. Secondly, the work of a concordance and lexicon should be completely unbiased to be above reproach. Still, I do not believe the man James Strong published this lexicon maliciously. He imputed what was generally accepted doctrine from the daughters of the Holy Roman Catholic Church, the Protestant belief system and the acceptance of a trinity, albeit nowhere to be found in Scripture implied or otherwise!

In 1870-1890 C.E., the American landscape saw an expanding west, class separation, subjugation of the American Indian, increasing wealth and poverty, multiple economic depressions, a false god was erected in New York City Harbor, populations began moving from farms to cities, and spiritism was becoming popular while social Darwinism took root in America.

Paying close attention, we can see, in all of these social issues above, a need to tame the people and produce an American exceptionalism policy which began to unfold and was united by common Protestant doctrines. Yet, back then, everyone was still willing to listen and be told what to do by family tradition or pastoral authority.

In 1890 C.E., Strong's Lexicon was welcomed, and a reader could now find out that God the father and God the son and God the Holy Spirit were all one and in three. Yet not one person could explain this doctrine then and still cannot logically explain to this day. This imputed theological doctrine of the trinity taught that Jesus had equality with Yahweh (Father) and was the Word. Breaking this down, the doctrinal influence implied that because of the trinity, one can assume that Jesus was with God (Yahweh) from the beginning of time, in other words eternal. This poses a real problem in our belief system's roots in that we have one God not two or three. The idea that Jesus was with Yahweh at the beginning automatically makes him co equal with God (Yahweh). If we accept this erroneous belief, then the equality with Yahweh gives Yahshua all authority to create what we see and live today. The second issue with this theological doctrine is that of Jesus being the Word.

How can Jesus be the Word before there was the Word? As in the case of being eternal with God.

How can something be called something when it is not called that something until the end of the book?

And in that thought, where it was the promised something that was being spoken about at the beginning of the book!?

The Bible is a historical timeline of humanity, and we learn to keep things in chronological order so we have that perspective. When we read the Scriptures from cover to cover, we see at the end of the book that Jesus (Yahshua) is coronated King and called Faithful and True, The Word. Rev 19:11-14. This has not happened yet, as we can see that this scene happens literally right before his second coming to usher in the 1000-year reign. Right now, our beloved Messiah is our intercessor or mediator performing priestly duties in the temple for us. With this in mind one must ask why would a coequal God, separate but one, be creating all of this and then having to give a law for remediation of sin? Come in the form of a demigod and die for us, only to be sent back to heaven to be a priest until he is crowned our king, all the while being this coequal deity? Simply put, Jesus (Yahshua) is not called the Word until the end of the book and never was the Word at any time before except in thought only by the One True God (Yahweh).

There is an adage in psychology that states you can only do what you know, and you cannot do what you do not know. That is what Strong and his team could only do – what they knew. I still do not believe Strong had ill intent when he published his lexicon. He merely created a tool in the best way he knew how.

In this chapter, we have investigated whether this Gospel of John was written in Hebrew or Greek. We found through culture, archeology, and linguistically, that yes, we can say that this gospel was most likely written by John, inspired by Yahweh's Holy Spirit in Hebrew.

Later, he then translated the same gospel into Greek to convey his thoughts to more people. As we dig into the verses, we will shore up this understanding even more. We reviewed the origins and new findings in the scientific communities concerning alphabets and the written word in human history. We discovered historically that thoughts lead to words expressed, spoken, or uttered, and that thoughts lead to words being written in picture and then with an alphabet. We took a deep dive into the Greek and Hebrew for the word *WORD*, discovered some very important understandings of what the word selection means, and what is being conveyed by the author in this way. What *word* means in these different languages cannot be misconstrued until someone puts an eisegesis doctrinal statement in the meaning.

Is that the end all?

No, of course not!

Let's go further and really peel back the text to see what John is expressing, here in his first chapter.

CHAPTER 2
PRE-INCARNATE, PRE-EXISTENT, AND DUALITY
THE JOHN 1:1 FACTOR

YAHSHUA IN JOHN 1:1

In the beginning was the Word,

and the Word was with God, and the Word was God.

In the	Beginning	Was	The	Word
Ἐν	ἀρχῇ	ἦν	Ἐν	λόγος
G1722 en (a preposition) – properly, in (inside, within); (figuratively) "in the realm (sphere) of," as in the condition (state) in which something operates from the inside (within).	**G746 arxé** – properly, from the beginning (temporal sense), i.e., "the initial (starting) point"; (figuratively) what comes first and therefore is chief (foremost), i.e., has the priority because ahead of the rest ("preeminent").	**1510 eimí** (the basic Greek verb which expresses being, i.e., "to be") – am, is. 1510 (eimí), and its counterparts, (properly) convey "straight-forward" being (existence, i.e., without explicit limits).	**G3588 ho** - the, the definite article.	**G3056 logos** something said (including the thought); by implication, a topic (subject of discourse), also reasoning (the mental faculty) or motive; by extension, a computation; specially, (with the article in John) the Divine Expression (i.e., Christ)

IN THE BEGINNING WAS THE WORD

O ur goal is to take each word one by one and make sense of what this verse is telling us. There have been centuries of confusion regarding this section of the first verse. I broke out the text showing the English translation, the Greek, the Greek transliteration, the Strong's reference number, and a definition.

IN, as we all know, is a preposition and basic to understand. In this case, it is used to direct you to, with the article attached – In the beginning.

THE BEGINNING means simply the top, the chief, the initial starting point. Of what? Of you and me, us, the world in which we live. We should pause right here, as this is where a lot of brothers and sisters freeze and would rather be led than study what is going on in Genesis. You have two points of view or schools of thought here. The first view: this is the beginning of everything, period! All of it, the angels, the universe, heaven, Yahweh, and the creation of earth, with nothing existing before. The second view is that this is the beginning of *our* story. This is not Yahweh's story. This is about our daddy creating us and our environment in which we live.

We must remember Yahweh is omnipotent and omniscient. He was and is forever! (Deuteronomy 33:27, Job 36:26, Psalm 90:2) Eternal means lasting or existing forever; having no beginning or end. With our chronologically linear thinking, this is very difficult to wrap our minds around.

Why? Because we have a beginning and an end, and we know this within our beings. We are created individuals living within the confines of time. This is preprogrammed into our DNA from the onset of our creation. Since we are not gods nor designed to be gods, we have a beginning and an end. Having the ability to think and reason, a functioning limbic brain, and the idea or belief of a supreme being assists us in fighting death and striving for life. Otherwise, the sheer anxiety of everyone would be immense.

As we continue in our study, please realize Genesis 1:1 was not the beginning of Yahweh, nor the kingdom of heaven nor the angels. Yahweh predated the events in Genesis. Additionally, why would Yahshua be created prior to Gen. 1:1?

We must return to our roots and understand Yahshua came to be for us. Not for Yahweh and not for the angels. John 3:16 does not say sent His only son; it says He *gave* His only begotten son. Meaning that Moses, Joshua, the prophets, the high priests, and John the Baptist were not sons that Yahweh specifically called out as His only begotten. They were sons because they believed in His name – big difference!

What is a son? How did Yahweh *send* his son? Well, my friends, it never says in the sense of sending you, me or us from one place to another. In other words Yahshua was not sent from heaven, he was sent out on a mission. A mission to give us the good news of salvation. That is the Greek understanding of John 3:17 where the word *apostello* is used. The word is used to send out into the world. This is the whole reason for the verses saying Yahshua was poured out as a sacrifice. That Yahshua was that thought in the beginning. The Greek word *didomi* used in John 3:16 is not sent. Don't be alarmed. I understood the same thing for fifty years. So, for what reason would a son be needed if there are no humans to be saved? It was a family. Simply meaning that a dual God (Yahweh and Yahshua before the creation story) in truth really does not fit, as there is not a family of humans to be saved. However, IT, being the family of mankind in a state of declension, certainly needs someone to save them from their missing of the mark. This is a portion of what John was trying to reiterate!

Now we can peel back the word: **WAS**. Here, we have the tricky little word, *was*. Theologians love to place this simple past-tense word to line it up with ideas of being, such as *I exist* and *I am*. Theologians and preachers alike take this to mean this is Yahshua, due to the definite article being Word, and then we create the whole paganized misunderstanding incorporated into our belief system with little or no regard to the consequences.

What do I mean by this? Notice above, in the Greek you see the word *was*. The Strong's reference is **G1510** in Bible Hub's Interlinear. However, in Strong's direct lexicon and the Codex Sinaiticus, you see **G2588** *(ane)*. This is the imperfect form of **G1510** used as *I was* (wast or were), be. This is a huge difference.

The translations of the Interlinear are trying to use the perfect tense to take you on a goose chase to corroborate a denominational or sectarian doctrine. This is another reason I do not believe Strong was flippant in his lexicon. Well, if this is true, what do we do with the Interlinear? Nothing.

Instead, we must look at the Greek and verify the words within to be sure. Because the word in the diagram above (*en*) is the exact same spelling. The difference being the word is *ane* instead of *eimi* due to the usage of the verb.

What is interesting is we can say "am the word, to be the word, or was the word" all three of these choices fit the context perfectly. However, none of these are grammatically correct in English or Greek, and that is why Strong's alerted you to the imperfect verb usage.

At this point, one could say, "Thanks, but I do not have time to do all this referencing and studying."

Yet I would reply in this way: "Your Dad gave you a document, a map for life, a map to explore, and you are willing to keep the map and glance at the map. However, you are not willing to study the map?"

Folks, this in-depth analysis comes with the territory. We do not need to be biblical scholars, but we should take the time to study. We do not have to say we have read the whole Bible, but we should be able to say we have a true relationship with our heavenly Father who has shown us what's revealed by His word.

This is the summary for the word: **WAS**. **WAS** is in the beginning and was the word! The best way to look at this is the Word existed in the beginning and that Word was not a created Being, or a Divine Being. It simply **WAS**, being the existent Word that Yahweh uttered.

We defined **WORD** in the previous chapter, but let us refresh our memory. In Greek, the word for Word is *logos* (**Strong's G3056**) defined as a word (as embodying an idea), a statement, divine utterance, or an analogy.

In Hebrew, it is *davar*, דבר (**Strong's H1697**) defined as word. The parent root of the word davar is *dor*, דר (**Strong's H1755**). It means generation, as in a generational order not just generation, the base meaning of this word is *order*. There must be an order to things and that requires intelligence. That is how we see good and bad (function and dysfunction or chaos and disorder).

I believe we can agree on the definition of this as a Divine thought or idea uttered. Can we say Yahshua is the Word? I do not believe so, as this word, *davar*, דבר in this verse could be translated as a thought uttered. We make plans to build something. We make plans in our head about finances. We also have thoughts about our children and how we will react to any situation in which they find themselves. So far, none of these have been anything other than a thought or an idea. The chosen word used here is *logos* which tells us this is proved as an utterance.

Now, at this point, we create something of a vision. Some of us are better at that than others; however, we all do this to some extent. Most of us typically write or draw the thought or idea so we can realize it and then make it a goal to accomplish. A smaller group of people are able to think up a plan, see it in their head, and then put it together all according to the plans in their head.

I do believe at this juncture, in this Genesis Scripture, we can say Yahweh did indeed envision Yahshua, you, me, the cross, and so on. Yet this was John writing this gospel and describing the moments right before the beginning of time as we understand it. Since Yahweh has no embodiment, John is describing the hope of Yahweh which is to be mankind's gift.

"In the beginning was the Word" is a parallel verse, and John used this to correlate with Genesis 1 as this is the beginning of humankind. This is the first reason why I believe this gospel was written in Hebrew. John captured the Hebrew language in a beautifully poetic display.

Though, we must understand something at this crossroad.

Let's examine Genesis 1:1-5:

Genesis 1:1-5: In the beginning God created the heavens and the earth. Now the earth was formless and empty, darkness was over the surface of the deep, and the Spirit of God was hovering over the waters. And God said, "Let there be light," and there was light. And God saw the light, that it was good: and God divided the light from the darkness. And God called the light Day, and the darkness he called Night. And the evening and the morning were the first day.

LIGHT, WORD, AND TORAH

In Genesis 1:1, when Yahweh decided to create the world, we must understand our Father is all-knowing and sees things in a circular pattern, not linear. Yahweh knows the beginning and the end. Otherwise, things would happen in human history or angelic history that surprised Yahweh.

And this is not so.

Think about the implications of a God surprised by human activity. Or one who has a son residing with Him in heaven, and suddenly, Yahweh says "J.C., can you get down there and straighten out these humans, please?"

This makes absolutely no sense and can only make sense if we keep Yahweh in a box of man's making, in other words make Him into a mean, threatening old man from the old world and old writings as a God. However, in Genesis 1:1, Yahweh, in all His glory, hovers over this sphere and contemplates what He will embark on and sees the layout, sees the sin, sees the downfall of all of this (*logos*), and then Yahweh says, "I will give them salvation, hope, because they will fail, they will fall."

The idea or the thought relayed is this: the thought of providing a savior existed at the beginning because Yahweh could see how history played out, as though it had already happened.

The WORD is the hope uttered. This hope is a blessed hope, and this blessed hope had to make the choice to carry the mantle (the logos). This role being accepted was where we were heading, where we had to arrive. That is why John wrote: *In the Beginning was the Word.*

Now we must give Strong some credit for his lexicon. When you look at the word Logos in the lexicon. The last piece of the definition or his exegesis is (with the Article in John) which is Word, The Divine Expression, for example The Messiah. All the lexicon says is the definite article in John which is Word is the Divine Expression of the Messiah. It does not say Yahshua was standing right there next to

Yahweh. In some English translations, we can find Yahshua was right there or He actually assisted in the creating.

This is blasphemy, as this would make Yahshua equal with Yahweh. This concept did not come out of Yahshua's mouth. We can see Yahweh separated the light out of the darkness. We can also see this was Yahweh creating order for us when He spoke the Word. We can also, through Scripture, see where Yahweh separated the light out of darkness, thereby creating Torah (Word). What does this mean?

When we look at the Hebrew word *DawBaR* דָּבָר (**H1697**), this means order, as in an arrangement or placement of something creating order.[1] Word is an order of a thought uttered. English translations of DawBaR result in *WORD*.

Yahweh said, "Let there be Light." For us, as humans, we need light to function. Not the luminaires of heaven, as they were not yet created and did not exist at this point in scripture. Instead, we would need something foundational to the basis of living, as Yahweh knew we would suffer declension and suffer consequences to our free will choices.

Proverbs 6:23 tells us *Torah is Light*. This is the first thing Yahweh created, hence, Yahweh said, "Let there be Light." If we have the Light, the basis of living, then we have Torah which is the way of the Light.

If the pathway is illuminated by Light for life, then this is a well-led life, then whom have we just described? None other than the thought uttered by Yahweh, which is the foundational basis for all creation, or chiefly us, so we may be saved and have everlasting Life! This would be the reason for statements made such as, "He was slain from the foundation of the world," "before Abraham was, I am," and "I and my Father are One."

Yahshua the Messiah at this point was not created physically, but he was uttered as a prophecy, intended to become the full embodiment of Torah so we may, by his blood, live blamelessly within Torah.

Remember, Torah cannot be done without the Law; however, Torah can be done without the Law if we have accepted Yahshua as our Messiah who gave up his life as a blood offering once and for all.

Was Yahshua not sent as an example for us all?

Was he not sent as a lamb of Yahweh?

Yes! Then Light =Torah = Messiah.

In fact, He said, *I am the Way, the Truth and the Life* John 14:6. It really does not get much simpler than this.

Torah is the foundation of our life between Yahweh and Man, Man and Man, and Man to himself, and this is how to function. Torah is function. When I write the words, "Torah is functional," that is because order is in place when we observe and do Torah. Not as works to earn salvation!

Torah is the guidelines to healthy living for Yahweh, others, and ourselves. The Hebrew word for functional is *tov* **טוֹב** (**H2896**), as in to be good such as in being functional.[2] Thus, when we accept and live Torah, we become children of Light and have knowledge of the Father of Lights (James 1:17).

Now we can understand, Light is another form of order for us. Why? Because Light is not darkness, and light allows us to see. With too much light, we become blind, and too much darkness, we become blind. Function and order must prevail, as Yahweh is the pinnacle of order, thus everything has an order and purpose, otherwise too much or too little can have consequences. Our Father knows when and where the Messiah must come along in human history in order for all things to be fulfilled. The thought (Logos) set forth in motion by an utterance of reason. As an act of order and as an act of function, so that a Messiah would appear in the ordained time (Moedim) chosen by Yahweh.

Let's support this with scripture! First, there is a thought (Logos) that is a divine idea which became a divine utterance. "Let there be light", the Logos, is where the apostles and prophets and Israel (Jacob) is speaking of a Messiah to come, the world was created through, by, and for him (John 1:3, Colossians 1:16) and slain from the foundation of the world (Revelation 13:8).

Now the foundation is not a concrete pillar(s), but we are witnessing your Elohim in His Glory! Seeing all in all, from A to Z, the completion of His plans. That is the foundation, and the Messiah is the foundation which holds it all up. There must be a foundation to the idea (Logos), in order for Yahweh to accomplish what He knew were going to rebel!

Fathers and mothers see and know their children, and they know when their child has a propensity toward a particular action. Is Yahweh any different? We are made in His image and likeness. So, the motion began, and the Word (Logos) became flesh in verse 14, at the birth of Yahshua. Secondly, light in Hebrew is *owr*, **אוֹר** (**Strong's H216**) defined as light or illumination. A commandment is directives in Hebrew (*mitsotai*), and these are guideposts to direct you in which way to go.

Proverbs 6:23: For a commandment is a lamp and the Torah is light. - Thus, for a guidepost is a lamp, and your Torah is light.

Psalm 119:105: Your word is a lamp to my feet and a light to my path. – Thus, your commandments are a lamp to my feet, and a Torah to my path.

On day one, Yahweh did not create the luminaries which gave off a light and lesser reflected. He created first Light, not sunlight, on that first day. The implications are astounding because I personally believe this is where the Torah is created.

This is also where the thought of Yahshua and of Him being slain from the foundations of the world came from Yahweh! One can see that both were, are, and will be a light for all mankind and his creation. Then, when the *moedim* (appointed time) comes for the Messiah to be born, He will bring the embodiment of Torah or the Light of the world into the world.

In Galatians 4:4-5, we read: *But when the fullness of time had come, God sent forth his Son, born of woman, born under the law, to redeem those who were under the law, so that we might receive adoption as sons.*

Hence, John 1:14: *And the Word became flesh and dwelt among us and we beheld His glory, the glory begotten of the Father, full of grace and truth.*

And John 1:7: *This man came for a witness, to bear witness of the Light, that all through him might believe.*

THE GREAT BIG LIE

Now, of course, in Yahshua's case, He was the promised offspring, Shiloh, or Messiah, and the Heir to the throne of David. Though, He was not an eternal god or even day-one creation except in thought only. Mary was chosen to carry the Messiah, a man, not a god placed in her womb, nor formed by copulation with divinity. The overshadowing by Yahweh's Holy Spirit upon Yahshua occurred, which simply means the human egg from a female combined with a prophetic word, the breath of Yahweh, which is the seed, became a man.

The event did not include a teleportation device like those imaginations of Star Trek, where one-minute Yahshua is in heaven with Yahweh and then he is an embryo in Mary's womb. Now Yahweh's Holy Spirit did speak those words to Mary and within Mary's uterus an egg was spoken to with Torah, being function and order. Thus, the Logos became flesh, the blessed hope, the wonderous joy, and the Prince of Peace. So, I submit, through etymology and scrip-turally—which is most important, that the Torah is the Word, and Torah is Light (Proverbs 6:23, John 1:1, Genesis 1:3, Luke 1:35).

In Luke 1:35, we see where the power – *dynamis* (**G1411**) is translated as power. This is interesting because this describes Elohim very well: powers. This verse says the most High "Elohim" will overshadow you. This word overshadow is *episkiazó* (**G1982**) to overshadow or envelop, and part of the word comes from *skia* (**G4639**), shade caused by the interception of the light.

We know what Light is, and we know what the Word is, and yet here it is being given to Mary. The Word is Light, and the Word is Yahweh. Yahweh spoke and all things were created by his Word. Torah, being the Word, became flesh. The Word was the seed because the Father spoke the Word to Mary's womb, and her womb responded to make it so. This allowed for the Torah to be made flesh, born of a woman through a birth canal. He was not a preincarnate divine being that gave up His place in heaven to inhabit a womb for nine months, then live as a little boy, and then a teen.

This is pagan belief!

This is from Greek and Roman mythology. Also, it comes from a Chaldean myth concerning Ishtar. Look, if Yahshua came from heaven to earth to be born of a woman, and then die, then our salvation is bunk, dead, not accepted. This is a pagan concept, not a biblical concept.

Why? A man had to be born from a virgin, and He then had to make the choice to be Yahweh's salvation, make the choice in his humanity to submit to do the will of Yahweh, choose to be the Lamb, so we might by all accounts have an example to live by, search by, and die by!

While preexistence is a pagan concept, meaning, outside Judaism or early Christianity, one cannot necessarily say it was borrowed from other religions. The virgin birth is a truly unique story. Most other accounts are either sexual acts of a god with a human woman where they still call the woman a virgin, even though semination has occurred, or these human women had children previously and then swore celibacy, so they were allowed to be called virgins. All of these stories postdate the Christian account by one to three centuries.

Other virgin birth stories are similar yet include thought-only births or other tools for impregnation. Yet within these stories, the women have often had children before this focal point birth. A few of these stories, however, did predate the Christian virgin birth. Some people will show the vestal virgins as evidence of this fact. However, this argument is null and void because some of these women had children and because they also took a vow of celibacy, so they could be considered virgins once again.

Zoroastrianism came from western Media, present-day Iran, and in all accounts looks as though this was the precursor to the seed of Satan fable and the Divine Right principle. If we remember, in the first chapter, we discussed the timeline of the Israelites being moved back in time from 1400 B.C.E to 2000-1900 B.C.E.[3]

I bring this up because most scholars will say this religion "might" have its roots in the second millennium B.C.E. This would be around the time Abraham left Chaldee and there was more than likely a remnant of people who held onto the old faith: one true God.

Zoroastrianism is interesting because it shares much of the same belief systems as Judaism and many of our Christian belief structures, such as monotheism, messianism, free will, judgment after death, an afterlife concept of heaven, hell, angels, and demons. It is believed this religion was started around 1200 BCE by Zarathustra. However, most scholars and historians place the beginning around the sixth to seventh century B.C.E.[4]

This makes it possible to be heavily influenced by the Jewish captivity in the first Babylonian siege, thus Jewish captives also influenced Zoroastrianism, as both religions are extremely close in ideology and beliefs. Nebuchadnezzar II was in control of all the Middle East at this time, including Israel, who paid tribute to this king. It must be a little of both scenarios, as Zoroastrianism was entered into historical record in the middle of the fifth century B.C.E. This religion, along with Judaism, heavily influenced the Gnostic teachings in Christianity, Northern Buddhism, Greek philosophy, and Islam.

In the Avesta, it states the prophet Zarathustra came into being by conjugal relations of his parents. Later, this was changed to his mother being a virgin and being impregnated by a shaft of light that came from the god Ahura Mazda.[5] This later addition came in the Common Era or AD.

With this knowledge, we can negate the idea the virgin birth came from this religion, as it happened after the fact of the Messiah Yahshua. To be clear, the Abrahamic religions did not in any way take borrowings from Zoroastrianism. This religion was influenced by Hebrew nomads beginning with Abram, and then Zarathustra took teachings from Hebraic thought and altered them to fit Zoroastrianism systems of belief. A source from Muslim scholars tells us Zarathustra was an inhabitant of Israel and a disciple of Jeremiah. There was a falling out between master and disciple, and Zarathustra left for modern-day Afghanistan and subsequently founded the Magian[6]. This most likely explains the Biblical mention of the Magi coming to give gifts and worship the two-or three-year-old year old Yahshua as they knew this was the promised Messiah.

In Buddhism, the Buddha descends from the heavens or the Tusita Body into a mother's womb. Now this heaven is described as one of six heavens. These stories were written at different times from B.C.E into C.E., comprised of seventeen books which describe the lives of the twenty-eight buddhas. Still, there is no actual historical evidence of anyone meeting a buddha; yet there are archeological finds pointing toward some men being a buddha in name only.

So, this appears to be men, intelligent men with strong discipline and morals who were highly regarded and then reached "enlightenment," or the social construct of enlightenment in their time.

How is this an issue? We could all use enlightenment on a subject or two!

There appear to be elements of Judaism in Buddhism, and this should be further explored and understood. Yet this should not be treated as a way to everlasting life. In Hinduism, we see a similar story to Judaism/Christianity, where Vishnu descends into the womb of Devaki. Here, though, Devaki was already married and had borne seven children. Thus, Devaki was not a virgin. We also find a trinity in Hinduism as well.

In the Greek and Roman gods or mythology, we see multiple gods each having a realm to care for. These ancient stories had their roots in at least the sixth century B.C.E. A father god who is a titan appears, and then sons and daughters take the mantle, such as Zeus and the progeny of Zeus. Zeus can come down and visit human women and make half-human/half-god men and women (demigods), often creating heroes.

Personally, this appears to be the forerunner to all major religions, as this perfectly lines up with a post-flood world and all the stories told of heroes who were created to defeat 'giants' on the earth. These stories were modified over time and then created to suit the god systems of Egypt, Armenia, and Babylon.

The Greeks held on to the old stories to a huge degree and encapsulated them in their flourishing culture. Persephone and Danae are just two famous virgins, yet after reading these tales, you find there was no act of intercourse whatsoever. A shaft of light came through a completely bronze structure and the other a child was taken and put into Zeus's thigh and was considered half god. Some of these women in the Greek myths were supposed virgins, yet penetration had already occurred or some of these women had children already.[7] The only story out of Greek mythology that has any similarity to the Biblical account is that of Perseus. I only compare these two stories due to what we established in the first chapter of this book, based on Proverbs 6:23 and that is Light =Torah. In that the power of Yahweh's Holy Spirit spoke Torah to Mary's egg as we discussed in the paragraph above. Perseus's mother was visited by Zeus in the form of a golden shower of gold. There was no copulation described at all. Interestingly, this story is believed to have come from pre-Greek peoples north of Greece called proto-Indo-European. This would make perfect sense, coming from the Scythians or Baghars of the central Asian steppes as they pushed west and south into

India-Persia. However, the Baghars had converted to Judaism as a kingdom around 300 B.C.E. With this kingdom conversion, we see the Hebrew account of Yahweh's prophetic word of the light and virgin birth. Both of these concepts coming directly from Hebrew nomads and the prophetic scriptures within Judaism. In light of this information, it appears without doubt that these stories all came from the post flood world when exiting the ark, thus flourishing around the world.

The Hebraic source of creation shows us that when light was made, the Messiah was the prophecy of mankind's saving grace. Here, we see a perpetuated story in several cultures descended from Noah and the prophecy given to Noah, told generation to generation. In the Mithra myth, the god of light was also known as the "Light of the World" and the mediator between heaven and earth. This same god was adopted by the Romans and Greeks in the first century B.C.E. He was the soldiers' god.

True Islam, not the media or the religious right's version of Islam, tells of Mary's miraculous virginal conception of Yahshua.[8] This is interesting because it verifies the Jewish and Christian accounts of this supernatural historical event via the Prophets, the Torah, the apostles, the Magi (Zoroastrianism), and Josephus. It's truly amazing Yahweh's promise to mankind was fulfilled, and we were given eyewitness and historical accounts, historical evidence of four major religions, and five secular eyewitnesses. The five secular accounts are Publius Cornelius Tacitus[9], the Talmud[10], Josephus[11], Mara bar-Serapion[12], and Pliny the Younger. [13]

In all cultures across the earth pre-common era, we see a god for a particular emotion, realm, or facet of life here in this world and our universe. Friends, these stories line up with the Genesis six account all too well, revealing the ancient Hebrew belief system as the originator—not today's Judaism, as that religion came later.

Also, the other belief systems all depict these gods in human form or variants of anthropomorphism. I have not listed Judaism nor Islam, as both of these came from the Hebraic belief system or Abrahamic faith and are similar.

To be clear again: I am not saying that the stories of Perseus and Zarathustra are proof of virgin births. What I am highlighting is that these were what appear to be prophetic stories of pre-flood origin which were made into stories of actual god men who would help or save mankind. It's intriguing that neither of these two stories led to a path of redemption or eternal life.

They are stories of might and enlightenment which lead to the thought of humans making their way into salvation by their own human power and enlightenment, instead of a true savior showing the way to salvation through their power and enlightenment.

The truly beautiful aspect of this story is that the Bedouin herdsmen were given the gift to deliver this Torah to Jacob the patriarch, to Moshe, and then through the prophets, the word, and then finally as a man who fulfilled all things to become the Messiah - all by a miraculous conception.

This is Yahweh's Word, and that Word is light. He spoke it, and this is not advanced brain science. What we all do as humans is forget this book is about a father-and-son relation-ship. This Bible is not solely about Yahweh.

This canon of books is, for a large portion, about us and our story, our relationship with a loving Father and how we relate to the Kingdom of Heaven. A loving Elohim who wanted us; He did not need us, yet He wanted us!

Then what was going to make us happy, full, and complete? Torah! What we immediately do as children because we have an innate nature, that Yahweh gave us, is to think about the eternal.

What was before us? Where did we come from? Where did God come from?

I say this because the Genesis beginning is our beginning, our environment Yahweh made for us. Not the angels, not Satan, not Yahshua. Now, in our Creator's infinite wisdom, He knew we would choose our own way and not His way. We were given free choice. We were also given two trees to look at but not touch. The beginning of our world and envi-ronment as Yahweh was creating or about to create, first things first. Whether you are perfect or whether you choose to be imperfect, you must have Torah. Because Torah is Light, it is instruction. Here are some scriptures for reference:

Light: John 1:9, John 8:12, John 12:46, 2 Corinthians 4:6

Word: John 1:4, 1 John 5:10, Revelation 19:13

In the beginning was the Word,

and the Word was with God,

and the Word was God.

And	The	Word	Was	with	-	Yahweh
καί	ὁ	λόγος	ἦν	πρός	τὸν	Θεόν
2532 kaí (the most common NT conjunction, used over 9,000 times) – and (also), very often, moreover, even, indeed (the context determines the exact sense).	**G3588 ho** the, the definite article.	**3056 lógos** (from 3004 /légō, "speaking to a conclusion") – a word, being the expression of a thought; a saying. 3056 /lógos ("word") is preeminently used of Christ (Jn 1:1), expressing the thoughts of the Father through the Spirit.	**G2258 ane** Imperfect of G1510:-I (thou) was (wast or were)	**4314 prós** (a preposition) – properly, motion towards to "interface with" (literally, moving toward a goal or destination).	**G3588 ho** the, the definite article.	**2316 theós** (of unknown origin) – properly, God, the Creator and owner of all things

TORAH VS. LIGHT?

The second piece of the text is bringing home a very important understanding. We can see that **AND** at the beginning of the phrase is easy enough to figure out. Following a comma and elaborating, as in "moreover," information in the form of a conjunction.

We can see **THE** as the definite article for **WORD**.

WORD in this section of the text is interesting because the definition has varied slightly in exegesis, revealing the thought of the Father through His Holy Spirit who was actually doing the creating in the beginning of Genesis.

Try not to get ensnared in the concept that Yahweh's Holy Spirit is the same as Yahweh Himself! In short, the Father's thought of the Messiah, His son, was expressed through Yahweh's Holy Spirit who was hovering or fluttering in the beginning (Genesis 1:1).

Does this mean Yahshua was in existence there? Not at all, as neither text shows us this nor implies that idea. The thought or vision of the Messiah for this world is implied. After all, since the fall, that day in the garden, does the creation not groan? We know that the whole creation has been groaning as in the pains of childbirth right up to the present time. Romans 8:22.

Here we have **WAS** (**G2258**) *ane*, again, and this word is simply **WAS**.

WITH (**G4314**) *pros* is a preposition, and in this case, is the end result. Not as in the manifestation or embodiment of the Messiah, but the end goal is always with Yahweh, purpose is always in the forefront of His mind.

Now this creates a beautiful picture here! A waiting expectant father is in anticipation of His only son who will be created. On the flip side of that thought, we have the Father's anticipation that we will be accepted in the kingdom based on this thought after it will be manifested.

What is incredibly exciting here, stay with me, Yahweh is an excited expectant father waiting for us as well. (John 1:12, Galatians 3:26, Romans 8:14, 2 Corinthians 6:18)

That is hope, a blessed hope. An eventuality only Yahweh can provide under His direction and guidance and one that only Yahshua can deliver by being an obedient son.

The word *ho* (**G3588**) without an English translation is used because Yahweh is in direct relation to the preposition *pros* (with). This is the accusative case and is also used here because it answers the question "Who was with the Word?"

Finally, Yahweh is Yahweh. This cannot be Yahshua since we are speaking of the Creator in this line of text. We have already established that Yahweh's Holy Spirit hovered over creation – not Yahshua. Yahshua is the idea or thought upon which all this is being created.

Yahweh is complete, and all things will work properly or perfectly to create a symbiotic balance, an order or functional balance of systems. For examples of this playing out, look around you.

Because Yahweh spoke the Word, it was with Him. Because He spoke it, it was Yahweh's Word, His Light, His Instruction. Hebraically, it is often said that this is a concept of the Aleph-Bet. Specifically, each letter represents creation on some level, and each letter of the Hebrew Aleph-Bet was spoken by Yahweh to create our environment. This is a fascinating idea, and when we dig deeper into the language, we begin to see this concept played out. If the environment is being created for us, then the Torah would be right there with Him as He created. When we input Torah in place of Word, it gives amazing depth here: *In the beginning was Torah, and the Torah was with Yahweh, and the Torah was Yahweh.*

Allow me to explain more. The environment is being created for us because we need the sky, we need the land, we need the rivers and streams and oceans. All of the birds in the air, the fishes of the sea and all the land animals, all of the different flora that goes with each region, all of the ocean and river flora along with the forest, these all work together in perfect harmony as they are functional or **TOV**. That is to say: they are good.

Every animal kingdom listed above has animals which feed on their dead, and these animals are typically listed as nonfood. Why? Because they clean the earth and the waterways.

Most Christians believe that because of Yahshua, and with a complete misunderstanding of what He said, we just can eat what we want. It is incredible when we sit back and wonder why all these diseases and cancer exist, could this be the main culprit? Of course, we need to remember that this is not the only reason diseases or cancers abound. There are many cases where perfect diets have been followed yet cancer still struck with tragedy. Perfectly fit people with diets that meet biblical guidelines for food were followed, only to suffer a massive heart attack. When we take no regard of what our creator shared with us what is actually considered food for consumption and then eat all the bottom feeders, thereby allowing for the pollution of our environment to take place, we end up making our environment dysfunctional, or **RAH:** bad.

Anytime Yahweh the Father, not Yahshua, gives us a guidepost to follow, this is Torah.

Torah is not a list of laws. It is a set of guideposts in how to live a life toward Yahweh, others, and yourself.

This is supported by **Matthew 22:37: "Love Yahweh your Elohim with all your heart and with all your soul and with all your mind."**

Matthew 22:39: "Love your neighbor as yourself."

1 Corinthians 6:18: "Flee sexual immorality. Every sin that a man does is outside the body, but he who commits sexual immorality sins against his own body."

Isaiah 64:6: "We are all infected and impure with sin. When we display our righteous deeds, they are nothing but filthy rags. Like autumn leaves, we wither and fall, and our sins sweep us away like the wind."

If Torah is truly meant to be our guideposts for living, then they are Yahweh's words. If they are Yahweh's words, then they would be instructions.

As we have already discovered in Proverbs 6:23, instruction is a light.

That Light is Torah. The first light is Torah. Torah is Word! Then Light = Torah = Messiah, and the Messiah is the only way we can get to our Father (John 14:6, 1 Timothy 2:5).

Thus, Torah, not Yahshua, was right there with Yahweh at the beginning.

In the beginning was the Word, and the Word was with God, **and the Word was God.**

And	The	Word	Was	Yahweh
καί	ὁ	Λόγος	ἦν	Θεός

2532 kai (the most common NT conjunction, used over 9,000 times) – and (also), very often, moreover, even, indeed (the context determines the exact sense).

G3588 ho the, the definite article.

3056 lógos (from 3004 /légō, "speaking to a conclusion") – a word, being the expression of a thought; a saying. 3056 /lógos ("word") is preeminently used of Christ (Jn 1:1), expressing the thoughts of the Father through the Spirit.

G2258 ane Imperfect of G1510: I (thou) was (wast, were).

2316 theós (of unknown origin) – properly, God, the Creator and owner of all things (Jn 1:3; Gen 1 - 3).

CONCRETE HEBREW OR ABSTRACT GREEK?

This is a Hebraic idea, not a Greek idea. Greek thought would have us believe because Logos and the word Theos are joined by the word *ane* (**WAS**), that the text is saying: The Word was Yahweh.

However, *ane* (**G2258**) is "has been" or "was" in an imperfect past tense. What John conveyed was pretty direct and straightforward. He conveyed that while Yahweh's word is His own, now something is happening, something prophetic is coming to pass. Even today, the words we choose are our own, it is who we are.

Do actions speak louder than words? Yes! Case in point: having Yahshua there at creation makes no sense, as Yahweh spoke salvation and then created the action at the time of Mary, the cross, and the resurrection. Being Yahweh, this was manifest in His infinite wisdom and foresight at His timing. Thus, we have the scriptures Revelations 13:8 and Hebrews 1:1-3.

Does the thought of Yahshua at the creation of this world makes sense? No! Why does this not make any sense?

Having the Messiah at creation, who was chosen for a specific time, creating the world with Yahweh only to see it fall really makes the preexistent Messiah redundant.

Taking the phrase "slain from the foundation of the world" and apply to Yahshua omnipresence would equate Yahweh and Yahshua. This simply is nowhere to be found in the Scriptures.

When understanding Revelation 1:3, we must look to the Greek to see that the Logos is a thought uttered and is still encapsulated in a timeline of fulfillment by the Messiah.

Of course, the obvious reason is because the statement John is making is similar to how we should read Revelation in three parts to have a proper understanding of that book.

John is giving you a timeline in the typical writing style of John. John is in no way, shape, or form saying Yahshua was in existence before Genesis 1:1 or before Genesis 1:5. As I said earlier in this book, choosing our words carefully should be our top priority. Remember, since the translators took a Greek text from a translated Hebrew text to an English text, this functional concept put into Greek, Latin, and English thought created an issue.

However, the Hebrew thought is "the WORD was Yahweh," as in past tense. When this was translated, it seemed to the translators that the Logos and the Theos were the same. Wow, this was almost a translated Hebrew thought of John, but not quite because paganism took over. How?

Christian paganism, throughout church history albeit not all denominations, will tell you a god and his word (Logos meaning the divine expression that is, the Messiah and the first-person singular with Theos which is the supreme deity) means they, being the Logos and Theos – that is Yahshua and Yahweh—are the same or equal in power and authority. While there is truth that Yahweh is outside of time, we must not get confused in thought, as Yahweh created time, therefore He is time. Yahweh is all in all, and that simply means He is everything because He created it. Since the dispersion of mankind at Babel these trinitarian or dualistic beliefs have flourished. As mankind got further from the ark, the stories, dialects, and concepts changed like a game of telephone. The most influential and powerful cultures, such as the Chaldean and Babylonian, furthered these concepts, and we can see them expressed in Hinduism, Egyptian mythology, and other various religions in world history. A quick search on these religions and myths will reveal these concepts.

In understanding the scripture in the Greek, the word *logos* was chosen because of its root **(G3004)** *Lego* – to lay forth, generally referring to an individual expression of speech, shew, speak to utter. The word *Logos* **(G3056)** is something said by implication a subject, reasoning, or motive, concerning doctrine, speech, utterance, word, and work. Even further back **(G2036)** *epo* – command, **(G5346)** *phemi*-to show or make known one's thoughts, **(G5316)** *phaino*-to lighten as in shine, and then **(G5457)** *phos*-from an obsolete to shine or make manifest. The word **WAS** in the Greek takes you to **(G2258)** *ane*- I was (wast or were) Imperfect of **(G1510)** *eimi*-first person singular present indicative, leading to **(G1498)** *eien* present of. *Theos* **(G2316)** of uncertain affinity; a deity especially the supreme Divinity with **(G3588)** *ho*-the definite article.

So, what is being read here is:

The Word (the speech, utterance, by reason or motive, to show or make known one's thoughts, to lighten or to shine, The Torah)

was (present of, I, first person singular)

Yahweh (of uncertain origin, a deity, especially the Supreme Divinity, the definite article (part of speech that identifies a specific noun).

Idea (the utterance reasoned that shone present of the first-person singular the Supreme Divinity)

Thought (The Torah/the Word – I will send a son/ slain from the foundation of the world was Yahweh's thought of his son)

At this point, we should see the expressed thought uttered by the Father was a word. That word is clearly the remediation to the creation and its steward that has fallen which is mankind. That remediation is Yahshua! However, not in a physical form co-creating with Yahweh, otherwise that would be redundant for a few reasons. The first reason is the one I expressed earlier (a god cannot save mankind by death). There is not one scripture where Yahweh says that He will come down as a man born of a virgin, nor is there a scripture that cites where Yahweh says that a God must be the atonement for mankind's sin. This is a pagan concept which has never worked or come to pass which is another concept of saving mankind that has surfaced in multiple religions, cults, and belief systems.

The idea that a half-human/half-god, a Greek concept, never produced any results on saving anyone except a few men because one hero happened to have great genes and was really brave, yet not one ever offered eternal life! Secondly, if Yahshua created the creation then had to come and save us, then are you sure Yahshua could do it a second time and not fail again? And then should we say a third time because the law given at the mountain in Leviticus is a growing belief that this was Yahshua is actually the Yahweh of the Old Testament. Sounds like this Yahshua character sure did have a lot of bad plans for saving humankind.

Thirdly, when you knowingly put a man in the position of equality with the King of the Universe, you have just blasphemed Yahweh's Holy Spirit who is Yahweh.

In **Genesis 1:26**, we read, **"And Elohim said, 'Let us make man in our image, and our likeness: and let them have dominion over the fish of the sea, and over the fowl of the air, and over the cattle, and over all the earth and over every creeping thing that creepeth upon the earth.'"**

In this verse, we can see something that has perplexed a lot of men and women over the millennia. What is image and what is likeness? I propose that image is not how we are *shaped*, as this would be heresy since Yahweh is not form. Now, this may come as a shock to most readers, as we have been taught since 200 B.C.E. that Yahweh is in the form of a man. This is false doctrine and has no Biblical basis whatsoever. Yahweh is majesty, pure energy, and power. He is and was and is still.

People read Genesis and assume when Moshe described Adam and Eve walking in the garden with Yahweh that Yahweh was walking. What the text actually says is that Adam and Eve walked, and Yahweh was there with them. Not in a bodily form. Yahweh's Holy Spirit is Yahweh, not a separate member of a trio. Yahweh and His Holy Spirit are the same being, not two distinct beings and certainly not a third person.

Let us take a look at this concept, as this is a major dividing point for two reasons. The first being it was borrowed from belief systems of old. Additionally, the Roman Catholic Church incorporated this as a way to make the Roman Empire more inclusive. By 800 A.D., this was just ignorance of our roots and the lack of personal study time within the word due to illiteracy and the rules set up by the church.

Now we need to search the Old Testament to find the truth. The Old Testament is not about the Jews, per se; it is about us as believers being adopted into the commonwealth of Israel and how the Jewish faith had an impact on humanity, cultures, and the Hebraic mindset. This led to Christianity becoming a major religion when, in fact, it is simply a belief system in whom the true God is included!

Isaiah 11:1-2 reveals the seven spirits of Yahweh — wisdom, understanding, counsel, strength, knowledge, fear. Wait, that seems to be only six. Where is the seventh? The first one listed is actually right there at the beginning of verse two, stating Yahweh's Holy Spirit is the spirit of Yahweh. Is your spirit apart from you? To answer this question, we must understand we can control our spirit, and we can control our flesh. If our spirit was a separate being of ourselves yet emanated from ourself, we would be schizophrenic.

Schizophrenia is defined as: a mental illness that is characterized by disturbances in thought (such as delusions), perception (such as hallucinations), and behavior (such as disorganized speech or catatonic behavior), by a loss of emotional responsiveness and extreme apathy, and by noticeable deterioration in the level of functioning in everyday life.[14]

We also need to also understand the definition of multiple personality disorder: a personality disorder that is characterized by the presence of two or more distinct and complex identities or personality states each of which becomes dominant and controls behavior from time to time to the exclusion of the others and results from disruption in the integrated functions of consciousness, memory, and identity.[15]

What did our master Yahshua say? **Matthew 26:41: "Watch and pray so that you will not fall into temptation. The spirit is willing, but the flesh is weak."**

In Genesis 1:26, we see where man is made in the image and likeness of Yahweh. Yahweh's Holy Spirit is the mode in which Yahweh comes to this earth or executes an action. Yahweh, as an entity, is power, like an energy source. He is all in all and that is why it is abhorrent, an abomination, and sacrilege to draw or think of Yahweh as a human form. In the mode of spirit, that is His Holy Spirit, one cannot draw a spirit either!

The image, *tselem* צֶלֶם (**H6754**) is the mode, outline, or resemblance of Yahweh's Holy Spirit. This is the representative of our flesh to Yahweh, yet it is not a separate being, it is who we are. Your name defines this spirit and is your character and will be judged accordingly.

This is why, my friends, we must overcome the flesh, bringing it into submission, as it will overpower our spirit and we will account for our character. The likeness, *demuth* דְּמוּת (**H1823**) is to fashion or to be like, as this word is a verb, thus the way we think and utter, our reasoning. This solely comes from the likeness of our creator. We are given this to perform the tasks that we need to do to function. These are our mental faculties where we are given power over our flesh and spirit to be in control of who and what we are. We are in control of our own destiny (Genesis 4:7)!

In Genesis 2:7, we see that the breath of life is given to respire and then man became a living creature. Here, we see Yahweh's spirit blew into our nostrils the breath of life, thus activating the spirit and the flesh so that our bodily and mental faculties turned on for function.

This is also described in John 1:3. This life or the ability to respire was the light of men and this caused the "puffing up" of the man and the light in his eye. These items, all the same being with no difference, and that was Yahweh in the mode of His Holy Spirit that created man.

Who is the Holy Spirit? Yahweh, pure and simple.

Now go back to Isaiah 11:2 and reread the passage. The seven spirits of Yahweh are not eight beings, as that would cause issues for trinitarians. Then we would have multiple gods and that is not Hebraic, Judaic, nor Christian. Isaiah 11:2 also shows emphatically and prophetically that Yahweh's Holy Spirit infilled Yahshua at his baptism. This is one of the most important scriptures concerning the Messiah that a Christian could ever have. That Messiah was a man, not a god, demigod, nor God himself. He was a man that willingly gave up his manhood to be a sacrifice for us and fulfill the role of Messiahship.

Here is the other heresy with the trinitarian doctrine: Yahweh is a person. Preposterous. Yahweh is Divine and not one of us. Why Elohim, then? Why this big deal about *Us* in the text of Genesis 1:26. Two simple reasons. the first being Elohim is powers. That's it!

He is the majesty and the power of this divine, supreme

being. Who is Yahweh speaking to? To the Earth, as in the dirt, his creation. Simple! Something like, "Hey, you and me, you have the matter and I have the know-how."

This verse does not show Yahweh speaking to His Holy Spirit and to Yahshua to create life or man. Elohim being powers is plural.[16] Not as in multiple gods but all empowering. When you see Abraham using my Elohim, he is not using this word to describe multiple gods, he is using this word to describe the powers that drive Abraham's life. The Powers that encompass who and what Yahweh is! Of course, you can use this in a singular, such as My Elohim, however you might consider using "My Eloah" instead. The Hebraic concept is such that a people or group, man or woman or anyone who picks this book, whether they be Jewish, Muslim, Christian, atheist, agnostic, or whatever they may believe, Elohim is used as a plural where a group of people, men or women is the plural aspect, not Yahweh. This was accepted and changed during the early years within the kingdom of Judah.[17] The identity of Yahweh is powers, not multiplicity. Again, this word is not God or gods, thus the plural ending is actually incorrect in its current understanding of the word Elohim (God). As Maimonides said: "I must premise that every Hebrew [now] knows that the term Elohim is a homonym, and denotes God, angels, judges, and the rulers of countries."[18] The Hebrew language has several nouns with -im (masculine plural) and -oth (feminine plural) endings which nevertheless take singular verbs, adjectives, and pronouns. Some examples of these are: Baalim, Adonim, Behemoth. This plural form is known as the "honorific plural," in which the pluralization is a sign of power or honor.[19]

Now back to the main point of: "What is image and what is likeness?"

Image is character and *likeness* is the ability to have a thought and formulate that thought into words to speak and write. When I use character for image, you have to understand that when you name something, you have authority over that person or thing until you die, marry, or relinquish that authority. However, this is not prevalent in our culture anymore.

This is why names are so important, and that is why names are changed biblically in certain situations and in certain applications. That name is your character, not an identifier.

Thus, we have a character just like Yahweh has a character. The image is not hands, feet, ten fingers, and so on. The image is our process of thought and intelligence, the ability to live forever, and the ability to know good and evil. These points are very important to understand as we progress in the following chapters.

Jews, or better yet Hebrews, never once thought of Yahweh in human form until the Greek empire came along. Egypt, Babylon, Persia, all had human-form gods, yet the Jews rejected that idea, as it was abstract and an abomination. By the time the Greeks took over, the Hebrew people were tired of their captivity, and they adapted so they could assimilate and live in peace in their land. This was the beginning of a huge divide religiously, politically, and socially, unlike what the world had ever experienced to that point.

Early Christians knew this, as did the Jews, and were divided, and this still continues to this day.

Yahweh appeared to Abraham, the finger of Yahweh appeared to Moshe to write the commandments, the elders saw brass feet and stared at what appeared to be Yahweh. Does this make Yahweh a human form because he manifested a hand or that the *malak* that is a messenger angel that Yahweh chose?

Yahweh's Holy Spirit, who is Yahweh, filled the Angel of Yahweh and chose that messenger to deliver a Word to Abraham, to Moshe, and to the elders. Now what about when Moshe hid in the crevice of a rock as Yahweh went by? Pretty clear to me that Yahweh in His absolute state passed by Moshe and His presence was so great that Moshe glowed afterward.

What about Jacob and the angel? There was no angel, text never says that. The text says a man wrestled with Jacob. Yahshua? Can't be Yahshua, as he was not in existence yet due to John 1:1. Besides, if Yahshua was preexistent, then he would not be a man, would he?

To go back and forth between heaven and earth indicates a divine nature. Now we are back to our salvation question, and if it is possible, Yahshua went between earth and heaven since we have the thought that Yahshua was divine or preexistent.

Instead, we understand Jacob wrestled himself. This is a major psychological lesson from our creator in how we think, behave, and react to stressful situations, and how you can overcome and overcome in a righteous way.

What happened to Jacob? He crossed the river, and his

life was changed forever that fateful daybreak. Even to the point of a name change which indicates a character change!

Again, we must slowdown in reading, highlight a questionable text, and then word-study that verse and word(s), look for the cultural application of the text, and then pray and seek Yahweh's understanding.

We must ask Yahweh's Holy Spirit to reveal what is being relayed.

In this way, we grow a deep meaningful relationship with our Father.

CHAPTER 3
DECLENSION, DOMINOES, AND A TIMELINE
THE JOHN 1:1 FACTOR

I n the previous chapter, we were able to look at each of the words in verse one and dig deep into the thought John was delivering. Of course, to the untrained eye, it seems as though anyone could have written this chapter. The Hebrew concepts discovered within the text allow us to become aware that John did indeed write this chapter in Hebrew and translate it to Greek. This occurred when John chose the word Logos. This idea came from the Word of Yahweh spoken in Genesis 1:3, and translated into Greek, the correct word used was Logos. This allowed John to stay in sync with Torah, Law, and Yahshua's teachings which complemented all three very well.

We also discovered Yahweh was alone in the making of our domain and, in His infinite wisdom, foresaw our fall, followed by the subsequent destruction of creation. John revealed Yahweh through a thought and then uttered a word. This word would eventually become a man, and our salvation promised of old. John also strengthened the idea from his forefathers that Yahweh was without form.

The last chapter also gives a strong indication the Torah was spoken here. The Word is Torah. Torah would be fulfilled one day by this thought, paving the way for our salvation and allowing us to walk Torah better, despite our mistakes.

This does not mean Yahshua was there the whole time with Yahweh (eternal, pre incarnate) nor does this mean that Yahshua was preexistent to his birth (pre-existence). This does mean Yahweh created the world beginning with Torah (Word), with the thought of the Messiah in His mind even then. Later, His son who would be slain for our fall and missing of the mark, and this *thought* is with Yahweh from the beginning of our created environment: to give His only begotten son to die for the world.

This is Torah, Word, Light. The Hebrew thought is a concerted idea, as in a marriage, an assembly, or two siblings, a father and son can be one, as in of one accord; however, not one in being! John never intended to equate Yahshua with Yahweh.

This is backed up by:

The same was in the beginning with Yahweh. John 1:2

He	was	in the	beginning	with	-	Yahweh
οὗτος	ἦν	ἐν	ἀρχῇ	πρὸς	τὸν	θεόν

He / οὗτος

G3778 Houtos - From the article G3588 and G846; the, he (she, it) that is, this, or that (often repeated) -- he

G3588 ho - The masculine feminine (second) and neuter (third) forms in all their inflections; the definite article -he.

G846 autos - From the particle au (perhaps akin to G109 through the idea of a baffling wind; backward; (1) self (emphatic) (2) he, she, it (used for the third person pronoun) (3) the same. Also, see G848 same. Also, see G848 hautou- a contraction for G1438; self.

G1438 heautou - him -self, alone.

was / ἦν

G2258 ane - imperfect of G1510, I (thou) was (wast or were).

G1510 eimi - Imperfect of eimi; I am (thou, etc.) Was (wast or were) -- + agree, be, X have (+ charge of), hold, use, was(-t), were.

in the / ἐν

G1722 en - A primary preposition denoting (fixed) position (in place, time or state), and (by implication) instrumentality (medially or constructively), i.e. A relation of rest (intermediate between G1519 and ek); "in," at, (up-)on, by, etc. -- about, after, against, + almost, X altogether, among, X as, at, before, between, (here-)by (+ all means), for (... Sake of), + give self wholly to, (here-)in(-to, on), while, X mightily, (because) of, (up-)on, one, X quickly, X shortly, [speedi-]ly, X that, X there(-in, -on), through(-out), (un-)to(-ward), under, when, where(-with), while, with(-in). Often used in compounds, with substantially the same import, rarely with verbs of motion, and then not to indicate direction, except (elliptically) by a separate (and different) preposition.

beginning / ἀρχῇ

G746 arxe - From G756; (properly abstract) a commencement, or (concretely) chief (in various applications of order, time, place, or rank) -- beginning, corner, (at the, the) first (estate), magistrate, power, principality, principle, rule.

G756 archomai - Middle voice of archo (through the implication of precedence); to commence (in order of time) -- (rehearse from the) begin(-ning).

with / πρὸς

G4314 prós - a preposition of direction; forward to, i.e. Toward (with the genitive case, the side of, i.e. Pertaining to; with the dative case, by the side of, i.e. Near to; usually with the accusative case, the place, time, occasion, or respect, which is the destination of the relation, i.e. Whither or for which it is predicated) -- about, according to, against, among, at, because of, before, between, (where-)by, for, X at thy house, in, for intent, nigh unto, of, which pertain to, that, to (the end that), X together, to (you)-ward, unto, with(-in). In the comparative case, it denotes essentially the same applications, namely, motion towards, accession to, or nearness at.

- / τὸν

G3588 ton the, the definite article.

Yahweh / θεόν

2316 theós - (of unknown origin) -- properly, God, the Creator and owner of all things

CULTURAL APPROPRIATION

Verse two must be understood correctly. What I mean by that is the Septuagint reads "this was," not He. This word Houtos is a demonstrative pronoun – nominative masculine singular. A demonstrative must point to something specific preceding the pronoun it is describing. The definition for demonstrative is serving as conclusive evidence of something; giving proof and (of a person) tending to show feelings, especially of affection, openly.[1]

Three grammar rules for demonstrative pronouns are:

• Demonstrative pronouns always identify nouns, whether those nouns are named specifically or not. For example: "I can't believe this." We have no idea what "this" is, but it's definitely something the writer cannot believe. It exists, even though we don't know what it is.

• Demonstrative pronouns are usually used to describe animals, places, or things; however, they can be used to describe people when the person is identified, i.e.: "This sounds like Mary singing."

• Do not confuse demonstrative adjectives with demonstrative pronouns. The words are identical, but demonstrative adjectives qualify nouns, whereas demonstrative pronouns stand alone.

The reason I bring this up is that it is the crux of the matter and where most readers get confused as to whose Word it actually is at this point. In translating this over to English, there was an assumption made by the translators that appears to be guided by an eisegesis. While "this" is a masculine form of the Greek demonstrative pronoun, the thought (Logos) is masculine, thus should not have been assumed it was "Yahshua." That is a doctrinal assumption made by the translator. As in verse one and two, we are speaking of the "word" which is masculine as well. This can only be describing "the Word," as Yahweh is already in place and is the accusative noun in the two verses. We also see the nominative case. The nominative case is the case used for a noun or pronoun which is the subject of a verb.

What is the verb in this text? It is **WAS (G1510)** *eimi*. This is also backed by verse one, and this word being the verb there as well. The subject is the Word, and we know this grammatically by following the rules of our language and the Greek language.

This is also confirmed by the masculinity of the pronoun and the subject in which it is describing. The issue becomes why the choice of "He" was used in translation. The Septuagint and the King James followed the rules of grammar to a T! They translated **(G3778)** *houtos* as "this." You can also use "such," as I believe it better fits what John is articulating. If John wanted to use "He" for the pronoun, then it would be **(G2076)** *esti*. This is a third person singular present indicative, as that would be making a statement about "He" being in the beginning with Yahweh. Yet that is not what is used.

For good reasons, Yahshua and his disciples were not well-liked by the religious leaders and the Roman authorities. In Judaism, around 200-100 B.C.E., we see a change in ideas about the nature of Yahweh. The influx of Western thinking invaded Judaism to a degree that changed Judaism altogether. John, being a disciple of Yahshua, would not have put Yahweh into a manly form, as this was sacrilege to orthodox Judaism.

Thus, the modern-day religious and government authorities, whose idea was to keep peace at all cost, did not appreciate Yahshua's message of getting back to the root of their belief system. My point here is that John would never have equated Yahshua with Yahweh.

John is telling us that Logos was the Hope, the Light, and the Truth. This was the Messianic promise to come stated in Genesis 1:3. Why do most translations use He? This is solely to put into your mind, based on a doctrine, that this Yahshua was a blue-eyed, blond-haired, white, European-dressed man. Coupled with the fact this white man was in the heavens with Yahweh and created the known universe with his dad.

This is a racist, economical, emotional, philosophical, institutional, cultural, and theological statement to the rest of the world that the white European power base is in control. Even though Isaiah 53 described what the Messiah would look like, the religious power base shaped for centuries what Jesus was and would look like to propagate control locally and internationally through an accepted belief system.

The King James version of the translation has the best rendering of the text: "The same was in the beginning with God." In the Greek Interlinear, the chosen text reads, "This was in the original toward the God," and in The Scriptures translation, the text chosen is: "He was in the beginning with Elohim." Even within the Hebrew Roots movement we see Catholicism and Protestantism baggage being carried over.

I chose to use what Bible Hub uses, as it still works, and it is close to all of these examples. Checking the text utilizing Bible Hub, different scripture translations, and older manuscripts will also prove the main point that the thought is the Logos and not Yahshua at this point. So often this is translated as "He was in the beginning with Yahweh."

These translators inserted a doctrine created by the Catholic church and Protestant reformation, not the actual meaning of the word! This is problematic at best, as it is a pagan concept.

Look, if Yahshua was eternal with Yahweh, then there are two Gods. If Yahshua is preexistent with Yahweh, then he is divine. If God or a divine being (son) was conceived by insemination in Mary's womb by that God, then our salvation is useless, it is bunk. Why? Because we must have a brother completely in the flesh be perfect, be the Word, be the Torah in order to be the spotless Lamb of Yahweh to be the perfect sacrifice to atone for our sins!

Read the Law in Leviticus chapters 1-8. In the law you see the sacrificial system which allowed for a man or woman to be brought back into grace. Hence, Yahshua had to fulfill this blood atonement once and for all. Otherwise, this would be another story from every other manmade pagan religion ever created since before the flood. In John 1, verse two is a complete reiteration of the first verse. This often happens in Hebrew text and is indicative of a very intense idea. Using repetition, the writer is telling you a very important piece of information in a very forceful literary way.

Let's prove that! Taking the word *Houtos,* we can see that it is a pronoun. Strong's goes further to say **G3778** *Houtos* – a demonstrative pronoun typically rendered as *that, he, she, it.* This changes some things already, however, let us continue. Houtos sends us to **G3588** *ho* - a definite article the, this, that one, he, she, it.

Houtos also sends us to **G846** *autos* – from the particle *au* (perhaps akin to the base of G109 through the idea of a baffling wind; **G109** *aer* – from *aemi* (to breathe unconsciously that is respire; by analogy to blow); air (as naturally circumambient – air. Compare **G5594** *psucho* – a primary verb; to breathe (voluntarily but gently; thus, differing on the one hand from **G4154** which is to breathe hard that is a breeze: - blow; and on the other from the base of **G109** which refers properly to an inanimate breeze) that is (by implication of reduction of temperature by evaporation) to chill (figuratively); - wax cold.

In short, this thought was now reiterated and confirmed by Yahweh. This is also revealing that this thought was basically put on hold until the proper time. In no way is this text saying Yahshua was given life or breath. It is saying Yahweh's Holy Spirit will give life to this idea at the appointed time, and this idea or thought (Logos) will be a male, and it will breathe like you and me.

This (the thought that was uttered) **was** (expresses being) The word "was" is used again, and you can see how this particular word is being used just like it was in verse one in a place of time or at a point. **In the** (the realm of) **beginning** (is just revealing the summit, the starting point).

This verse alone knocks out the idea once and for all that Yahshua existed before Genesis 1:1. Why? Clearly, we can see with the Greek words chosen by John this was an idea from the beginning of the creation. This was not a thought before the creation of our domain, therefore impossible for Yahshua to be alive or existing before Genesis. **With**, the word chosen *pros* is a great choice by its definition. In the genitive case with Yahweh and same for the dative case under the beginning. In the accusative case, this would be a causative case in Greek, so the rendering is the beginning with respect to the destination of Yahweh at the appointed time. The relation or destination is the fallen into decay or decline (whither) being predicated by Yahweh's appointed time. *Theos* is understood as **Yahweh**, the owner and creator of all things. A more in-depth translation of this verse would be: ***This same thought uttered was expressed or given in the beginning with that is inline and constant with Yahweh.*** This verse is strictly a reiteration of verse one revealing the Messiah, that is Yahshua, in word only as in a prophetic sense.

This also allows for the hitting home that our El is one. **Deuteronomy 6:4 *"Hear, O Israel: Yahweh is our ELOHIM, Yahweh the one and only. (Shema Israel Yahweh Elohenu Yahweh echad.)"***

All things through him came into being; and without him came into being not even one thing that has come into being. **John 1:3**

All things
Πάντα

G3956 panta /pas ("each, every") means "all" in the sense of "each (every) part that applies." The emphasis of the total picture then is on "one piece at a time." 365 (ananeóō) then focuses on the part(s) making up the whole – viewing the whole in terms of the individual parts.

through
δι'

G1223 dia preposition -through, on account of, because of, properly, across (to the other side), back-and-forth to go all the way through, "successfully across" ("thoroughly"). 1223 (diá) is also commonly used as a prefix and lend the same idea ("thoroughly," literally, "successfully" across to the other side), is a root of the English term diameter ("across to the other side, through").

Him
αὐτοῦ

G846 autou (1) self (emphatic) (2) he, she, it (used for the third person pronoun) (3) the same. Usage: he, she, it, they, them, same. In itself it signifies nothing more than again, applied to what has either been previously mentioned or, when the whole discourse is looked at, must necessarily be supplied. From the particle au (perhaps akin to G109 through the idea of a baffling wind, space).

came into being
γίνομαι

G1096 ginomai – properly, to emerge, become, transitioning from one point (realm, condition) to another, means "to become, and signifies a change of condition, state or place. means to come into being/manifestation implying motion, movement, or growth" (at 2 Pet 1:4). Thus, it is used for God's actions as emerging from eternity and becoming (showing themselves) in time (physical space).

And	without	Him	came into being
καὶ	χωρὶς	αὐτοῦ	γίνομαι

G2532 kai – and (also), very often, moreover, even, indeed (the context determines the exact sense).

G5565 chōris - (a preposition, also used as an adverb which is probably derived from 5561 /xōra, "an open or detached space") – properly, apart from, separated ("without"); (figuratively) detached, rendering something invalid or valid.

G5561 chora through the idea of an empty expanse; room that is space or territory (more or less extensive, often including its inhabitants)

G5117 topos a spot (generally in space but limited to occupancy; whereasG5561 is a larger but particular locality that is location.

G846 autou -From the particle au (perhaps akin to G109 through the idea of a baffling wind; backward; (1) self (emphatic) (2) he, she, it (used for the third person pronoun) (3) the same. Usage: he, she, it, they, them, same. In itself it signifies nothing more than again, applied to what has either been previously mentioned or, when the whole discourse is looked at, must necessarily be supplied. Also, see G848 hautou- a contraction for G1438; self.

G1438 heautou - him -self, alone.

G1096 ginomai – a prolonged and middle form of a primary verb; to cause to be (generate) that is to be (generate) that is (reflexively) to become (come into being) used with great latitude (literally, figuratively, intensely etc.) arise, be assembled, be (fall, come, have self) be brought (to pass), to emerge, become, transitioning from one point (realm, condition) to another, means "to become, and signifies a change of condition, state or place. means to come into being/manifestation implying motion, movement, or growth" (at 2 Pet 1:4). Thus, it is used for God's actions as emerging from eternity and becoming (showing themselves) in time (physical space). God forbid, be ordained.

| Not even | one thing | that | has come into being |
| οὐδέ | ἕν | ὅ | γίνομαι |

G3761 oude – ("neither indeed," "nor indeed") introduces a statement that is negated factually and deductively (it occurs 137 times in the NT). That is, the negation rules out (invalidates) the statement that precedes it, and what naturally extends from it. This is analogous to the following: Because 100 is not enough, then neither are 90, 80, or 70 because they are all included in 100. Thus if "A" (100 in the previous example) is invalid, so is what necessarily follows (statement "B" – 90, 80, 70).

G1520 hen - one. a primary number

G3739 ho a demonstrative pronoun, this, that. usually rel. who, which, that, also demonstrative this, that, usually rel. who, which, that, also demonstrative this, that

G1096 ginomai – a prolonged and middle form of a primary verb; to cause to be (generate); that is (reflexively) to become (come into being) used with great latitude (literally, figuratively, intensely etc.) arise, be assembled, be (fall, come, have self) be brought (to pass), to emerge, become, transitioning from one point (realm, condition) to another. means "to become, and signifies a change of condition, state or place. means to come into being/manifestation implying motion, movement, or growth" (at 2 Pet 1:4). Thus, it is used for God's actions as emerging from eternity and becoming (showing themselves) in time (physical space). God forbid, be ordained

DOMINOES FALLING

Firstly, there are two questions begging to be answered, since this verse is the basis for believing this is Yahshua and also that Yahshua co-created with Yahweh at Genesis 1:3. The two questions are: Who is him? and why is him not capitalized?

Secondly, we need to make sure we notice the semicolon after the first six words of this verse. The semicolon is very important and tells us something. A semicolon is used to split what could easily become a run-on sentence. In this case, the semicolon is being used to link two independent clauses which are closely related in thought. When a semicolon joins two or more ideas in one sentence, those ideas are given equal rank. This is extremely important, as there are two ideas here and each one is as important as the other. While there is not an upside-down question mark in the Greek text to signify a semicolon, there is a comma.

The English language would have not allowed this; hence, the semicolon. Therefore, this verse is a dual thought and not actual duality, as is often misunderstood from this verse. Why do I know this?

Theos is still the direct object in this sentence. Even if you argue that it is *Logos*, you would have to explain how because *Logos* would be the Word or Torah and *Theos* would be who is creating. *Theos* is the supreme Deity—who is Yahweh. The Word at this point is *Logos* which is speech or utterance. So, through the Word were all things made and without The Word nothing was made that was made.

Now, I can and will agree that Yahshua was the ultimate thought here as the definitive final purpose. I am not equating Yahshua to Yahweh, but Yahshua the thought of saving grace for humanity, the Hebrew Aleph-Bet, and the heir apparent. This is still not Yahshua because the text does not say the Word was made flesh yet.

All things (**G3956** – *declension which is the variation of the form of a noun, pronoun, or adjective by which its grammatical case, number, and gender are identified and a condition of decline or moral deterioration.*) **Were made** (**G1096** *ordained or come to pass.*) **by** (**G1223** *channel of an act – through*) **him** (**G846** *baffling wind*) – *ruach?* Is this the Holy Spirit?

Dissecting this first sentence, we see **all things** (that is the human timeline, you, me, and every living thing affected by declension), associated with this thought (the Messianic plan) **through** (act or channel or diameter) **him** (Yahweh's Holy Spirit) **came into being**, (emerged or was made).

We should pause here and have a discussion concerning the word declension. The Greek word *pas* is an adjective in a nominative case, neuter gender and plural. This is pertaining to all things, or all kingdoms on the earth hence, the neutered gender and plurality. When I speak of kingdoms I am not speaking of different nations, peoples and tongues although that is included. The idea here would be kingdoms as in mankind, the animal kingdom, plant kingdom - the earth itself. This can be backed up with Scripture: **"*For we know that the whole creation groans and labors with birth pangs together until now. Not only that, but we also who have the firstfruits of the Spirit,*** *even we ourselves groan within ourselves, eagerly waiting for the adoption, the redemption of our body."* **Romans 8:22-23.** Upon further study one could also see this idea expressed in the garden where there was a state of function not disfunction until the disobedience of mankind. Why did the rest of creation suffer this disobedience? Well, because mankind was put in charge as a steward of this created realm.

The word declension is not in the actual text yet we can see where the Greek word *pas* is in a state of declension grammatically. Interestingly enough, the second definition of declension is a moral or ethical decline, slope downward. Given the scripture above and the 'state' of the garden itself, until affected by mankind, we have seen the continual downward slope both ethically and morally. I took some time and looked in all four gospels, the Book of Acts and Romans and discovered that each time this Greek word *pas* is used by the author it denotes declension (moral and ethical decline) within the context of the speaker, subject, or narrative. Furthermore, this choice of word in this tense, construct and form is only used in twenty seven percent of the verses utilizing the word *pas* in both definitions in all four gospels. This is incredible and I believe that this something that has been staring us in the face this whole time!

Understanding declension in its full form and only in the nominative neuter plural case as an adjective is crucial to our faith. This has major implications for the Jews and Muslims as well. I say that because when we understand the omniscient, omnipresence and omnipotence of the one true God we see that the Messiah was *born* at the right time and at the right place for humanity. This also shows the majesty of Yahweh in that He is One and acted alone in creation and 'all things' were made for Messiah with the end result being – that we can have a redeemed, restored relationship with our Creator.

The idea being expressed is the creation, not Yahshua or even the idea that all of creation was created by him. What the text is saying is that Yahweh's Holy Spirit created all of this with the thought of the Messiah to rescue this that which would suffer by declension. There are no capital letters in Hebrew. In English, we differentiate with the use of capitals for proper nouns. This is why some later versions of the text will have a capital for Him and earlier versions will not. *His Holy Spirit* would be proper English, as this is Yahweh's Holy Spirit. Him is correct as well because Yahweh is the Holy Spirit, not a separate entity of Yahweh. Hence, the reason Yahshua says in John 16:7: "Nevertheless, I tell you the truth; It is expedient for you that I go away: for if I go not away, the Comforter will not come unto you; but if I depart, I will send him unto you."

When we break down verse three, we see Yahweh knowing that declension (a decline or moral deterioration) would happen which was ordained to pass a channel of an act (the thought of a son (Messiah)) by a baffling wind (Yahweh's Holy Spirit.) All things were made by him (Yahweh's Holy Spirit), **and** (because of the semicolon the use of "and" is for the same thought process carried forth to present another idea) **without** (separately or apart from) **Him** (baffling wind Yahweh's Holy Spirit) **came into being** (God forbid, ordained to come to pass). **Not** (not!) **one thing** (not even one). **That** (that which pointing to the article). **Has come into being** (God forbid, ordained to come to pass.) So, as importantly as the aforementioned, apart from this idea of a son (messiah) this baffling wind (Holy Spirit) God forbid not anything, not even one thing that God forbid. Thus, and without him was not anything made that was made. In other words, Yahweh's Holy Spirit was the only One doing the creating!

We must keep in context what John is speaking about, the beginning of our time and how we will be impacted and how our Father (Yahweh) will remediate this for us and His creation. His Holy Spirit created all of this and that is Yahweh and it hovered or fluttered, and that fluttering is a baffling wind. All these conditions were ordained by an act or through His Holy Spirit.

Basically, Yahweh by His Holy Spirit allowed the conditions to develop to reveal the need for a Messiah, and there was in no way anyone or anything was getting in the way! An elaborate version of the text: *Everything that was ordained to come to pass came under declension through the action of Yahweh's Holy Spirit; moreover, apart from Yahweh's Holy Spirit forbid ordained to come to pass nothing not even one was allowed to come to pass.*

Allow me to create a scenario in your mind's eye. When we read the Genesis 1 creation account, we see Yahweh's Holy Spirit hovering. Yahweh thought, "I will create life on this sphere," so he begins making plans and imagining what this will look like upon completion.

Now picture, if you will, someone who has created an elaborate domino setup, complete with all kinds of interesting and intriguing moves for these dominoes. Now we are looking at billions of dominoes all lined up and ready to fall to create a beautiful picture after all the dominoes have fallen. So, at the moment Yahweh's thought to create comes into play, the dominoes tip, beginning with the first one. Is Yahweh everlasting? Isaiah 40:28, 1 Timothy 6:16, Psalm 33:6, Psalm 90:2. These dominoes are you, me, Sally, and George. Yahweh sees the moral and ethical decline, and then the thought of salvation comes to mind and emerges (**G1096**). This thought *is* the Messiah, i.e. "I will send a son so they may be saved." They can accept or decline.

This is the answer to the two trees in the garden. The age-old question: "If Yahweh knew we would rebel, then why did He put them in the garden in the first place?" which boasts a most common answer: "I do not know." Well, the reason those trees were put there was a gift. Not a gift for the future use of those trees. Yahweh could have done that at any time!

He purposely put those trees to offer the saving salvation of a Messiah. Why? In Hebrews 12, we see Yahshua is the author and finisher of our faith. This alone is given to Yahshua by Yahweh's Holy Spirit who gave that power, glory, and character (Hebrews 1:1-6). Here is the thought uttered in John 1:1: Yahweh is the author and finisher of our faith through the Messiah. That is why Yahshua is the one mediator between Yahweh and man (1 Timothy 2:5).

The two trees were divinely put in the garden to give mankind, at some point, both knowledge of good and evil and life everlasting. However, we took the bait and ate of the tree of good and evil.

This opened our eyes to declension, and our accuser resulting in a decision, causing a world of turmoil and setting in place a timeline of events which only Yahweh's Holy Spirit could discern. In 2 Peter 1:2-4, we see this expressed in the fact that Yahweh's Holy Spirit was given the ability, through the Messiah, to call us into glory and virtue and is given to us with exceedingly great and precious promises: that you may be partakers of the divine nature having escaped the corruption that is in the world through lust. Yahweh showed himself through Messiah Yahshua by His Holy Spirit who filled Yahshua with the promise of the Word spoken in John 1:1.

In him was life; and the life was the light of men. *John 1:4*

In
ἐν

G1722 en (a preposition) – properly, in (inside, within); (figuratively) "in the realm (sphere) of," as in the condition (state) in which something operates from the inside (within).

Him
αὐτοῦ

G846 autou - From the particle au (perhaps akin to G109 through the idea of a baffling wind; backward; (1) self (emphatic) (2) he, she, it (used for the third person pronoun) (3) the same. Usage: he, she, it, they, them, same. In itself it signifies nothing more than again, applied to what has either been previously mentioned or, when the whole discourse is looked at, must necessarily be supplied. Also, see **G848 hautou**- a contraction for G1438; self.

G1438 heautou him -self, alone

Was
ἦν

1510 eimi (the basic Greek verb which expresses being, i.e. "to be") – am, is. 1510 (eimí), and its counterparts, (properly) convey "straight-forward" being (existence, i.e. without explicit limits).

Life
ζωή

G2222 zoe – From 2198; life (literally or figuratively) Compare G5590

G2198 zao – a primary verb: to live (literally or figuratively) life (-time) (a-) live (-ly) quick.

G5590 psuche – From G5594 breath that is (by implication) spirit abstractly or concretely (the animal sentient principle only; thus, distinguished on the one hand from G4151 which is the rational and immortal soul; and on the other from G2222 which is mere vitality even of plants; these terms thus exactly correspond to H5315, H7307 and H2416 Nephesh, Ruach and Life respectively

And καὶ	life ζωὴ	was ἦν	the light φῶς	of men ἀνθρώπων
G2532 kai – and (also), very often, moreover, even, indeed (the context determines the exact sense).	**G2222 zoe** – From 2198; life (literally or figuratively) Compare G5590	**1510 eimi** (the basic Greek verb which expresses being, i.e. "to be") – am, is. 1510 (eimi), and its counterparts, (properly) convey "straight-forward" being (existence, i.e. without explicit limits).	**G5457 phos** – From an obsolete (to shine or make manifest especially by rays; compare G5316 and G5346; luminousness	**G444 anthropos** – From G435 and countenance; from G3700); man faced that is a human being.
	G2198 zao – a primary verb; to live (literally or figuratively) life (- time) (a-) live (-l-y) quick.		**G5316 phiano** – prolongation for the base of G5457; to lighten (shine) that is show (transitive or intransitive literal or figurative): - appear, seem, be seen, shine, think.	**G435 aner** – A primary word (compare G444); a man (properly as an individual male): - fellow, husband, man, sir.
	G5590 psuche – From G5594 breath that is (by implication) spirit abstractly or concretely (the animal sentient principle only; thus, distinguished on the one hand from G4151 which is the rational and immortal soul; and on the other from G2222 which is mere vitality even of plants: these terms correspond to H5315, H7307 and H2416		**G5346 phemi** – to show or make known one's thoughts to speak or say.	
	Nephesh, Ruach and Life respectively		**G3004 lego** – primary word properly to lay forth (relate in words) say, speak, call or tell.	

LIGHT, LIFE, AND FUNCTION

The verse in John 1:4 reads "In him was life; and the life was the light of men" can also be misconstrued as "him" being the Messiah. The focus has not changed in the Greek where it is still focusing on **him G846** which we have identified as the Holy Spirit. **In** (**G1722,** *this is where we got our word (In)- a preposition.*) **Him** (**G846** *baffling wind.*) This is in no way relating to Yahshua. This is Yahweh's Holy Spirit dealing with mankind. The next word **Was** (**G2258** *I, was (wast or were).* **Life** (**G2222** *to live (literally or figuratively) quick.*) **And** (**G2532** *(and) used in conjunction with the semicolon primary particle.*) **life** (**G2222** *to live (literally or figuratively) quick.*) **Was** (**G2258** *I, was (wast or were).* **The light** (**G5457** *phos-from an obsolete to shine or make manifest, (5316) phaino to lighten.*) **Of men** (**G444** *Anthropos man-faced that is a human being.*) Hence: In the baffling wind (Yahweh's Holy Spirit) was (past tense) life to be quick; and as importantly as the first sentence, the life quick was (past tense) caused to shine of those humans.

Yahweh's Holy Spirit had the life, to make quick, and that quickness caused the humans to shine. Blessed be John who made it very clear here in verse four that two humans were given life, and they did shine. This is for both male and female and all mankind. This appears to be speaking, that for these humans, the light was the hope of redemption through this thought of a Messiah. In other words, the hope was the light in mankind. Wait! What about Adam and Eve? They were perfect people in a perfect garden. This is truth.

Or is it? Nowhere in the Hebrew does the word "perfect" show up in describing the environment of Eden. This is a manmade thought added to teachings and biblical text.

When we are in a dark situation, what is the first thing we look for as humans? So, we are in a dark field at night, or looking for one of our livestock in a dark pasture and the flashlight goes out. It's dark. What do we look for? A star? Find the north star and—*boom*—you have direction. Find the light of your security pole, and you can find your way home. Look for the light of your house or TV on in the house.

Light for humans is hope; of course, too much light and you are blind, and no light causes blindness as well. The right amount of light is ideal and creates a sense of well-being which is hope or security. Not excitement. When we find the light, there is hope. The first order of business was "Let there be light" yet the luminaries were not created until the fourth day. The hope was the first thing put out there into the expanse for this creation. As Yahweh knew according to the laws of physics that declension would have its way.

Yahweh also knew that the stewards of this creation filled with intelligent emotion would make choices that would further the declension of this creation. What was just described is hope, mercy, and grace in the introduction of our story, the Bible, before we were even made or stood up on the ground, Yahweh's mercy and love toward us was revealed.

The Word of Yahweh says that it was good. Good in Hebrew is **tov** – agreeable, pleasant, good, or functional.

Now I believe they were in a different state of being than we are now. The creation story tells us this concerning the consequences of our actions when we ate the fruit. The earth also suffered from our actions as well.

Thus, we all became dysfunctional. The point being made is that Yahweh's Holy Spirit, in his loving kindness, placed within us from the very first breath the hope of a Messiah. That hope is the light of men, and that hope would one day become Yahshua Ha Messiach.

And the light shineth in darkness; and the darkness comprehended it not. John 1:5

And καὶ	the light φῶς	shineth φαίνει	in ἐν	darkness σκοτίᾳ
G2532 kai – and (also), very often, moreover, even, indeed (the context determines the exact sense).	**G5457 phos** – From an obsolete (to shine or make manifest especially by rays; compare G5316 and G5346; luminousness	**G5316 phiano** – prolongation for the base of G5457; to lighten (shine) that is show (transitive or intransitive literal or figurative): - appear seem be seen shine think.	**G1722 en** (a preposition) – properly, in (inside, within); (literally or figuratively):- dark (ness).	**G4653 skotia** – From G4655; dimness obscurity (literally or figuratively):- darkness.
	G5316 phiano – prolongation for the base of G5457; to lighten (shine) that is show (transitive or intransitive literal or figurative): - appear seem be seen shine think.		**G1722 en** (a preposition) – properly, in (inside, within); (literally or figuratively) "in the realm (sphere) of," as in the condition (state) in which something operates from the inside (within).	**G4655 skotos** – From the base of G4639; shadiness that is obscurity (literally or figuratively):- darkness.
	G5346 phemi – to show or make known one's thoughts to speak or say.			**G4639 skia** – Apparently a primary word; shade or shadow (literally or figuratively [darkness of error or an adumbration]):- shadow.
	G3004 lego – primary verb properly to lay forth (relate in words) say, speak, call or tell.			Obscure:- the state of being unknown, inconspicuous, or unimportant, the quality of being difficult to understand.
				Adumbration:- foreshadow or symbolize, overshadow

And καὶ	the darkness σκοτίᾳ	comprehended κατέλαβεν
G2532 kai – and (also), very often, moreover, even, indeed (the context determines the exact sense).	**G4653 skotia** – From G4655; dimness obscurity (literally or figuratively): - dark (ness). **G4655 skotos** – From the base of G4639; shadiness that is obscurity (literally or figuratively): - darkness. **G4639 skia** – Apparently a primary word; shade or shadow (literally or figuratively [darkness of error or an adumbration]): - shadow. _Obscure:_ the state of being unknown, inconspicuous, or unimportant, the quality of being difficult to understand. _Adumbration:_ foreshadow or symbolize, overshadow or oversight.	**G2638 katalambano** – From G2596 and G1983; to take eagerly that is to seize, posses (I. or F): - apprehend attain come upon comprehend find obtain perceive (over-) take. **G2596 kata** – primary particle; (preposition) down (in place or time) (according to the case [genitive, dative or accusative case with which it is joined): - about after against among as (according as) (to) after against. frequently denotes opposition distribution or intensity. **G1983 episkopeo** – From G1909 and G4648; to oversee; by implication to beware: - look diligently take the oversight.	**G1909 epi** – A primary proposition properly meaning superimposition (of time or place order) as a relation of distribution [with the genitive case] that is over upon etc.; of rest [with the dative case] at on etc.; of direction [with the accusative case] towards upon etc.; - about (the times) above after against among as long as (touching/at beside X have charge of [be-[where-]] fore in (a place as much as the time of – to) (because) of (up-) on (behalf of) over (by for) the space of through (-out) (un-) to (-ward) with. In compounds it retains essentially the same import as upon etc., (I. or F) **G4648 skopeo** – From G4649; to take aim at (spy) that is (figuratively) regard: - consider, take heed, look at, (on) mark. Compare G3700 **G4649 skopos** – From G4649; (scope) to peer about G4626 through the idea of concealment; compare (G4629); a watch (sentry or scout) that is (by implication) a goal: - mark. **G4626 skapto** – A primary verb; to dig **G3700 optanomai** – The first (middle voice) to gaze that with eyes wide open as at something remarkable. **G4629 skepasma** – a covering, clothing raiment.

it

αὐτό

not

οὐ

G846 autou - From the particle au (perhaps akin to G109 through the idea of a baffling wind; backward); (1) self (emphatic) (2) he, she, it (used for the third person pronoun) (3) the same. Usage: he, she, it, they, them, same. In itself it signifies nothing more than again, applied to what has either been previously mentioned or, when the whole discourse is looked at, must necessarily be supplied. Also, see

G848 hautou - a contraction for G1438; self.

G1438 heautou him -self, alone

G3756 ou - A primary word; the absolutely negative (compare G3661) adverb; no or not: - +long nay neither never no (X man) none. G3364 G3372

G3361 me - a primary particle of qualified negation

G3364 oo me - A double negative.

G3372 mekos - length (L or F)

A TIMELINE REVEALED

We must remember where we are in the timeline at this point. In the first part of the verse, as Yahweh says, "Let there be light." As we read, we are hovering above the deep with Yahweh's Holy Spirit. We also know Yahweh's Holy Spirit gave life to mankind and gave them light. This light is what? What is light in the Bible? Proverbs 6:23 tells us plainly that the commandments are lampposts and your (Yahweh) Torah is light! Light is the Word.

Yahshua is not the Word yet. The Word was just spoken prophetically, thus the Torah on day one was created. (Psalm 119:105). Light = Torah. As most of you have heard, there is a conscience within us, even when we are little children when we do something we shouldn't. Who is that? That is the light of Yahweh's Holy Spirit imprinted within us.

The verse states in the Greek: **And** (indeed) **the Light** (the promise, the hope, or the Torah: we know this because the word *phos* - to light, then to make luminous, to make known in that light Yahweh's word by the uttering of His thought.) **shineth** (made bright, appeared) **in** (within the realm of) **darkness** (obscurity, in the shadiness and then foreshadowing).

This is clearly a double image. When I say a double image, I mean this is John showing us two points on the timeline: Genesis 1:3 and Genesis 3. The Word was uttered in the obscurity and Light filled the space God (Yahweh) was in, and this happened in the darkness.

John 1:5 is also showing us a scene in the garden at the trees where Adam and Eve have partaken of the fruit of the tree of knowledge of good and evil. The serpent is trying to seize the light which is in mankind (Adam and Eve), believing, by doing so, he has won and defeated this plan of Yahweh. Not so! The enemy was actually outwitted.

Yahweh already knew the choice would be made. We can see this truth in the word study of verse one of John one, that Yahweh, with a confident harangue, made it known what the word was and that the word would be accomplished. In verse five, we see this is the Word (Torah) and darkness could not comprehend or discern the light. As the Word was not made flesh until verse 14 so, the parameters were set in place for this creation that was about to unfold by the Creator's hand. This is a timeline from the beginning—or Gen 1:1. This is the only way Yahshua's words which he spoke in ministry—I am the way, the truth and the life, (I AM the way (law), the truth (Torah) and the life (the one designated to deliver it and made it accessible)—could have worked.

Moving along in the verse, we have a semicolon. Remember: a semicolon tells us this next part of the sentence is just as equal in thought and emphasis. **And** (**G2532** *primary particle*), **the darkness** (**G4653** *obscurity, in the shadiness, and then foreshadowing*), **comprehended** (**G2638** *katalambano take eagerly, that is to seize takes us to* **G1983** *episkopeo (to oversee or look diligently to take the oversight)*, **it** (**G846** *autos a baffling wind*), **not** (**G3756** *oo absolutely negative.*) So, this becomes: and the light that shone did shine in obscurity and the obscurity could not seize and oversee Yahweh's Holy Spirit.

In this text, the intriguing part is the word comprehend. When we break down this word, we go from *katalambano* **G2638** take eagerly, that is to seize, to *episkopeo* **G1938** to oversee or look diligently to take the oversight. From there, the root of *episkopeo* **G1938** takes us to *epi* **G1909** which means this within the genitive case that the darkness could not come upon it, in the dative case could not move with it or in its direction, and in the accusative case could not move toward the darkness. Or simply put, the darkness could not be upon, in, on, unto Yahweh's Holy Spirit.

From there, we see referral to the word *skopeo* **G4648** to take aim at or spy. This leads to the root *skopos* **G4649** to peer about in concealment, with the related word *skapto* **G4626** to dig. *Optanomai* **G3700** is to gaze at with eyes wide open, as at something remarkable. Finally, *skepasma* **G4629** as in a covering, clothing, or raiment.

This darkness desperately was trying to snuff out though gazing in amazement, spying, and coverings of raiment which sounds oddly familiar to Matthew 7:15, Ezekiel 22:27, Colossians 2:8, 2 Peter 2:1. John chose these words clearly to express the idea that the Spirit of Yahweh cannot be thrown off its course. The Spirit of Yahweh will accomplish any and all thought and words originating from Yahweh. Though, the darkness will try, and *did* try, to overtake it, and clearly it failed then, and it will fail again.

In summary, within these four verses, we see Yahshua is a thought, conceived by his Father from the beginning. We saw pre-incarnate theology cannot be possible due to verse two being at the summit or beginning. If Yahshua had existed at that time, there would be no need to discuss the "word" because Yahshua would have been there to begin with! We need to realize Logos is not a physical manifestation of Yahshua but an idea uttered.

Clearly, we can see our God is one—Yahweh is One!

Nothing was created without Yahweh's Holy Spirit, and Yahweh's Holy Spirit *is* Yahweh, not one of two distinctive entities. Light is Torah as Torah is Word, which means Light is Word, and we proved this with scripture.

Nothing came into being without Yahweh's Holy Spirit, and with Yahweh's Holy Spirit, the promise, word, and prophecy of the Messiah, we can understand why this world was created through, by, and for Yahshua. Now we can also perfectly understand Paul when he wrote in **Hebrews 1:1-5: "In the past God spoke to our ancestors through the prophets at many times and in various ways, but in these last days he has spoken to us by his Son, whom he appointed heir of all things, and through whom also he made the universe. The Son is the radiance of God's glory and the exact representation of his being, sustaining all things by his powerful word. After he had provided purification for sins, he sat down at the right hand of the Majesty in heaven. So, he became as much superior to the angels as the name he has inherited is superior to theirs. For to which of the angels did God ever say, 'You are my Son; today I have become your Father'? Or again, 'I will be his Father, and he will be my Son'?"** Herein is the Glory, Power, and Authority of

Yahshua given to him by God (Yahweh). The darkness is constantly trying to seize or take light to try and understand, or misunderstand, Yahweh's word. We are all awaiting our blessed hope, who is the Word, and will return as our King.

In the next chapter, we will visit the next verses and dig into John the Baptist.

CHAPTER 4
JOHN THE BAPTIST
THE JOHN 1:1 FACTOR

*There was a man sent from God,
whose name was John. John 1:6*

There was	a man	sent	from
Ἐγένετο	ἄνθρωπος	ἀπεσταλμένος	παρά

G1096 ginomai – a prolonged and middle form of a primary verb; to cause to be (generate) that is (reflexively) to become (come into being) used with great latitude (literally, figuratively, intensely etc.) arise, be assembled, be (fall, come, have self) be brought (to pass), to emerge, become, transitioning from one point (realm, condition) to another. means "to become, and signifies a change of condition, state or place. means to come into being/manifestation implying motion, movement, or growth" (at 2 Pet 1:4). Thus, it is used for God's actions as emerging from eternity and becoming (showing themselves) in time (physical space). God forbid, be ordained.

G444 anthropos – From G444 and countenance; from G3700); man faced that is a human being.

G435 aner – A primary word (compare G444); a man (properly as an individual male): - fellow, husband man sir

G3700 optanomai – The first (middle voice) to gaze that with eyes wide open as at something remarkable.

G649 apostello – From G575 and G4724; set apart that is (by implication) to send out (properly on a mission) literally or figuratively - put in, send (away forth out) set [at liberty].

G575 apo – primary particle; off, that is away (from something near) in various senses (of place time or relation; L or F): -(X here); after, ago, at, because of, before, by (the space of) for (-th) from in (out) of off (up-) on(-ce) since, with. In composition (as a prefix) it usually denotes separation departure cessation completion reversal etc.

G4724 stello – Probably strengthened from the base of G2476; properly to set fast (stall-Figuratively) (to repress reflexively) abstain from associating with:- avoid, withdraw self.

G2476 histemi – abide, appoint, stand, bring continue, covenant, establish, hold up, lay, present, set (up) stanch, Compare G5087.

G5087 tithemi – fix, establish, ordain.

G3844 para – with the genitive; and as in Greek prose writings always with the genitive of a person, to denote that a thing proceeds from, the side or the vicinity of one, or from one's sphere of power, or from one's wealth or store. From, beside (L or F)

Yahweh

2316 theós (of unknown origin) – properly, God, the Creator and owner of all things (Jn 1:3, Gen 1 - 3).

Θεός

whose

αὐτῷ

G846 auto -From the particle au (perhaps akin to G109 through the idea of a baffling wind; backward; G3685); a name (l or F) (authority character)) - called (+ sur -) name (-d).

G846 auto -From the particle au (perhaps akin to G109 through the idea of a baffling wind; backward; G3685);
(1) self (emphatic) (2) he, she, it (used for the third person pronoun) (3) the same. Usage: he, she, it, they, them, same. In itself it signifies nothing more than again, applied to what has either been previously mentioned or, when the whole discourse is looked at, must necessarily be supplied. Also, see G848 hautou- a contraction for G1438; self.

G1438 heautou - him -self, alone.

name

ὄνομα

G3686 onoma – From a presumed derivative of the base of G1097 (compare G3685); a name (l or F) (authority character)) - called (+ sur -) name (-d).

G1097 ginosko – A prolonged form of a primary verb; to know (absolutely) in a great variety of applications and with many implications (as shown at left with others not thus clearly expressed):- , allow be aware (of) feel (have) known (-ledge) perceive be resolved can speak be sure understand.

G3685 oninemi – as in notoriety.

was John

Ἰωάννης

G2491 Ioannes – Oh Hebrew origin H3110 Ioannes (that is Jochanan the name John.

H3110 יוֹחָנָן – Yahweh has graced

PRIESTLY DUTIES

In verse six, we finally see John the Baptist entering the picture. Of course, John the Baptist and John the Apostle are two different individuals altogether. What makes John the Baptist so unique is that John's appearance was prophesied in the Old Testament in several locations.

We see one of these in Isaiah 40:3. "The voice of him that crieth in the wilderness, prepare ye the way of Yahweh, make straight in the desert a highway for our God." Moreover, I would highly recommend reading all of chapter forty, as this is an in-depth description of John the Baptist's work, Yahweh's word from Genesis 1, and Yahshua's fulfillment of that word in the gospel accounts. Malachi 3:1 gives a description as well: "Behold, I am sending my messenger, and he will clear a path before Me; suddenly the Master whom you seek will come to His sanctuary, even the messenger of the covenant, for whom you yearn, behold, he comes, saith Yahweh, Master of Legions."

The resulting issues with the understanding of these two texts result in two viewpoints within Christendom as follows: One viewpoint takes this to mean Yahshua came from heaven to earth. The other viewpoint sees this as Yahweh coming to earth and being announced by prophets. Well, what both viewpoints are seeing here is the *Logos - a word as embodying an idea, a statement, divine utterance, or an analogy.* This is Yahweh's word coming to pass at the appointed time. Yahweh is sharing throughout the prophets: the coming of this Word is soon!

In Luke 1:13-15, John is announced by an Angel of Yahweh. "But the angel said unto him, Fear not, Zacharias: for thy prayer is heard; and thy wife Elisabeth shall bear thee a son, and thou shalt call his name John. And thou shalt have joy and gladness; and many shall rejoice at his birth. For he shall be great in the sight of Yahweh, and shall drink neither wine nor strong drink; and he shall be filled with Yahweh's Holy Spirit, even from his mother's womb." Remember this verse, it will impact our study.

The most intriguing detail in all of John the Baptist's life is he was a Levite—the son of a priest, born of the tribe of Levi. John was proclaiming the mikveh ritual, what we call a baptism. John, the son of Zacharias, a priest of the temple but not the high priest, had every legal right according to Law to perform these baptisms. A priest could shake a reed dipped in the water and throw the water or sprinkle the waters of purification. Now this of course is a purification described in Torah. We can also see the double meaning of this statement by our Messiah where a person or people can be mesmerized by reeds on a lake swaying in the wind. Where people can be swayed or mesmerized by strange doctrines that come and go. "And as they departed, Jesus began to say unto the multitudes concerning John, what went ye out into the wilderness to see? A reed shaken with the wind?" Matt 11:7.

Hebrews 9:19 says: "For when Moses had spoken every precept to all the people according to the law, he took the blood of calves and of goats, with water, and scarlet wool, and hyssop, and sprinkled both the book, and all the people."

Since John was a firstborn son and a Levite, he was required to be set aside to minister to the congregation of Israel. "And if a Levite come from any of thy gates out of all Israel, where he sojourned, and come with all the desire of his mind unto the place which the Lord shall choose; Then he shall minister in the name of Yahweh his God, as all his brethren the Levites do, which stand there before the Lord." Deuteronomy 18:6-7.

John the Baptist was chosen by Yahweh to perform a divine service for Israel. This is evident later in John 1:33: "And I knew him not: but he that sent me to baptize with water, the same said unto me, upon whom thou shalt see the Spirit descending, and remaining on him, the same is he which baptizes with Yahweh's Holy Spirit." The fact a Priest of Israel (John the Baptist) is physically calling out to prepare the way for the future king – our messiah—is plain amazing.

So, where was John before he was born? Was he in heaven with Yahweh? I ask this question because the same English word is used in John 3:16, however it is a different Greek word. In most of our Bibles, the chosen word **G649** *apostello* is translated as sent. This translation simply comes from - to send away. Does this mean John was in heaven as well and was sent in an action for earth?

We must understand the word **G649** *apostello* to send out on a mission literally or figuratively. This is where our English word apostle comes from. When you break down *apostello*, you will find **G575** *apo,* primary particle *off,* that is away in various senses of place time or relation. *Stello* **G4724** is to stand, abstain from associating with: avoid, withdraw self. *Stello* sends us to **G2476** *histemi,* to appoint, establish.

Finally, showing **G5087** *tithemi* which is to fix, ordain, or stablish.

This shows John was commissioned by Yahweh to be the man to herald the messiah. John was ordained for this task, at this time, and this fits perfectly with the Levitical priesthood requirements and the first-born requirements. In Greek, these words are used to convey a message of ordained and established—which are all abstract thinking words, translated from Hebrew to take a concrete idea and make it comprehensible to all avenues of thought. Even with these truths about John the Baptist, John the Disciple chose his words wisely and carefully to convey the thought needed. John was not in heaven before his existence as he came from the womb of Elizabeth and was announced by an angel who expressed John would be filled with Yahweh's Holy Spirit even in the womb. This scenario is the same scenario for Yahshua. Born of humans and filled by Yahweh's Holy Spirit, these men were born for their appointed or ordained callings.

From our verse diagrams above, we see **There was** (came to be or emerged) **a man** (human being.) **Sent** (ordained, sent on a mission) **from** (in the sphere of) **Yahweh** (the Supreme being), **whose** (the breath of him) **name** (character or notoriety) **was John** (Yehochanan which is Yahweh has graced.) In the timeline of Scripture, we are still looking for Yahshua at this point.

*This man came for a witness, to bear witness of the Light, that all through him might believe. **John 1:7***

The same	came	for	a witness	to	bear witness	of
οὗτος	ἦλθεν	εἰς	μαρτυρίαν	ἵνα	μαρτυρήσῃ	περὶ

The same — οὗτος

G3778 houtos – From the article G3588 and G846; the, he (she, it) that (often with the article repeated): - he.

G3588 ho - The masculine feminine (second) and neuter (third) forms in all their inflections; the definite article; the.

G846 autos - From the particle au (perhaps akin to G109 through the idea of a baffling wind; backward), (1) self (emphatic) (2) he, she, it (used for the third person pronoun (3) the same. Also, see G848 hautou- a contraction for G1438; self.

G1438 heautou - him -self, alone.

came — ἦλθεν

G2064 erchomai – Middle voice of a primary verb (used only in the present and imperfect tenses, the others being supplied by kindred [middle voice] eleuthomai (el-yoo'-thom-ahee), which do not otherwise occur) to come or go (indicating the result. to or into) to come. Of persons: to come from one place to another, and used both of persons arriving and of those returning; to appear, make one's appearance, come before the public. Metaphor: to come into being, arise, come forth, show itself, find place or influence. be established, become known, to come (fall) into or unto to go, to follow one.

for — εἰς

G1519 eis – a preposition (properly) – From G1444, (unto) – literally, "motion into" which implying penetration ("unto," "union") to a particular purpose or result. to or into (indicating the point reached or entered, of place, time, purpose, result). Usage: into, in, unto, to, upon, towards, for, among.

a witness — μαρτυρίαν

G3141 marturia – From G3144, evidence given (judicially or generally): - record, report, testimony, witness.

G3144 martus – a witness (literally [judicially] or Figuratively [generally]); by analogy a martyr: - martyr, record, witness.

to — ἵνα

G2443 hina – Probably the same as the former part of G1438 through the demonstrative idea; compare G3588; in order that (denoting the purpose or the result): - albeit because to the intent (that) lest, so, as (so) that (for) to. Compare 3363

bear witness — μαρτυρήσῃ

G3140 martureo – From G3144 to be a witness that is testify (literally or figuratively): - charge give [evidence] bear record have obtain of good honest report be well reported of, testify give have testimony (be witness, bear give obtain) witness.

G3588 ho - The masculine feminine (second) and neuter (third) forms in all their inflections; the definite article -he.

G1438 heautou – (reflexive pronoun him -self, alone a witness (literally [judicially] or Figuratively [generally]); by analogy a martyr: - martyr, record, witness.

G3144 martus – a witness (literally [judicially] or Figuratively [generally]); by analogy a martyr: - martyr, record, witness.

G3363 hiname – in order (or so) that not.

of — περὶ

G4012 peri – From the base of G4008; properly through (all over) that is around; concerning, of, pertaining to, for sake.

G4008 peran – apparently the accusative case of an obsolete derivation of peiro (to pierce); through (as adverb or preposition) that is across: - beyond farther (other) side over.

The Light	that	all	men through	him	might believe
Φως	ἵνα	πάντες	δι'	αὐτοῦ	πιστεύσωσιν

G5457 phos – from an obsolete Phao (to make shine or make manifest especially by rays; compare G5316 and G5346); luminousness:- fire, light.

G5316 phaino - prolongation for the base of G5457; to lighten (shine) that is show (transitive or intransitive literal or figurative):- appear, seem be seen shine.

G5346 phemi – to show or make known one's thoughts to speak or say.

G2443 hina – Probably the same as the former part of G1438 (through the demonstrative idea; compare G3588; in order that (denoting the purpose or the result):- albeit because to the intent (that) lest, so, as (so) that (for) to. Compare 3363

G1438 heautou - (reflexive pronoun him self, alone

G3588 ho - The masculine feminine (second) and neuter (third) forms in all their inflections; the definite article -he.

G3363 hiname – in order (or so) that not.

G3956 pas – every, all manner of, Including all the forms of declension; apparently a primary word; all, any, every, the whole – all (manner of, means), always (-s), any (one), X daily, + ever, every (one, way), as many as, + no(- thing), X thoroughly, whatsoever, whole, whosoever.

G1223 dia – a primary preposition denoting the channel of an act; through.

G846 autos – G846 autou- From the particle au (perhaps akin to G109 through the idea of a baffling wind; backward, (1) self (emphatic) (2) he, she, it (used for the third person pronoun) (3) the same. Also, see G848 hautou- a contraction for G1438; self.

G1438 heautou - (reflexive pronoun him -self, alone

G848 hautou - Contraction for G1438; self her, of him (-self) his (own) of it thee their (own) them (-selves) they,

G4100 pisteuo – From G4102; to have faith (in upon or with respect to a person or thing) that is credit; by implication to entrust (especially one's spiritual well-being to Messiah):- believe (-r) commit (to trust) put in trust with.

WALKING IN TORAH?

Verse seven is packed with a lot of information, enough to preach a forty-five-minute sermon on this verse alone. One could argue, the crux of this whole chapter is right here in verse seven. This alludes to John's brilliance and demonstrates a Hebrew wrote this chapter. The Judaic ideas and the theology of the Torah and Prophets are contained right here. One can only understand this verse by knowing and working Torah in one's life.

The previous sentence may sound like a bold statement, yet so often the Torah is proclaimed to be done away with, that the old covenant is of the Jews and that Christ fulfilled all of those regulations. One of the main points of this book which you are reading now is this point I am making here. Torah is not done away with! This point should be reflected on, meditated on, and taken very seriously.

Yahweh did not give a set of instructions in the beginning, to then suddenly change midstream. That makes no sense whatsoever! Consider Hebrews thirteen and focus on verse eight: **"Jesus Christ is the same yesterday and today and forever."**

Who is Yahshua? A deity who came from above to visit our planet for thirty-something years and then went back home? This would be a good Steven Spielberg movie plot.

However, Yahshua is a man who laid down his life and accepted the mantle from Yahweh, and the light made him anointed. Was Yahshua not anointed? Isaiah 61:1, Matt. 3:16. Is he not the son of Yahweh? Matt. 3:16-17. Yahshua was filled with Yahweh's Holy Spirit, and he was given the Light. Acts 2:36, Romans 1:1-4, Isaiah 9:1-2. The Light which separated the darkness from the Light. Genesis 1:3, John1:1-9. This light, this word is the same today, yesterday, and forever. Hebrews 13:8.

This verse in Hebrews does not imply pre-existence nor pre-incarnation. This verse speaks plainly and states exactly what it means; Yesterday: from the day he was born to his death, today: right now, in the heavens as high priest being the intercessor between man and Yahweh, and Forever: from here onward. In a thousand years or perhaps tomorrow, Yahshua will be the same and lift up Torah because he is the living embodiment of Torah and he is the fulfillment of that light!

This is proven already because the Light = The Word = The Messiah, and the Word is Torah. Yahshua did fulfill the Law! Matt 5:17-19, Jeramiah 31:31-34, Ezekiel 36:26-27. What does this mean then?

It means that the recompense required when Torah is broken has been fulfilled by the Lamb of Yahweh, i.e., the Lamb of Yahweh paid this redemption price once and for all. Was this not the function of the Messiah? See Isaiah 42, Isaiah 61.

We are able to approach the throne due to his sacrifice and him being the living embodiment of Torah. We must follow or adhere to Torah. Torah is the path to living a life worthy of fellowship with the Father. Torah cannot be done without Yahshua, as Yahshua is the Light which draws men, otherwise you will need the consequences of law, the sacrificial system, to have atonement.

And now if you live without Yahshua, you are bound to the results of law as we read in Romans 7, being lost and without hope. Thus, the Messiah gives us cause to believe, and the Messiah, the embodiment of Torah, allows this to happen.

So, will following the Torah save us from death? *NO!* Our belief in Yahshua's sacrifice and resurrection saves us from destruction. Torah gives us the how—the commands, ordinances, and precepts—in which to live out our salvation with much fear and trembling. Philippians 2:12-13.

Torah is not a method for saving, nor does it provide salvation. Torah is the instructions which show how to live toward Yahweh, others, and ourselves.

We also see the first hints of Yahshua at the beginning of the second part of verse seven in the Light **G5457** *phos*, from an obsolete *phao-* to shine or make manifest.

What does the Light do? It reveals darkness. What does Yahshua do? He reveals the darkness in our lives and causes us to shine when we accept Him. Why? Because this is the Torah, and when Torah is evident in your life, the darkness cannot comprehend it.

Torah = Light = Yahshua.

Can you do Torah in the dark?

Can you read in the dark?

Can you see in the dark?

All three of these are the Word and all three of these are Yahshua! Now after his death and resurrection as the Son of Yahweh, he is all of these things. This is why, in Revelation, he is finally called the Word of God.

The promise or the word which Yahweh uttered is

Torah. It is how we should live, and the hope of this promise is how we can walk in Torah. If we have the hope of the Messiah, we are free indeed, **Genesis 26:5: "because Abraham obeyed me and did everything I required of him, keeping my commands, my decrees and my instructions."**

When we acknowledge the ten (commandments), the decrees (precepts), and the safeguards (ordinances), and we keep them, we walk down the path which is Torah. The path is lined with lampposts revealing the way. Accordingly, Yahshua said he is the way, the truth, and the life, John 14:6. Yahshua was filled with Yahweh's Holy Spirit, and the Light in him revealed the way to live Torah.

Sacrificing an animal because you fell short or missed the mark is not acceptable any longer. The messiah, Yahshua, died to fill that requirement. If you miss the mark you should recognize, turn and then realize why you are committing the error. The infilling of Yahweh's Holy Spirit into Yahshua gave us this ability. When Yahshua departed for heaven, our Father's Holy Spirit became our comforter, as it is a father's job to comfort his children! Wow, what a concept, isn't this what the Father wanted all along?

This is most wonderful news: Yahshua was the intended target since before creation. The miraculous conception, the temple scene when Yahshua was a boy, and the baptism by John the Baptist, John 1:32, were all ordained. Yahshua accepted his role while he was at the temple, fully became the role at his baptism, and then fulfilled the Law upon resurrection. Once coronation takes place in heaven upon his return, he will have completely fulfilled this role. The word being made flesh in John 1:14 is the promise, and the intended one would soon be human flesh.

John 1:32 further strengthens verse seven, as we can believe John is who John is and why we can believe in his witness. The idea that the light **G4547** *phos* is the light manifested **G5316** *phiano*, which we found back in verse two, shows up here again, and it is made apparent or allowed to manifest **G2064** *erchomai* by John's witness **G3140** *martureo*.

This word (*phos*) and John's witness (*martureo*) implies Yahshua was not alive prior to this chapter at any time and yet also confirms John 1:1; the light was luminous and was a thought uttered by Yahweh **G5436** *phemi*.

This verse can be viewed this way: **The same** (John alone) **came** (to come or go made public appearance) **for** (preposition to or into the purpose) **a witness** (to give testimony) **to** (in order to or for the purpose) **bear witness** (to give an honest good report) **of** (concerning) **The Light** (manifested that light to make known one's thoughts) **that** (in order to or for the purpose) **all** (forms of declension whatsoever and whosoever) **men through** (man faced through the channel of an act) **him** (John filled by the Holy Spirit) **might believe** (by implication to entrust).

He was not that Light but was sent to bear witness of that Light. John 1:8

He was
ῆν

G2258 ane –-Imperfect of G1510; I (thou) was (wast or were):- - agree, be, have charge of, hold, was, were

G1510 eimi - (the basic Greek verb which expresses being, i.e., "to be") – am, is, 1510 (eimi), and its counterparts, (properly) convey "straight-forward" being (existence, i.e., without explicit limits).

not
οὐκ

G3756 ou – A primary word; the absolutely negative (compare G3661) adverb; no or not:- +long nay, neither, never, no (X man) none, G3364 G3372 alone.

G3361 me – a primary particle of qualified negation

G3364 oo me – A double negative.

G3372 mekos – length (L or F)

that
ἐκεῖνος

G1565 ekeinos - From G1563; that one or G3778 affinity; there; by extension thither: - there thither (-ward) (to) yonder (place) alone.

G1563 (ekei - Of uncertain

G3778 houtos – From the article G3588 and G846; the, he (she, it) that is, this, or that (often with the article repeated):- he

G3588 ho - The masculine feminine (second) and neuter (third) forms in all their inflections; the definite article –he.

G846 autos - From the particle au (perhaps akin to G109 through the idea of a baffling wind; backward; (1) self (emphatic) (2) he, she, it (used for the third person pronoun) (3) the same. Also, see G848 hautou- a contraction for G1438; self.

G1438 heautou - him -self, alone.

Light
φῶς

G5457 phos –From an obsolete Phao (to make shine or make manifest especially by rays; compare G5316 and G5346); luminousness:- fire, light.

G5316 phiano - prolongation for the base of G5457; to lighten (shine) that is show (transitive or intransitive literal or figurative):- appear, seem, be, seen, shine.

G5346 phemi –-to show or make known one's thoughts to speak or say.

but	was sent to	bear witness	of	that Light
ἀλλ'	ἵνα	μαρτυρήση	περὶ	φωτός

but — ἀλλ'

G235 alla – Neuter plural of G243; properly other things that is (adverbially) contrariwise (in many relations): - and, but, even, howbeit, indeed, nay, nevertheless, no, notwithstanding, save, therefore, yea, yet.

G243 allos – A primary word; else that is different (in many applications): - more one (another) (an-some an-) other (-s -wise).

was sent to — ἵνα

G2443 hina – Probably the same as the former part of G1438 through the demonstrative idea; compare G3588; in order that (denoting the purpose or the result): - albeit because to the intent (that) lest, so, as (so) that (for) to. Compare 3363

G1438 heautou - (reflexive pronoun him -self, alone

G3588 ho - The masculine feminine (second) and neuter (third) forms in all their inflections; the definite article -he.

G3363 hiname – in order (or so) that not.

bear witness — μαρτυρήση

G3140 martureo – From G3144 to be a witness that is properly through all over that is around; with the genitive case denoting the charge, give [evidence] bear record, have, obtain, of good report, be well, reported of, testify, give, have testimony (be bear give obtain) witness.

G3144 martus – a witness (literally [judicially] or Figuratively [generally]): by analogy a martyr: - martyr, record, witness.

of — περὶ

G4012 peri - From the base of G4008; properly through all over that is around; with the genitive especially by rays; compare G5316 and G5346); subject or occasion or superlative point: - concerning, of, on, over, pertaining to, forsake, by, in, with.

G4008 peran- Apparently the accusative case of an obsolete derivation of peiro to pierce; through (as an adverb or reposition) that is across: - beyond, farther, other side, over.

that Light — φωτός

G5457 phos –From an obsolete Phao (to make shine or make manifest with the genitive especially by rays; compare G5316 and G5346); luminousness:- fire, light.

G5316 phiano - prolongation for the base of G5457; to lighten (shine) that is show (transitive or intransitive literal or figurative): - appear, seem, be, seen, shine.

G5346 phemi – to show or make known one's thoughts; to speak or say.

John was not the Light. However, John was ordained and purposed to bear witness of that Light. Now we see that the Light is the Word and also that the Word is about to be manifest as foretold throughout the Prophets. If the word was spoken, can this not also mean something was planted? Are words seed? Are words prophetic? Can words kill? Can words bless?

If a word is spoken, then the word is uttered from a thought. We also see in a previous chapter that we are made in His likeness – How we think or reason, not how we look.

If I give a prophetic word to someone and it comes to pass, this can be seen as a seed being sown. If I give someone a blessing such as, "May your days be long and fruitful with an abundance of children and the fat of the land," then I planted a seed and a blessing in their life. Is there really much difference when we look at the world with spiritual eyes?

See Luke 8:11, John 6:63, 1 Peter 1:23, Galatians 6:7, Genesis 3:15.

In these scripture references, you can see the word or a word from Yahweh is a seed which will come to harvest. We can see how the word of Yahweh is sown and has a harvest of differing degrees. It also becomes clear words can give life. Sowing seeds of hatred, discontent, and malice from our mouths will bear the same fruit as love, hope, and peace.

The concept that there will be enmity between mankind's seed and a serpent's seed shows we and animals also carry seeds within us. John is beginning to tell us this Word spoken or uttered is light and is about to manifest on earth. There was a miraculous conception, and this event was not a sexual encounter.

For our Jewish and Muslim brothers, this conception was not the result of fornication or adultery of any sort. It was Yahweh selecting the bloodline of a woman who was blessed to be chosen to carry the Messiah, Luke 1:26-35. An Angel, not a messenger angel (*malak*), but an archangel, Gabriel, spoke to Mary. Gabriel specifically told her, "The Holy Ghost will come upon thee and the power of the Highest shall overshadow thee." Luke 1:35.

The words *come upon* **G1904** and **G1909** is *eperchomai* and is to supervene, that is to arrive or influence. This can also be used to mean attack, as in flanked or surprised.

Have you ever felt the presence of Yahweh's Holy Spirit? I have, and it is quite surprising, nearly overwhelming to say the least. This word leads us to *epi* which is toward, in the direction of, coupled with the word *erchomai*, to accompany, appear light, grow. If there was any kind of sexual connotation here in Luke, we would definitely have Greek words to know exactly what happened. When we look at the words overshadow **G1982** *episkiazo*, to cast a shade upon, to envelop in haze of brilliance, we begin to see a clue of what is happening.

There is a Hebrew word called *shekinah* which is the Glory of Yahweh. While this word is not in the Bible, it is coined by the Rabbis of old and means "he caused to dwell." This shekinah glory is described in Exodus 13:20-22, Exodus 33:9,10,20, Exodus 14:24-25. This is the brilliance which overshadowed Mary. Yahweh's Holy Spirit created or fashioned each one of us.

If He took a rib from Adam, shaped Eve, and gave breath to her, then why can't this same Holy Spirit take the Word and an egg from Mary to create a life?

Did Yahweh not speak all our world into existence? Was this not words used as seeds to produce all of this life around us? Pray tell, then, is it so crazy to imagine that a human egg and the Word from Genesis 1:3 (which we already know is Light and light is Torah and Torah is the Word) can fertilize a human ovum?

This is not a huge theological understanding of Divinity. This is straight forward. No other religion on this planet since day one has ever had this concept. That concept being, where a creator does not have sexual relations but takes His creating power, the spoken word, and speaks to the ovum to create life. That life becoming a Messiah, a savior for mankind. We have been sold a bill of goods by the mother church who took in pagan cultures to expand the economic and political base of the Holy Roman Empire emanating from Rome.

ARE THE ANGELS OF THE OLD TESTAMENT YAHSHUA?

There have been questions raised with the idea that angels in the Old Testament were actually Yahshua. Not all the angels mentioned, of course, but quite a few in stories such as the tent meeting with Abraham, Jacob's encounter at the river, and other mainstream teachings point out that this is an incarnation of Yahshua (more on this in a moment). Were these angels being used by Yahweh actually Yahshua? Then what happened here? Using this idea and if this were the case, then let's use this here with Gabriel. Was Yahshua announcing his own birth to Mary? Why Gabriel? Was Yahshua being deconstructed at a cellular level so he could be transported to Mary's womb? Not at all.

The miracle of a virgin birth that took place was announced by the archangel Gabriel, known for announcements. He gave notice that Yahweh's Holy Spirit, the creator and giver of Light to men, had selected this virgin to carry the Messiah for mankind. Remember: Yahweh is the Holy Spirit, and they are not two distinct entities.

The thought or theology in which Yahweh and the Holy Spirit and Yahshua are three distinct persons in one is false doctrine, a pagan concept with no roots in the Bible whatsoever.

There is a huge debate amongst Christians about the Old Testament angels and why the different translations read differently. Genesis 16: 7-12, 21:17-18, 22:11-18, Exodus 3:2, Judges 21:1-4, Zechariah 1:12.

The issue arises from both simple translation and, more importantly, a flourishing doctrine of ignorance that Yahshua is "the Angel of the Lord." Firstly, Yahshua cannot be an angel because Yahshua is not an angel. He is human! Hebrews 2 explains this very clearly. Secondly, Yahshua did not preexist. The angels had awaited this Word made flesh for a few thousand years. Thirdly, if Yahshua was divine before his birth as a man, he would not be an angel, as he would be co-equal with Yahweh, and which means Yahshua would utilize the Holy Spirit to manifest in a messenger angel to give that word which needed to be given. Follow?

The answer here is that Yahweh's Holy Spirit does the communicating. Yahweh's Holy Spirit fills an individual, like John the Baptist or Yahshua or a messenger angel or you or me.

This is another point in this verse. John the Baptist is the designated individual bearing witness to the Light, and that Light can inhabit all of mankind, not just the Temple any longer!

When people who subscribe to this belief system say, "Then what has happened to these angels of Yahweh in the New Testament?" Do you not see them? Consider the time Peter, Paul, and others were freed and let out of prisons, or think of those men who were visited by angels who were filled by Yahweh's Holy Spirit to accomplish a mission. These angels cannot be Yahshua, as he was in heaven giving intercession for us at the right hand of the Father.

In the New Testament, we understand that this was accomplished by the movement of Yahweh's Holy Spirit. This was not understood because false doctrines came into Christianity and prohibited the understanding of Yahweh's Holy Spirit as in John 1:1.

A commonly held belief is Yahweh cannot come to this earth because it is filled with evil. If this is true, then we must ask: Who is this Holy Spirit and how can he be in any one of us, let alone fill the Messiah to accomplish the greatest work of all, if he cannot be present around evil?

If Yahweh cannot be near or around sin, then what about Isaiah 1:18? What about the fact we have all sinned and fallen short? Yahweh is opposed to sin. The idea that Yahweh cannot be around sin makes no sense or else why would He go to all these great lengths in which to save us? If Yahshua was God, and he could not be around sin, then that pretty much negates the theory of preexistence and of him being Yahweh because he dwelled as a man on earth among evil men.

Verse eight reiterates the importance of verse seven. Just like John did in verse two for verse one of the first chapter of John. If we recall, these reiterations are a repetitive style of writing in the Hebrew and conveys the importance of an idea. To repeat an idea is a way to accentuate it in the mind of the hearer.

It is intriguing that Isaiah tells us Elijah will come to announce the coming of the Messiah. Clearly, what is often misunderstood when reading Isaiah is that the spirit of Elijah will herald the coming of the Messiah. The word tells us when John was asked by the priests and Levites if he was Elijah, he answered honestly without negating either the prophet or the word, possibly because John the Baptist was asked the wrong question. Elijah clearly was filled by Yahweh's Holy Spirit himself. John was also filled, since the womb, with Yahweh's Holy Spirit.

We must, as a body of believers, understand the role of Yahweh's Holy Spirit—which is Yahweh filling us, Yahshua, Elijah, John and so on. Yahshua's redemptive work allowed for the indwelling of Yahweh's Holy Spirit for anyone who accepts the Messiah, who is the thought uttered, the Word given.

Can this verse also now answer the age-old question: "What is blasphemy of Yahweh's Holy Spirit?"

An in-depth look at this verse would be: **He** (John) **was** (being) **not** (absolute negative, never) **that** (from, himself) **Light** (manifested to show thoughts spoken or said) **but** (nevertheless) **was sent to** (he was purposed, in order to) **bear witness** (to testify or give testimony) **of** (pertaining to the piercing of) **that light** (from, manifested to show thoughts spoken or said).

That was the true Light, which lighteth every man that cometh into the world. John 1:9

That was / Ἦν	the true / ἀληθινὸν	Light, / φῶς	which / ὃ	lighteth / φωτίζει
G2258 en – Imperfect of G1510; I (thou) was (wast or were): - agree, be, have charge of, hold, was, were.	**G228 alethinon** – From G227; truthful: - true.	**G5457 phos** –From an obsolete Phao (to make shine or make manifest especially by rays; compare G5316 and G5346); luminousness: - fire, light.	**G3739 hos** – Probably a primary word (or perhaps a form of the article G3588); the relative (sometime demonstrative) pronoun, who, which what, that: - one (an the) other, some, that, which, who (+ -m -se) See also G3757.	**G5461 photizo** - From G5457; to shed rays that is to shine or (transitively) to brighten up (l. or F): - enlighten, illuminate, (bring to give) light, make to see.
G1510 eimi – (the basic Greek verb which expresses being, i.e., "to be") – am, is, 1510 (eimi), and its counterparts, (properly) convey "straight-forward" being (existence, i.e., without explicit limits).	**G227 alethes** – From G1 (as a negative particle) and G2990; true (as not concealing): - true, truly, truth.	**G5316 phaino** - prolongation for the base of G5457; to lighten (shine) that is show (transitive or intransitive literal or figurative): - appear, seem, be seen, shine.	**G3757 hou** - Genitive case of G3739 as adverb; at which place that is where: - where (-in) whither (soever)].	**G5457 phos** –From an obsolete Phao (to make shine or make manifest especially by rays; compare G5316 and G5346); luminousness: - fire, light.
	G1 alah – Of Hebrew origin; figurative only, the first.	**G5346 phemi** –to show or make known one's thoughts to speak or say.	**G3588 ho** - idiom): - the, this, the definite article; the (sometimes to be supplied, at others omitted, in English that, one, he, she, it, etc.	**G5316 phaino** - prolongation for the base of G5457; to lighten (shine) that is show (transitive or intransitive literal or figurative): - appear, seem, be seen, shine.
	G2990 lanthano – Prolonged form of a primary verb which is only used as an alternative in certain tenses; to lie hid, be hid, be ignorant of unawares, in order (or so) that not.			**G5346 phemi** –to show or make known one's thoughts to speak or say.

every man / πάντα ἄνθρωπον	that / πάντα	cometh / ἐρχόμενον	into / εἰς	the world / κόσμον

G444 anthropon From G435 and ops (the countenance; from 3700; man faced that is a human being: - certain man

G435 aner – A primary word (compareG444; a man (properly as an individual male):- fellow, husband, man, sir.

G3700 optanomai - to look at, behold to allow one's self to be seen, to appear

Tie together with every and that.

G3956 pas – every, all manner of. Including all the forms of declension; apparently a primary word; all, any, every, the whole -- all (manner of, means), always (-s), any (one,) X daily, + ever, every (one, no[-thing],) X thoroughly, whatsoever, whole, whosoever.

G2064 erchomai – Middle voice of a primary verb (used only in the present and imperfect tenses, the others being supplied by kindred [middle voice] eleuthomai (el-yoo'-thom-ahee,) or [active] eltho (el'-tho), which do not otherwise occur) to come. to come. Of persons: to come from one place to another, and used both of persons arriving and of those returning, to appear, make one's appearance, come before the public. Metaphor: to come into being, arise, come forth, show itself, find place or influence. be established, become known, to come (fall) into or unto to go, to follow one

G1519 eis – a preposition) – properly, into (unto) – literally, "motion into which" implying penetration ("unto," "union") to a particular purpose or result. to or into (indicating the point reached or entered, of place, time, purpose, result). Usage: into, in, unto, to, upon, towards, for, among.

G2889 kosmos – Probably from the base of G2865; orderly arrangement that is decoration; by implication the world (in a wide or narrow sense including its inhabitants literally or figuratively [morally]): - adorning world.

G2685 kolumboa – From a primary word kolumbos (to tend that is take care of); properly to provide for that is (by implication) to carry off (as if from harm; generally, obtain): - bring, receive.

EVERY ONE OF US HAS THE LIGHT

Our Messiah was not hidden or kept quiet in heaven only to show up every now and then to accomplish something Yahweh did not feel like doing himself.

In the first part of this verse, we read, "That was the true." We need to make sure we keep in step with John and begin our study by understanding what "That" is referring. The word *that* is a definite article, as it is defining or indicating what we are already speaking of: the Light.

Why is the word *was* being used? John is still conveying from the first part of his chapter that the hope of the Messiah from the thought uttered is still very much in existence—the hope and thought exist as a promise. Not in a fleshly existence but in a set-in-course action, a prophetic word, and a hope for mankind.

Is this a mystery? Yes, and Paul describes this beautifully as we see in Colossians 1.

In Colossians 1:25, we see that this "word of Yahweh" is describing this thought perfectly. Make sure to read the whole chapter for context.

In verse 26, the mystery was hidden for ages and generations but is now revealed to his saints. We must recognize this current idea we have of Yahshua being preexistent crept into Christian doctrine shortly after 100 AD and paved the way for the concept of the trinity to be widely accepted. Here in John 1:9, we see that "the true" is the one and only, the first, being hidden, not concealed but unawares, ignorant.

We can see this still holds true in our assemblies and in

the world who intentionally or unintentionally refute Yahweh's Holy Spirit. Who woos you and me to the Messiah?

In John 6:65, our messiah stated, "And he said, Therefore, said I unto you, that no man can come unto me, except it were given unto him of my Father." Given, draw, gave, or cause are excellent words used to describe how Yahweh draws man or gives men that Light—the Light we need to remember is the manifestation of the thoughts shown by words. The Holy Spirit, who is Yahweh, draws us to the Messiah.

Why? Because that is the true Light!

What is the Light? The same definition of Light we established Biblically in this and the previous two chapters of this study. A thought manifested to show by speech, that is the Logos.

This is a very interesting verse. John is telling us that this thought was **G2990** *lanthano* to lie hid, ignorant of, unawares. Not that Yahshua is the Light just yet, but that Yahweh's intention was hidden, a mystery, and now John reveals the Messiah is on the way, will soon be present on this earth.

Remember: a word **G3506** *logos* is defined as a word as embodying an idea, a statement, divine utterance, or an analogy. This thought is brought by Yahweh's word which was "Let there be Light." This was order - light and darkness, day and night. The word Light is defined through Biblical context—using Scripture to define Scripture—as Torah.

We know that this was all brought about by Yahweh's Holy Spirit. This same Holy Spirit overshadowed Mary in

Luke 1:35 revealing how and why the power, **G1411** *dunamis* and **G1410** *dunamai*, might be possible. These two words imply the miracle. That miracle is the Word spoken (which is Light which is Torah) was spoken to Mary's womb.

Yahweh's Holy Spirit spoke the Word (which is Torah), thus speaking order and a generational order into being, thus Light was given to Mary's womb. This Light from Yahweh's Holy Spirit is also given to every man, and this why we will have no excuse. This Light is a piece of Himself, and this is the only way we can respire or exist. It is that simple. The Torah is the Light that lighteth every man which comes into the world because it is life! Until we reject that light, that is until we reject Torah.

Every man is given a piece of this hope or Light when they come into the world. Even in their sin nature, they still have this hope.

Think about this for a moment. What do people say who believe or are on the fence or have no belief at all? The most common question from them all is, "Why would God allow that to happen?" They ask because that is something in their spirit screaming out, and they are internally contemplating (though not always consciously) the need for and hope of a Messiah to fix this broken world. How do we know this? Well, the words chosen in the text are very clear. The text reads, "That was the true light which lighteth." This is what I am referencing.

This is **G5461** *photizo* and this word means to shine or to brighten up. This word comes from **G5457** *phos* which means to make shine or make manifest, especially by rays.

In an open-casket funeral, this concept becomes very

clear. The life or the light is removed from the individual. When someone dies in our arms, we can literally watch their light slip away. The skin begins to chill and deflate, and the eyes lose their light as they change.

From there, the word you will be referred to is **G5346** *phemi* which is to show or make known one's thought; to speak or say. Grammatically, this make sense which is understood and translated as a relative pronoun for the word light.

Which light? The true light. And it does what? "The true light lightens."

Now, when we add every human who comes into the world to the text, we see the true light lightens every man. Thus, giving us further proof that this true light is given to every human who comes into the world—not by Yahshua, but by Yahweh's Holy Spirit.

The phrase *comes into the world* is intriguing in itself, as is the word translated as *world*. The word given in Greek is **G2889** *kosmos* and that word is typically defined as an orderly arrangement. This implies that Yahweh has an orderly arrangement in this world, and we are to adorn the world to which he sends us. Not that we were in heaven and he sent us out, but that we are part of his master plan, and our Messiah will be given, sent, and appear at the allotted time.

The word adorn is defined as to make more beautiful or attractive.[1] What was our mission when we were created? In Genesis, the Word of Yahweh never says we are to worship Him. Our mission was to be stewards of the garden and take care of it, to make it reproduce and flourish. We were also to rest on the seventh day and be fruitful and multiply.

Nowhere in the Word does Yahweh command us to worship him. This idea of a forced worship is a pagan idea. People all over the world thought they had to sing and scream and kill and cut and dance and all these things.

What is true worship? To present ourselves as a living and holy sacrifice, Romans 12:1-2. This is obedience and living a peculiar life—or a set-apart life. We are to obey and be mindful of Torah. Folks, the Torah was given to the Israelites to give to the world. They did not do that, and now we have Judaism unable to discern who the Messiah is, and we have Christians running amuck, claiming Torah is dead to them and is only for the Jews.

My beloved brothers and sisters, the Torah was given in the garden, and the law was given at Mount Sinai to a people who were to deliver the Torah to the nations. The law was inserted into Torah as the book of Leviticus for recompense or remediation of our sin, for when we miss the mark, for when we break Torah.

As you read this, if you are unfamiliar with Torah because you have been taught all your life the Torah was done away with or that the Law and Torah are the same, I urge you to speak with someone who understands the Messiah's role in this world. Don't settle for a canned response which makes absolutely no sense.

Breaking down this verse in depth shows us: **That was** (the hope of the Messiah, exists) **the true** (the one and only truth) **Light** (manifested to show ones thought to speak or say) **which** (that) **lighteth** (to brighten up and make unhidden) **every man** (all man faced appearing) **that** (through all forms of declension) **cometh** (making an appearance) **into** (penetrating) **the world** (the circle of the earth and all it aggregates.)

As a final note for this chapter, I encourage you to reread 1 Peter 1.

Pay special attention to these important verses **1 Peter 1:18-21**:

"For as much as you know that you were not redeemed with corruptible things, as silver and gold, from your vain conversation received by tradition from your fathers; But with the precious blood of Messiah, as of a lamb without blemish and without spot: Who verily was foreordained before the foundation of the world, but was manifest in these last times for you, Who by him do believe in Yahweh, that raised him up from the dead, and gave him glory; that your faith and hope might be in Yahweh."

CHAPTER 5
WHO MADE WHO?
THE JOHN 1:1 FACTOR

**He was in the world,** and the world was made through him, and the world knew him not. _John 1:10_

He was
ἦν

G2258 ane – Imperfect of G1510; I (thou) was (wast or were):- agree, be, have charge of, hold, was, were.

G1510 eimi - (the basic Greek verb which expresses being, i.e., "to be") – am, is, 1510 (eimi), and its counterparts, (properly) convey "straight-forward" being (existence, i.e., without explicit limits).

in
ἐν

G1722 en (a preposition) – properly, in (inside, within); (figuratively) "in the realm (sphere) of," as in the condition (state) in which something operates from the inside (within).

the
τῷ

G3588 ho - The masculine feminine (second) and neuter (third) forms in all their inflections; the definite article -the.

world
κόσμον

G2889 kosmos – Probably from the base of G2865; orderly arrangement that is decoration; by implication the world (in a wide or narrow sense including its inhabitants literally or figuratively [morally]):- adorning world.

G2685 kolumboa –From a primary word kolumbos (to tend that is take care of); properly to provide for, that is (by implication) to carry off (as if from harm; generally, obtain):- bring, receive.

IT'S ALL IN THE PRONOUNS!

If given enough thought and without any preconceived assumption in our thinking, John 1:10 will most certainly cause one to have a crash course in Greek structure of pronouns. Without boring readers and writing a book about Greek pronouns, it is safe to say the Greek system of pronouns is much like our own.

That is the easiest way to say it and should be; after all, we did get our language from Latin and in turn from the Greeks. Most people like myself read this line of scripture and immediately think of Yahshua. I did this for years and had no additional questions about it at all.

Our friend **G1510** is present again in this line of text and glares like a thumb hit by a hammer. It is imperative we find out who this is. As we see in the English translation, "He was" – *ane*. As a refresher, *ane* in English is wast (this word is an archaic form of *was*) which is a third-person singular past indicative of be.

In this case, we see He (Yahweh) was in the world. The Greek, though, asks us to look at **G1510** which is interesting because we saw the same thing in verse one. First person singular present indicative – imperfect of **G2258**. The choice of using *ane* **G2258** is grammatically correct. However, we must keep in mind that **G1510** is applicable in this context.

If we understand this concept and description, we know that **G2258** is imperfect to **G1510** which is *I exist* or *I be*. Who is I AM or I EXIST? Yahshua? No. There is no scripture to support this, nor did Yahshua proclaim this about himself either. *I be here today* is incorrect English and Greek. Thus, you have the imperfect word forced to get the point across.

In this case, as before, John is speaking of Yahweh's Holy Spirit. Yahshua is not born yet, so it cannot be him. As the rest of the text tells us, combined with what we have also discovered in previous verses, this cannot be Yahshua. John used the third person in Greek correctly – the author is not referring to himself but to the first-person imperfect verb I AM!

Third person singular in this case is why the translator chose He. Because of the imperfect tense "He" corroborates the "I AM." The imperative, indicative moods convey actuality, as in indicating an action as a command for the verb was. He, as in Yahweh's Holy Spirit and is being the only one—as in Yahweh is *echad* (one unit). Essentially what happened here in translation was a proper grammar issue ironed out. The text should read "I BE was in the world," "I EXIST was in the world," and "I AM was in the world," though neither of these really are proper English, and the translator made this verb an imperfect indicative active third person singular. When we compare the Septuagint, we find the same, and it is often translated "He was in the world." There is not a voice for the verb "was" because it was indicative (actuality) and imperative (command). Thus, "He" is correctly chosen, keeping in line with the pronoun context of this chapter and that context being Yahweh's Holy Spirit. The I AM or I EXIST is Yahweh, and the Holy Spirit is Yahweh, not a separate entity. In other words, His Holy

Spirit was in the world at the beginning when He made the world, he was in the world for the last four thousand years, and now at this juncture, with John the Baptist screaming out that the kingdom of Yahweh is at hand, was still in the world. Hopefully you can see the present and past in one concept just explained.

Who is He? – Yahweh's Holy Spirit. And who is the Holy Spirit? – Yahweh's Spirit. How is it Yahweh's Holy Spirit? Scripturally we can prove that it is Yahweh's Holy Spirit as He was in creation making both man and creation, Genesis 1:2, 26, Psalm 33:6, Gen 2:7, Job 33:4.

Now that we have discussed pronouns and have this discussion out of the way, we can further know that this is Yahweh's Holy Spirit by keeping the text within context of the chapter and especially the prior verses.

The text clearly speaks in verse ten about the same individual in verses seven through nine: the Light. Who is the Light? At this point, it is Yahweh's Holy Spirit, as we have already proposed, questioned, and proven Yahweh's Holy Spirit is the Light.

Yahweh's Holy Spirit gives us light when we are being created as we saw in verse four. In verse seven, we see John was purposed to give testimony and be a witness of that Light. Who is the comforter? Yahweh's Holy Spirit. And what comfort do we have in receiving the Holy Spirit? Hope! That the Logos will be manifest for us. The promise will come to be.

The promise is the Messiah, sent to reconcile us when we believe in him. When Yahweh's Holy Spirit descended upon Yahshua, that Light was fulfilled, as in Yahweh's word made flesh. This fulfillment of the Light made manifest in Yahshua is the sole function of the prophetic word concerning the Messiah. So, when we are reading the pronouns in the text, we must keep in step with the author or we will get lost. Up to this point we see Yahweh's Holy Spirit is the Light as stated in the text calling us to Torah. Soon we will see how the promise of a Messiah will become the Light of the world calling us to Torah.

Knowing Yahweh and His Holy Spirit are one, in verse ten, we see Yahweh can be on the earth and move amongst men. Yahweh was and is in the world seeking, watching, and waiting, John 4:23.

The people who are searching scripture to learn how to do the right thing and to be on the right path are true worshippers. Yahweh, who is the father, has actually moved about this earth since creation. The typical assumption amongst Jews and Christians is that Yahweh cannot be amongst men on the Earth due to sin. This is nowhere to be found in scripture.

Since there are detestable things or abominations on this earth, how does Yahweh know this if he is not amongst us? His angels tell him? No! Yahweh's Holy spirit moves, seeking out who is on the correct path and who is not. Can you grieve Yahweh's Holy Spirit? Certainly! Anytime we walk outside of Torah which is His instruction on how to live. Is Yahweh not in you? Of course! We all have a piece of Yahweh in us, however a life accepting Yahshua is a covenant of residence.

TO SEE OR NOT TO SEE!

How then can we compute Genesis 12:7? Yahweh appeared before Abraham. Well, the word רָאָה **H7200** *rawah*- to see, look. This is a looking; seeing; appearance, form; vision as granted to the prophets, and preeminently to Moses, the vison of God. The definition seems basic. However, when we plug in the definitions, a new idea emerges.

Yahweh did appear unto Abram. Yet, not as we English speakers use the word appear. When we use the word appear, to us, this means suddenly showed up as in a visible manifestation. Hebraically, this word conveys looked upon, as in Yahweh looked upon. This word can be used in numerous applications literally or figuratively, direct and implied transitively, intransitively and causatively. Two things happened in this passage.

When we look at the word *rawah*[1] and its meanings, we learn: to see or perceive something or someone. To see visions. See, look, behold, shew, appear, consider, seer, spy, respect, perceive, provide, regard, enjoy, lo, foresee, heed.

Is it not interesting that most of these words are a vision or prophetic word? Now read the whole passage again and you will see Yahweh is prophesying over Abram that He will give all this land to Abram. Why? Because Abram listened and obeyed! Hence, the word appeared as in consider, seen, saw, perceived, provided, enjoyed, foresaw, heeded. After Yahweh called Abram out of Ur and upon the arrival to the appointed destination, Yahweh revealed unto Abram His plan for Abram's life and legacy.

So, the word chosen is *rawah*, meaning: appear, consider,

prophecy, foresee, lo, and provide. The author of Genesis is painting us a picture of Yahweh's exuberance concerning Abram's continuous display of steadfast faith. Abram listens and obeys. He trusts Yahweh, and Yahweh gives Abram a vision of his plan (Yahweh's vision).

Thus, Transparent English Bible reads, "And Yahweh was seen toward Abram and said…"

The Tanach version reads, "Hashem appeared to Abram and said…"

The KJV reads, "And the LORD appeared unto Abram…"

Stated simply, it is: Yahweh looked upon Abram and gave him a vision of what is to come for being obedient.

With this being said, I am not discounting the existence of the old Hebrew idea of angels and what purposes some of the angels of the Old Testament served, such as Genesis 16:7-11. I do believe in this and subsequent examples of Yahweh's Holy Spirit filling an angel to accomplish His task. That is why we see in the Septuagint, Tanach, and English translations the term "Angel of the Lord," "angel of Hashem," and for sacred name denominations, "Angel of Yahweh." This is why these angels are called messengers of Yahweh. Yahweh is clearly in this form and not present Himself or else that form will bring death to the individual being presented to!

Often, we love to overcomplicate things and make nuances in which unwittingly box in our Yahweh. Let's keep it simple.

THE GREAT I AM

In John 8:58-59, the Jews were appalled and angered when Yahshua uttered those famous words which have since been bent out of context: "before Abraham was, I AM."

For many years, I misunderstood these words as well, and for a long time, I used this phrase as an anchor for my beliefs —almost like an anthem. One day, I listened as some friends discussed this topic. Up until that time, I was on a completely different path, learning about the difference between Torah and the Law. I would never in a million years have thought my attention would be diverted to this statement of when Yahshua came into existence. That day, truth caught my attention as I heard them both defend their respective points.

As I paid attention, I discovered neither knew the truth of what they believed. Each side could only repeat what they had been taught. Now this statement I just made seems very arrogant or presumptuous, yet one could deduce that no scriptural evidence was supplied to accommodate a cultural perspective. When the same rhetoric we have heard for thirty, forty, fifty years, which is accepted theology from both of these individuals, caused me to pause. Now the fact of the matter is: you can only do what you know and cannot do what you do not know. At this point I interjected my beliefs, as the conversation was beginning to get heated. Maybe if I give another viewpoint perhaps, the discussion could begin to simmer again instead of coming to a boil. Another discussion participant present, upon hearing my original beliefs, that Yahshua was actually created or came in to being at Genesis 1:3, called me a Syriac believer. I was not spurned but spurred into action, since none of us like to be called names, especially if we have no understanding of what those names imply. These back-and-forth statements hit me hard, and my quest began the next week. That quest turned into a journey, and the result is this book. What hit me hard is, if I am to be intellectually honest, the fact is that I had this all drawn out and it had made the most sense. The truth is there are not many Christians who believed the way I did. I was amazed when I discovered this and could see almost immediately that the Logos was pronounced at the pinnacle of creation. For Us! This is why Yahshua was slain from the foundation of the world. 1 Peter 1:19, Revelation 13:8. Not the physical or spiritual embodiment of Yahshua but the thought uttered to give a Messiah for our benefit. This is the most loving act. Throughout the timeline of humanity, Yahweh saw you and me in a fallen world hurting and offered a way out.

In this scenario I just described above, we can see it is easy to take different meanings from one sentence. In English we tend to see things in an abstract thought, whereas in the Bible, these ideas are Hebraic and are very much concrete in thought. The Hebrew language is an action language that focuses on the verb, where English is noun focused. Extrapolating the understanding can sometimes get cloudy, thereby producing different interpretations. While others will understand the first time exactly what was being communicated or intended.

While this is nowhere near the work of the Word of Yahweh, I felt driven to show where some of these discrepancies can come from. When reading several chapters of scripture at a time, we can have information overload and really not retain what we just read and can barely recall a timeline. This is called Sunday newspaper Bible reading, or reading the Bible like a Sunday newspaper, based on your environment and culture. This is not meant to be taken in a derogatory manner. As I stated above, "You can only do what you know and cannot do what you do not know." If we take bite-size chunks of the scripture and study those words, look at the culture of those bits of information, all the while keeping it simple, very basic, a whole world of under-standing will occur. My friends, you must study the words within Scripture, actually study as though there will be a final test someday! Not just reading the words five times and then maybe looking up a couple of reference scriptures. We do not need to have hours upon hours of study time in a setting. Read the verse, discover the context, explore the culture of the time, look at the Hebrew or Greek, ask Yahweh's Holy Spirit to reveal His word to your heart and mind.

This will not take a lot of time if you prepare. Have your reference material ready, as most of us have phones now that are faster and hold more technology than the Apollo astro-nauts had to get to the moon. Find the chapter you want to explore, or topic, and Yahweh's Holy Spirit leads us to some-thing interesting again and again. Some of us will give up and flip onto someone's YouTube channel who has just as much information on the topic as you do. I would like to encourage you, though, to stay the course, keep trying. There is nothing wrong with investigating some of our brothers' and sisters' opinions or facts that they have discov-ered – just beware and rely on your relationship with

Yahweh's Holy Spirit. I say this because a lot of these channels are not our brothers and sisters. Most of these modern-day wolves have been regurgitating the same worn-out older misconceptions and doctrines which have no Biblical truth in it whatsoever. Words have meanings, and these meanings are often modified by cultures. We see this today in the cultural movement to redefine a great many terms.

Yet Yahweh is amazing, and how he maintained language translations over millennia is absolutely astonishing.

When Yahshua used the words, I AM in John 8:58, he was stating before Abraham that the LOGOs was! In other words, I AM the Messiah Prophesied and uttered by Yahweh. I AM the embodiment of the hope of the long-known promise. The Logos was a thought uttered by Divinity (Yahweh); it was the promise of a Messiah.

Yahweh's Holy Spirit carried this promise and gave a little bit of this promise to every human being on this planet. Remember this Light was the promise uttered by Yahweh Himself. It's this Light, this promise, which makes us alive. This is the promise we have in Yahweh - John 1:12. It is *our* Light. When Yahshua accepted his role as Messiah, Yahweh's Holy Spirit filled him, and he became that Light which Yahweh uttered. Yahshua became the Messiah, and when the Messiah fulfilled his role as our sacrifice, was raised from the dead, and then became our advocate, we can have Yahweh's Holy Spirit in us. Not as mini messiahs but as sons and daughters of Yahweh, learning Torah, residing in grace and working out our salvation with much fear and trembling. Hence, before Abraham, I was (I AM). There is nothing complex about it and nothing ever mentioned about Yahshua being with Yahweh in heaven as more than a thought or intention or equal to Yahweh himself.

It's ironic that modern-day Christians now believe like the Jews did back then. In other words, the Jews saw this as an affront—the equating of oneself to Yahweh. In evangelical Christianity, they see that Yahshua is, by this declaration, equal to or the same as Yahweh. The only difference being the assumed equality factor, that is to say one sees this as outrageous while the other sees this as a trinitarian or duelist belief.

As I have learned throughout preschool, grade school, middle school, high school, and so on, how we read and comprehend information is crucial. It is vital to our understanding and being able to act on our beliefs. As studiers of scripture, we must learn to lay down all we have been taught by doctrine and by man to allow Yahweh's Holy Spirit to instruct us. We must always watch and discern the fruits of all men who wish to teach. Otherwise, when we do not, strange doctrines come into our faith and our lives.

I have since repented of my previously wayward thinking as I have come to understand that believing Yahshua is Yahweh, existed with Yahweh as Divinity, or that Yahshua existed prior to his birth is of the anti-Messiah or more commonly called the antichrist.

Our Messiah cannot be a God or else the sacrifice is not any good. The sacrifice must be made wholly by a human being, fully man, who emptied himself to walk in the Torah perfectly and give his own life as a ransom to all who will accept.

On the other hand, those that claim Yahshua has no glory, power, or authority given to him by Yahweh are also in danger of being anti-Messiah/antichrist.

He was in the world, **and the world was made through him,** *and the world knew him not.John 1:10*

and καὶ	the world κόσμον	was made ἐγένετο	through δι'	him αὐτοῦ

2532 kai (the most common NT conjunction, used over 9,000 times) – and (also), very often, moreover, even, indeed (the context determines the exact sense).

G2889 kosmos – Probably from the base of G2865; orderly arrangement that is decoration; by implication the world (in a wide or narrow sense including its inhabitants literally or figuratively [morally]): – adorning world.

G2685 kolumboa – From a primary word kolumbos (to take care of); properly to provide for that is (by implication) to carry off (as if from harm; generally), obtain): – bring, receive.

G1096 ergento or ginomai – a prolonged and middle form of a primary verb; to cause to be (generate) that is to become (come into being) used with great latitude (literally, figuratively, intensely etc.) arise, be assembled, be (fall, come, have self) be brought (to pass), to emerge, become, transitioning from one point (realm, condition) to another; means "to become, and signifies a change of condition, state or place. means to come into being/manifestation implying motion, movement, or growth" (at 2 Pet 1:4). Thus, it is used for God's actions as emerging from eternity and becoming (showing themselves) in time ("physical space). God forbid, be ordained.

G1223 dia preposition - denoting the channel of an act; after, always among, at, to, avoid through, on account of, because of. properly, across (to the other side), back-and-forth to go all the way through, "successfully across" ("thoroughly"). 1223 (dià) is also commonly used as a prefix and lend the same idea ("thoroughly," literally, "successfully" across to the other side), is a root of the English term diameter ("across to the other side, through").

G846 autou - From the particle au (perhaps akin to G109 through the idea of a baffling wind; backward; (1) self (emphatic) (2) he, she, it (used for the third person pronoun) (3) the same. Usage: he, she, it, they, them, same. In itself it signifies nothing more than again, applied to what has either been previously mentioned or, when the whole discourse is looked at, must necessarily be supplied. Also, see G1438; self.

G848 hautou - a contraction for G1438; self.

G1438 heautou him -self, alone

WHO MADE WHO?

In this part of the text of verse ten, a lot of people get mixed up with whom John is speaking of. One reason is due to the word "him" and all the doctrines thereof.

The current English rules regarding pronouns taking the place of proper nouns and which proper nouns the *him* refers to can also confuse the issue. Remember: English is not the original language of this document.

The second reason is the translation word choice by King James and his translators for the word *dia* **G1223**. For some reason, the English word "by" is chosen for *dia* – channel of an act – best described as *through*. In English, this word "by" implies not only through or through a medium, but by can also mean in proximity to, as in nearby. Also, it can mean borne or caused. As with my sons by marriage to my wife or I made the chair by my hand, respectively.

This word *by* implies that the creation of the world was the result of Yahshua's hand in conjunction with Yahweh. Instead of *by*, using the word *through* gives us a better understanding of what occurs and does not cause any problem within the grammar of the original language.

This should be cause for pause when reading because him in this text is **G846**. As we know through the whole of John 1:1-10, **G846** has not changed. The author is still speaking of the same third person singular. This is Yahweh's Holy Spirit, as each verse has only shifted from Yahweh's Holy Spirit to John the Baptist, and John the Baptist did not create the heavens and the earth.

In chapter one of this book, we learned Yahweh's Holy Spirit created the heavens and the Earth along with man. He created all of creation. Yet made through *who*? Yahweh and His Holy Spirit did the creating. One of the mind-blowing truths we miss because Hebrew has been translated into English is that Ruach Ha Kodesh (Yahweh's Holy Spirit) is a feminine word. Technically Spirit "ruach" is feminine, however we are discussing Yahweh's Spirit, and it is Holy. Yahweh is a masculine word. Yahweh's Spirit who formed us and gave us life, being in the female form is rather interesting in regard to a woman who carries the child to term. We grow from embryo to baby in our mother's womb. This seems so basic, yet our desensitizing violence and disregard for human life has left us unable to appreciate the miracle of life in all forms. The masculine side of this equation is Yahweh uttering his Logos which, as we learned in an earlier chapter, can be a seed. The Holy Breath, which is coming from Yahweh, is not a separate entity of Yahweh. This is His Holy Spirit. Just as our breath isn't a separate entity from us, because Yahweh breathed into the man when he created Adam.

Here is another reason to make a careful, thoughtful, and concerned approach to abortion. Not only are we snuffing out the Light given by Yahweh's Holy Spirit, we also basically reject the portion of the creation process given to us by our creator.

Having a child is a male and female process which requires both participants, and this creation should not be a woman's decision alone, unless the father has disappeared. However, keep in mind that even a child brought into the world by rape is still a child who was thought of before the ground dried under the fluttering of Yahweh's Holy Spirit. Let us quickly "reason out" this statement. In Genesis 1 we know that the "Divine Presence" which is Yahweh's Holy Spirit did the creating. We also see in this first chapter of Genesis that all of us were thought of when Yahweh said "Let there be light" in Genesis 1:3. The need for a Messiah, as Yahweh saw the declension that would occur. In Genesis 1:2 we will find Yahweh's Holy Spirit hovering. This word comes from the Hebrew word *rachaph* **H7363**, to brood; by implication to be relaxed: flutter, move, shake. We can see the translator used the word hovering at his own discretion and rightly so, as hovering is never used as a meaning or synonym by Strong's Lexicon. The actual word here is to flutter[2] and this is why I used the phrase "before the ground dried under the fluttering of Yahweh's Holy Spirit."

When we lose sight of scripture, or when we lose sight of Yahweh, we end up in an isolated and hurtful place which can seem lonely and can lead to doctrines which do not honor Yahweh.

THE SEED OF SATAN DOCTRINE

We should always take the time to understand words and their meanings in context of the scripture. Just like listening to a speaker or receiving directions or even hearing a boss give a set of goals to reach for the day; if we do not make careful consideration of these thoughts uttered to us, then we can offend, get lost, or even get fired due to our own ignorance.

Through these last five chapters, we begin to see how strange doctrines can spring up because of the lack of careful consideration and meditation on the Word and because word choices can have a deep and consequential impact on our beliefs and the world around us.

People will often be willing to die on a hill for a belief system whether they were taught it, read about it somewhere, or learned it as their culture. These belief systems can often create strife, hatred, war, and racism.

One common doctrine which runs rampant is the serpent seed theory. This theory states Eve had sex with Satan, and Cain was the result, and then Eve had intercourse with Adam and another egg was fertilized, becoming Abel. When we come to a realization that Cain and Abel were twins this becomes very clear and come into focus. This double fertilization is called heteropaternal superfecundation or superfetation. While these two scenarios are possible, they are both exceedingly rare. As we discussed earlier in this chapter, here is a prime example of a Sunday newspaper Bible reading.

The most glaring problem with this idea is it negates man's choice to be bad or be good, i.e., Cain couldn't choose because of his genetics.

Secondly, this doctrine places blame on someone else for Cain's choices, instead of his taking responsibility for his own missing of the mark. This negates the need for a Messiah as well.

Thirdly, Cain and Abel were twins born right after the other, which negates superfetation and makes superfecundation even less likely to have occurred.

Fourthly, Cain is the older brother, and his name means "acquired." The root of this word is man. Abel means "empty," as in vain or vanity, empty of substance. In these names alone, there is a complete misunderstanding of the scripture surrounding the serpent seed doctrine theory. Why? In the Hebrew mindset, names are one of the most important items of discussion, assisting in understanding the character of the person. This is evidenced by how often inscriptive names were given, the promise given, before babies were born, and names were changed as significant aspects of persons were changed (such as Jacob, Abram, Sarai, and even Naomi). As we learned in an earlier chapter, the character is your image.

Fifthly, Cain took the work of his father, as the eldest son normally would. Cain was doing the right thing thus far.

Sixthly, why were they performing sacrifices? Or were they giving offerings to Yahweh? Because Yahweh had instructed Adam and Eve to abide by Torah. Not Law but Torah! How can a seed of Satan perform or keep the Torah? Why did they do a sacrifice anyway? Mount Sinai had not yet occurred. Therefore, something else must be going on here. Could there have been a struggle or did some sin demand atoning? I personally believe this was Pentecost or Shavuot, as they were supposed to bring in the first fruits for these sacrifices or offerings. That would be following Torah which all of us who follow Yahshua as Messiah should be doing, so we can watch the prophetic timeclock/calendar of Yahweh! While Cain's sacrifice was not accepted, being the oldest, he was told to do better and keep his temper in check.

Let's look at one of my favorite scriptures: Genesis 4: 6-7. Here, we can see that based on the masculine and feminine forms of the words in this text that "his" is Abel. Most see the "his" in the text meaning sin, however the word for sin in Hebrew is a feminine word, so it cannot be sin but Abel. This is an almost identical passage to Genesis 3:16.

Seventhly, as the elder of the two, Cain was to lead Abel, as is the custom in most cultures around the world, especially in Biblical culture. We see a strange cut-off in the text at verse eight. What did they speak about? Did Abel flaunt his ambitions? Seems very suspicious. We do not know and will not know until Yahweh settles all arguments Isaiah 2:4. Yet Yahweh remains gracious toward Cain, the supposed seed of Satan up to this point. Who has not been annoyed when someone tries to one-up you or make you look bad in front of another person, boss, teacher, pastor, or friend? Suddenly, Abel is dead, killed by his brother Cain.

Eighthly, why did Yahweh show mercy to Cain if he was the seed of Satan? He allowed him to live after committing a capital offense. Yahweh allowed a mark to be placed on Cain so no one touched Cain. Then Yahweh put a curse on anyone who killed Cain! Pretty cushy scenario for a seed of Satan!

Finally, the Hebrew does not allude to this seed scenario whatsoever, not in Aramaic Hebrew or in the Ancient Hebrew. This story is about not being allowed to overcome a usurper by murder, slander, or contempt.

Even when the cause seems just, capital punishment may not be the sentence received. Though, transgressors will pay for their transgressions just as well. This may mean wandering, being hated, or an endless self-turmoil. This is not because there is a doomed line of seed fathered by Satan. We see proof for this in John 1:10.

Anyone who studies to understand scripture and takes the time to contemplate it will see that every human being that has ever existed has had the option to accept eternal life through the promised word uttered by Yahweh concerning His son Yahshua Ha Mashiach.

In no way, implicitly or explicitly, did Yahweh allow for a seed of Satan to be introduced into humanity. Besides, why would Satan who wants to kill, steal, and destroy undo his chance of winning this war against Yahweh by performing such a task?

He was in the world, and the world was made through him, **and the world knew him not.** *John 1:10*

and καὶ	the world κόσμον	knew ἔγνω	him αὐτόν	not οὐκ

2532 kaí (the most common NT conjunction, used over 9,000 times) – and (also), very often, moreover, even, indeed (the context determines the exact sense).

G2889 kosmos – Probably from the base of G2865; orderly arrangement that is a great variety of applications and by implication the world (in a wide or narrow sense including its inhabitants literally or figuratively [morally]): – adorning world.

G2685 kolumboa – From a primary word kolumbos (to tend that is take care of); properly to provide for that is (by implication) to carry off (as if from harm; generally, obtain): – bring receive.

G1097 ginosko – a prolonged form of a primary verb; to know (absolutely) in a great variety of applications and with many implications: – allow, be aware (of) feel (have) known (-ledge) perceive, be resolved can, speak, be sure, understand.

G846 autou - From the particle au (perhaps akin to G109 through the idea of a baffling wind; backward; (1) self (emphatic) (2) he, she, it (used for the third person pronoun) (3) the same. Usage: he, she, it, they, them, same. In itself it signifies nothing more than again, applied to what has either been previously mentioned or, when the whole discourse is looked at, must necessarily be supplied. Also, see G848 hautou- a contraction for G1438; self.

G848 hautou- a contraction for G1438; self.

G1438 heautou him -self, alone

G3756 ou – Also ouk, ouk, ook used before a vowel and oux, ouch, ookh before an aspirate. A primary word; the absolutely negative (compare G3361 [absolute denial]) adverb; no or not: - +long nay neither, never, no (X man) none. G3364 G3372

G3361 me – a primary particle of qualified negation.

G3364 oo me – A double negative.

G3372 mekos – length (L or F

A CHANGING WORLD

And the world knew Him not. Yahweh was here the whole time, moving about the Earth, watching mankind and seeking individuals for relationship. Those seeking a glimmer of hope in this now fallen world Yahweh's Holy Spirit created originally, now overshadowed by a corrupt religious system on one side and fallen empires of man's ambitions on the other. Here is the declension we discussed in chapter one of this book.

Now at the end of verse ten, Yahweh's Holy Spirit is still the object of discussion as Yahweh's plan comes together, resulting in the imminent announcement of the Messiah. The world Yahweh's Holy Spirit created, filled, and fattened is now in such a fallen state where it cannot recognize who He (Holy Spirit) is. Thus, this blindness reveals the despair and depravity of mankind.

On one hand, this seems strategic because the Jews had been subjugated to the Greeks and now to the Romans. The Roman Empire is known for its cruelty and ambitious appetite.

At this time in history, technology is not as simple as one might imagine. The Persians and Chinese had developed mathematics to a high degree. Astronomy had been improved on by the Greeks, and Persians had advanced the study tremendously. The Greeks' abstract way of thinking led to more and more civilizations relying on higher education and educated autonomy to dictate what nations and individuals can attain collectively but especially individually.

Through philosophy, scientific advancements in psychology, along with hedonism and nihilism, relying on oneself leads to what some would describe as a hole or deep pit in their abdomens. Whereby mankind is drifting further and further from their Creator.

This new Western thinking style has led to an assault on Eastern philosophy and theology, causing the human race to lean on spiritual self-awareness, resulting in the ongoing attempt by humanity and religions to justify one's sin or shortcomings.

Many do not realize the peace within and the already lost art of repentance is only one step away from all of us. However, due to men's haughtiness, they cannot begin to fathom who to call out to in order to turn away from these empty pursuits. Thus, the world knew Him not. The "systems" (**G2889** *kosmo*), as translated from the Septuagint, have been trampled in the name of progress. Mankind's systems of rules and their pseudo-semblance of order cannot recognize the simplest form of Torah. The self-determination of man has created a wall of deception, whereby creating an inability to recognize Yahweh's Holy Spirit, and this shows how out of touch mankind has become.

A more in-depth translation of this verse would be: **He was** (I Am, baffling wind, wast*)* **in** (in the realm) **the** (definite article) **world** (system or orderly arrangement, left to take care of) **and the world** (system or orderly arrangement, left to take care of) **was made** (ordained or dedicated to come to pass) **through** (a channel of an act) **him** (baffling wind) **and the world** (system or orderly arrangement, left to take care of) **knew** (aware of, perceived) **him** (baffling wind) **not** (absolutely not).

He came unto his own and his own received him not. John 1:11

He came	unto	his own	and
ἦλθεν	εἰς	ἴδια	καὶ

G2064 elthen

(erchomia – due to the tense with the pronoun) – middle voice of a primary verb (used only in the present and imperfect tenses the others being supplied by kindred {middle voice} word eleuthomai or eltho; which do not otherwise occur); to come or go (in a great variety of applications literally and figuratively):- accompany, appear, bring, come, enter fallout, go, grow, light, next, pass, resort, be set.

G1519 eis

a preposition) – properly, into (unto) – literally, "motion into which" implying penetration ("unto," "union") to a particular purpose or result, to or into (indicating the point reached or entered, of place, time, purpose, result). Usage: into, in, unto, to, upon, towards, for, among.

G2398 idios

of uncertain affinity; pertaining to self that is ones own; by implication private or separate:- his acquaintance when they were alone, apart, aside due his (own proper several) home (her our thine your) own (business) private (-ly) proper severally their (own).

G2532 kai

(the most common NT conjunction, used over 9,000 times) – and (also), very often, moreover, even, indeed (the context determines the exact sense).

his own	received	him	not
ἴδια	παρέλαβον	αὐτόν	οὐ

G2398 idios of uncertain affinity; pertaining to self that is ones own; by implication private or separate:- his acquaintance when they were alone, apart, aside due his (own proper several) home (her our thine your) own (business) private (-ly) proper, severally their (own).

G3880 paralambano From G3844 and G2983; to receive near that is used only as an alternate in certain tenses; to take (in very many applications literally and figuratively G1209 is rather subjective or passive to have offered to one; while G138 is more violent (to seize or remove):- accept + be amazed assay signifies nothing more than again, attain bring X when I call catch come on (X unto) + forget have hold obtain receive (X after) take (away up).

G3844 para A primary preposition; properly near that is (with genitive case) from beside (lit. or fig.) (with dative cause) at (or in) the vicinity of (objectively or subjectively) with (objectively) with accusative case) to the proximity with (local especially beyond or opposed to) or causal (on account of)). In compounds it retains the same variety of application:- above against among at before by contrary to friend from + give (such things as they) + that (she) had X his in more than nigh unto (out) of past save side... by in the sight of than (there-) fore with. In compounds it retains the same variety of application.

G2983 lambano A prolonged form of a primary verb which is primary akin to G109 through the idea of a baffling wind; backward); (1) self (emphatic) (2) he, she, it (used for the third person pronoun) (3) the same. Usage:- he, she, it, they, them, same. In itself it

G846 autou - From the particle au (perhaps akin to G109 (compare G3661) adverb; no or not:- +long nay neither never no (X man) none. G3364 G3372

G848 hautou - a contraction for G1438; self.

G1438 heautou him -self, alone

G3756 ou - A primary word; the absolutely negative (compare G3661) adverb; no or not:- +long nay neither never no (X man) none. G3364 G3372

G3361 me - a primary particle of qualified negation

G3364 oo me - A double negative.

G3372 mekos - length (L or F)

YAHWEH CAN AND DOES VISIT HIS CREATION

When drive-by reading occurs, most people will tell you this verse is strictly dealing with Yahshua and his people, the Jews. I thought and believed the same thing for many years because I was taught this within the Protestant sect of Christianity.

Yahshua did say he did not only come for the lost house of Israel, Matthew 15:21-28. Paul also backs this up in his direct mission to the Gentiles in Roman 1:16. The power of the gospel is to save, and it is for the Jew first and then for the Gentile. I am sharing this so we can understand that this is still Yahweh's Holy Spirit John is writing about. Yahweh's Holy Spirit is moving across the Earth, looking for relationship with us, his man-faced creation.

The first part of this verse, he came is *ethlen* **G2064**, this is aorist indicative active third person singular verb. Wow! A verb in the aorist tense is rare, and this choice by John to relay a Hebraic idea in a Greek mindset is brilliant.

Why is that? I am glad we asked.

The basic idea of this word is I come and I go or back and forth. The aorist tense is secondary and indicates past action and a single discreet action where the tense is simple. This tense states a fact which is that the action has happened. There is no time frame involved due to this being indicative (mood) and active (voice). The action has happened with no extra info about continuing or completing the action.

Now the verb is in simple form; thus, it is a simple action, or an action not marked regarding whether the results of the action are continuing. This is interesting as this implies that "He came," He being Yahweh's Holy Spirit whom as we are still speaking of, **him G846** *autos*. This subject nor the direct object has changed, so being in this tense tells us yes, Yahweh moved across the earth, back and forth, while looking and seeking.

Seeking what? To see if anyone would recognize their creator. It's a beautiful concept. Our creator searches for us —as he searched for Adam and Eve in the Garden of Eden Genesis 3:8-9. This cannot be Yahshua, as he is not born yet. Can humanity see the light? Will we recognize the light? Are we paying attention to seasons? The same thing happens in today's time, Ecclesiastes 1:1-11.

Does anyone recognize who their creator is today? Some do.

However, most people who believe in the blood atonement that Yahshua completed have replaced Yahweh, their creator, with Yahshua. With this bold statement, I offer a simple thought. The creator who knew we would fail, who knew we would miss the mark, gave us two trees and the promise of the Messiah!

Every step of the way, Yahweh's mercy has been made apparent by his hand through the ages. Then the promise was fulfilled, and the created esteems themselves above the creator. This is what the witches and new-agers do; this is mankind praising the creation, not the creator, and this happened first at the flood. There is nothing new under the sun.

Yahshua gave a stern warning about this type of thinking as we also recall the whole story of the flood, Matthew 27:34. Particularly, pay attention to the events leading up to the flood waters, Genesis 6:1-8, and then in times concurrent to Yahshua, Romans 1:18-32.

When we take a notion or a doctrine that a created being is equal to or above the one true GOD who created them, then destruction will surely ensue. Yahshua was created in the womb of Mary and set his humanity aside to fulfill his role of Messiah. Furthermore, Yahshua never once equated himself with His Father. He did say, "I and my father are one," meaning this as in a unit moving in a direction together along a human timeline.

I will bend the knee to Yahshua, and I will honor him in any way I can, and I know scripturally Yahshua will never ask me to do anything to violate Yahweh's sovereignty. For Yahshua to ask me to place him above Yahweh would negate all of the work on the cross. We see how this idea has taken root. The idea that a God died for our sins is so engrained in millennia of DNA that we accept this pagan belief and then dare to say it was Yahweh who died on the cross—thus, equating the creator and the creation. This is a frightening place to be, and I recommend believers abandon this idea and get in the metaphorical ark.

This aorist verb (*elthen*) is a moving back and forth, all through Old Testament, and it continues in the New Testament in John 4:23-24.

The Holy Roman Catholic church (mother church) began bearing down on the European kings and states with their doctrinal influence. Even at the time of the reformation, the Protestant churches (daughter churches) kept a lot of these pagan doctrines and rituals active—such as the doctrine of the trinity, as we discussed in an earlier chapter.

This equality with Yahweh is rooted deep within believers; thus, in some cases, believers replace Yahweh with Yahshua, leaving Yahweh as an old man on a throne waiting to strike vengeance upon mankind. Why is this familiar? Where have we heard this before? Oh yeah, Viking and Greco Roman religions. Imagine that! Odin and Thor, Cronos, and of course, Zeus and his many sons and daughters born of earthly women.

These pagan-sourced ideas, thoughts, and belief systems brought this idea into mainstream Christianity, and it stuck almost genetically it seems. Interestingly enough, the types of abominations[3] are defilement, perversions, and wickedness. These are found in topics such as food, sexual relations, idolatry, lies, weights and measurements, sorcery, and abortion. The word abomination is in modern day tied to epigenetics[4], realizing that this word means something close to genetic alteration. That is why eating non-food items as food will result in an abomination according to Yahweh. Did you know science has now proven that your sexual, substance, and eating activities can flip certain genes off? Then this changed genetic marker is passed down to your unborn offspring.[5]

Why does Yahweh say that homosexuality is an abomination? When we go beyond the original human design of sexuality, we encounter a plethora of pleasures that are not necessarily healthy as a result. These results or occurrences, when repeated, will become habits, and these habits will rewire the human brain by creating pathways geared for that specific way to intake pleasure. This can cause the fantasy realm of the brain (amygdala, limbic brain, and sexual templates) to be overstimulated and the release of hormones creates sensations of pleasure and reward. These can literally flip genes on and off. This can happen to an individual who becomes addicted to alcohol or drugs, as well. The overeating or undereating of foods can also complete this gene-altering cycle.

Why did I go here? The fact that thought processes, especially belief systems, can literally be so entrenched into our being that we can become genetically predisposed to that belief.

Can one overcome their predisposition? Certainly!

That is why Yahweh said, in **Ezekiel 18, "the son shall not bear the guilt of the father nor the father bear the guilt of the son."** It might be hard to reprogram our thought-habits and compulsions, but we can do this.

The first commandment states: **"You shall not make for yourself an image in the form of anything in heaven above or on the earth beneath or in the waters below. You shall not bow down to them or worship them; for I, the Lord your God, am a jealous God, punishing the children for the sin of the parents to the third and fourth generation of those who hate me, but showing love to a thousand generations of those who love me and keep my commandments." Exodus 20:3-6**

This particular translation, unfortunately, uses the word punishes. Now the word punished can be used here. However, this is in error, given the wording of the verse itself.

Oversee is the correct translation for פָּקַד H6485 *pawkad*, as in visit, oversight, charge, governor, commit. This changes the connotation to something better in keeping with the text as it appears in the first place.

Yahweh is not a mean or vindictive God. Yet this is what we have been taught over and over in the same regurgitated theology since 225 B.C.E. At about 300 A.D., the trinity comes into view and mixes with the mean Zeus-like God theology, and the damage has been done, leaving an imprint on Western culture for ages to come.

How can the church control us more efficiently or the government keep us in line? Put an unhealthy fear of God into the populace and use this fear of God to make multitudes obedient to the government. This, coupled with old wives' tales and superstitions, and we have a perfectly subordinate assembly, workforce, and culture.

So, yes, my friend, you are the captain of your own ship, if you so choose, and Yahweh's Holy Spirit is waiting for each of us to ask him to guide us into a life which will lead to peace and a great friendship with Yahweh.

In summation, the mother church set a doctrine in stone, and even after the reformation, the daughter churches retained this doctrine. To be clear, this doctrine is the idea that Yahshua is Yahweh and Yahweh is Yahshua and the Holy Spirit does the leg work as a third person in this relationship. Also, often included in this view, Yahshua is generally present as part of this trinity at the beginning of creation.

Strong, the writer of Strong's Concordance, and his team believed this doctrine within the Methodist denomination, and this is clearly visible in their exegesis under the **G2064** *erchomai* heading in his concordance. Strong's Concordance uses multiple examples of scriptures to point to one understanding of this particular word used in this particular passage, i.e., toward this being the Messiah. Now this doctrine exists in all sects of Christianity, including Roman Catholic, Orthodox Catholic Church, Protestant, and Hebraic Roots. Under most denominations of these sects, we can see why these eisegesis statements, sermons, and literature pressure one to accept or adopt this belief.

We see again, in this verse, there is a poetic nature in the Hebrew. This verse doubles down and repeats, to a degree, the first verse to show that this text is a very important thought being relayed here. As in verse ten where "he was in the world and the world knew him not," verse eleven makes the same basic statement, "he came into his own and his own knew him not."

Let's visit "his own," since it stares all of us in the face when we read this, unless we read through the verse on auto pilot. These two words, "his own," are as important as "he comes." This has probably made some of us question already what this was getting at or who "his own" really is.

Idios **G2398** belonging to, one own, distinct, and personal implies a nature of Yahweh's Holy Spirit which means we are his own, his personally, belonging to him as part of his creation, and that we are distinct to his creation.

What is certainly interesting here is the idea that Yahweh desires to be in communion with us.

However, all other religions or gods want mankind to go after them or require some strange form of worship. Yahweh does not require bogus, nonsensical acts as his true form of worship; he requires commitment, obedience to his Torah, and a relationship.

Yes, he offers a two-way relationship, and we are all the children of Yahweh. We can see, in a non-Biblical historical timeline, the progression of mankind socially and technologically.

This is evident with the Chinese, Persian, Egyptian, and Greek Empires. By the time Yahshua was born, mathematics and science had taken a huge leap. Ironically, the astrologers, alchemists, scientists, philosophers, scholars, historians, rabbis, and priests did not see this great event—the coming of the Messiah—in their near future.

There was a conjunction, and a certain set of stars formed constellations, appearing in the night sky. This should have certainly set off an alarm, at least to the priests and astrologers, that a human Messiah was to be born and soon.

"And his own received him not" is exactly what this text describes. Man, in all his wisdom and learning, cannot even tell what season it is and will not be able to discern the signs despite all of the prophecies of this appearance.

Paralambano **G3880** is acknowledge. However, it was translated as received, as in "to take from." It appears that acknowledge fits this line of text much more appropriately. The word *elthan* begs this word *paralambano* due to the act taking place and in the verb tense chosen. In other words, does mankind acknowledge that I am seeking or coming and going?

An in-depth rendering of this verse would be: **He came** (to come and go, back and forth) **unto** (toward or among) **his own** (one's own, creation) **and** (indeed) **his own** (one's own, creation) **received** (acknowledge, associate by relation or office) **him** (baffling wind) **not** (absolutely not).

CHAPTER 6
THE POWER, THE WORD, & THE FLESH
THE JOHN 1:1 FACTOR

But as many as received him, to them gave he power to become the sons of Yahweh, even to them that believe on his name:*John 1:12*

But

δὲ

G1161 dé - A primary particle (adversative or continuative); but, and, etc. — also, and, but, moreover, now (often unexpressed in English).

as many as

ὅσοι

G3745 hosos - By reduplication from G3739; as (much great long etc.) as:- all (that) as (long many much) [as] how great (many much) [in]] as much as so many as that (ever) the more those things what (great -soever) wheresoever wherewithsoever which X while who (-soever).

G3739 hos - Probably a primary word (or perhaps a form of the article G3588); the relative (sometime demonstrative) pronoun who which what that:- one who which what that:- one (an the) other some that which who (-m-se) See also G3757.

G3757 hou - Genitive case of G3739 as adverb; at which place that is where:- where (-in) whither ([soever]).

received

ἔλαβον

G2983 lambano - (from the primitive root, lab-, meaning "actively lay hold of to take or receive," see NAS dictionary) – properly, to lay hold by aggressively (actively) accepting what is available (offered). lambánō ("accept with initiative") emphasizes the volition (assertiveness) of the receiver.

him

αὐτοῦ

G846 autou - From the particle au (perhaps akin to G109) through the idea of a baffling wind; backward; (1) self (emphatic) (2) he, she, it (used for the third person pronoun) (3) the same. Usage: he, she, it, they, them, same. In itself it signifies nothing more than again, applied to what has either been previously mentioned or, when the whole discourse is looked at, must necessarily be supplied. Also, see

G848 hautou - a contraction for G1438; self.

G1438 heautou him -self, alone

When we study verse twelve, it appears this text is speaking of Yahshua. However, we soon realize that the him written of here is actually still the same him written about in the previous verses of this chapter. The subject is the Holy Spirit who is Yahweh. The primary particle "but" is being used in an adversative from verse eleven. Whereas verse eleven speaks about his own not receiving him, as in those of his creation not receiving Yahweh.

The primary participle, "but" *de* (**G1161**) is used here to convey another thought quite different from the prior thought and not as a conjunction. John is also confirming here that, though a minority, people of all circles of life anticipated this prophecy to unfold at any moment. The prophecy being the Logos (**G3056**), the promise, the light.

John 1:6-11 tells us, thus far, Yahweh's Holy Spirit has been moving and stirring up, which translates to preparing the way of the Logos or the Word to become manifest for no other time than this. Simply put, all were welcome to experience this marvel which was about to come to pass, hence the word, *hosos* (**G3745**) which is a pronoun. From the etymology of this word, its full definition includes ideas such as how much, how many, whosoever.

The next word translated as received is, *lambano* (**G2983**) to actively lay hold of, to take or receive, lay hold of aggressively and accepting what is available. To me, this is exciting. I see and accept Yahweh as a loving Elohim who wants a relationship with us, has mercy and grace toward us, teaching us his instructions.

So, when you are His and you know Him, *lambano* is the perfect verb to describe how believers are motivated. This also dispels any idea that this was a "dead time" or "dry spell" concerning Biblical or religious interactions with the creator in the world at large within the Hebrew, Greek, or Roman cultures.

There are people who say the Old Testament God of the Bible is mean, judgmental, and has no mercy at all. This could not be farther from the truth. Over and over again, we see this desire from Yahweh toward mankind for a relationship, Hosea 6:4-6, John 3:16-17.

We also see in other cultures, aside from the Jews, mercy delivered and cultures flourishing. Israel enjoyed a large volume of mercy when it came to obeying Torah, treatment of the sojourner, and sabbaticals toward people and the land. Yahweh desired a relationship with them.

Finally, understating and adjusting our bearings, we see that him is Yahweh's Holy Spirit who is Yahweh. In this profound statement in the first part of verse twelve, we see Yahweh openly accepting anyone who wishes to have a relationship with him to seize this gift.

This, my friends, is reminiscent of the times when we pick up our little son or daughter and the child gives us a great big hug, so tight and almost never-ending. Remember those days?

It is a beautiful picture!

But as many as received him, **to them gave he power to become the sons of Yahweh,** *even to them that believe on his name: John 1:12*

to them
αὐτοῖς

gave he
ἔδωκεν

power
ἐξουσίαν

to become
γενέσθαι

the children
τέκνα

of Yahweh
Θεοῦ

G846 autos - From the particle au (perhaps akin to G109 through the idea of a baffling wind; backward;) (1) self (emphatic) (2) he, she, it (used for the third person pronoun) (3) the same. Usage: he, she, it, they, them, same. In itself it signifies nothing more than again, more than again, has either been previously mentioned or, when the whole discourse is looked at, must necessarily be supplied. Also, see G1438; self.

G848 hautou - a contraction for G1438; self.

G1438 heautou - him-self, alone

G1325 edoken - A prolonged form of a primary verb (which is used as an alternate in most of the tenses); to give (used in a very wide application, properly or by implication Lor F, greatly modified by the connection); - adventure, bestow, bring forth, commit, deliver(up), give, grant, hinder, make, minister, number, offer, have power, put, receive, set, shew, smite (+with the hand) strike (+with the palm of the hand) suffer, take, utter, yield.

G1849 exousia (from 1537 /ek, "out from," which intensifies 1510 /eimi, "to be, being as a right or privilege") - authority, conferred power; delegated empowerment ("authorization"), operating in a designated jurisdiction. In the NT, 1849 /eksousía ("delegated power") refers to the authority God gives to His saints - authorizing them to act to the extent they are guided by faith (His revealed word). See 1832

G1832 exesti - Third person singular present indicative of a compound of G1537 and G1510, so also, exon; neuter present participle of the same (with or without some form of G1510 expressed); impersonally it is right (through the figurative idea of being out in public): - be lawful let X may (est).

G1096 ergento or ginomai - properly, to emerge, become, transitioning from one point (realm, condition) to another; means "to become, and signifies a change of condition, state or place. means to come into being/manifestation implying motion, movement, or growth" (at 2 Pet 1:4). Thus, it is used for God's actions as emerging from eternity and becoming (showing themselves) in time (physical space).

G5043 tekron - From the base of G5098; a child (as produced): - child daughter son.

G5098 timoria - From G5097, vindication that is (by implication) a penalty: - punishment.

G2316 theós - (of unknown origin) - properly, God, the Creator and owner of all things (Jn 1:3, Gen 1 - 3).

TO BE A SON

Moving forward, something begins to come into view. The idea that this verse is speaking of Yahshua is quite troublesome because, when reading verses one through eleven, we see John is speaking about the Promise which is the Word (Logos – a thought uttered).

This Word has been passed down for generations; this Word which is the Light, and it is Hope. When we see Light, there can be hope (Genesis 1:2-3). Now when we accept the Word from Yahweh our creator, we have received this, and therefore, lay hold of it to take or receive. This receiving is the power granted to us to take hold of our place in the kingdom of Yahweh, which is to be a child of Yahweh.

Within this section, we have *autios* (**G846**) yet what happened here? **G846** has been Yahweh's Holy Spirit this whole time and now it appears to be them which would be "as many as" as was the case in the previous verse.

If we will notice, on one hand, the Greek spelling is different, and the pronoun has changed for this group of people. We are not speaking about Yahweh's Holy Spirit. Now, on the other hand, we must also see these people or this group received Yahweh's Holy Spirit. Thus, **G846** is a perfect choice for describing this group of people who has received him, Yahweh's Holy Spirit.

Reminder: (**G2258**) in context to the text is *ane*. This word is imperfect of (**G1510**) *eimi*, which is first person singular present indicative: as in I exist or I am! Contextually, from John 1:1, we see the word "was" (*ane*) is an important word describing who, when, and what is the Word described. This word points directly to (**G846**). Who is he? He, in this case, still being the subject of the prior verses, interacting exclusively with this group of people, is Yahweh's Holy Spirit.

An interesting detail to mention is that this verb, *edoken* (**G1325**) to give, offer, put, place. Give is the word chosen and recorded by Strong's team of translators, yet, are all acceptable and very powerful in describing the degree in which this power was given. To be given power is quite a privilege.

This next word in the Greek, *exousia* (**G1849**) is used as a sense of ability which is expressly given by Yahweh. Not only is this a power, but it is freedom or liberty. This should cause one to pause and see this in relation to sin. When we realize we have been given power as children of Yahweh, we can begin to see our freedom from sin and practice this power to put sin away. This received power also gives a lawful sense that we have the right to rule over darkness. Is this easy? Not necessarily, as we all have some form of a habitual sin. The habit can be overcome by finding the root of the habit and then conquering the habit through the power received. A majority, if not all habits, come from a form of escape from a past hurt. Utilizing this authority allows us to seek the hurt, relive it, and conquer the hurt logically, not emotionally. All because we have the authority granted to us by Yahweh himself. Because we have this power at our disposal, we can overcome through the knowledge of who we are in Yahweh.

Ginomai (**G1096**) to cause to be or to become, is so trans-formative prior to Yahshua even being on this earth. Yahweh is literally laying out his plan, or His schematic if you will, to describe who and what we are on this planet and in this life!

Frankly, this is also the mighty hand of Yahweh sweeping in to free his creation. Rescuing those who choose to be his, to deliver them from the malevolence which is spiritually affecting the human mind due to the complex emotional system we were given when created. This also applies to evil and its effect on us as the human race. The power gives us the ability to overcome human tragedy, which is currently, or has and will, touch each one us at some point.

This is not a king or a pharaoh holding us in bondage, but that tragedy induced by evil puts our minds or self in a state of bondage. That beautiful ability as a child to put oneself in a construct[1] as a means for protection. This appears to be a defense system put in place by our creator, however we can unwittingly, as we mature, allow for ourselves to be placed in bondage if we do not deal with that hurt. This bondage can produce all types of mental instabilities if not dealt with. We must realize who and what we are by the power given to each one of us as a free gift via Yahweh's Holy Spirit.

However, we must choose to lay hold of or take by force the power to become *tekron* (**G5043**) a child, not as a penalty but by vindication. Vindicating ourselves as a human being and an individual who sins—or misses the mark.

For so long, we have been force-fed the idea which says when we sin, we are bad people. Bad humans! While, yes, sin is bad, the issue is not the penalty but the ability to fix it. The penalty is always going to be there, so if we miss the mark (sin), and we do nothing about missing the mark, we have become or are becoming dysfunctional from a functional biological being. This poses a plethora of issues for our internal systems and typically results in sickness and then death (Romans 6:23). Remember death can be complete death or the loss of a functional system within your body.

Missing the mark is an archery term and also comes from Hebrew. When one recognizes they are missing the mark (sin), *chattah* (**H2403**) an offence, from (**H2398**) *chata* to miss the mark or target. When we offend someone or miss a goal, most people will feel bad or have a regret. When this occurs, we are literally measuring the distance of where the true mark is to where we fell short. This is the very idea of *chattah* (**H2398**); when one realizes they are off the mark, they wish to understand and do better. The appropriate reaction to missing the mark is to measure against the correct action. In this way, Torah is the straight edge by which all our efforts should be measured.

Unfortunately, people love to heap on guilt and shame, especially those in power, and these two emotions have been used in Christianity to create a negative outcome. This abuse has brought about an attitude which causes people to give up, overlook, or completely ignore their missing of the mark.

When we look at the Messiah for a complete remediation of sin, as though he is a get-out-of-jail-free card, this mentality became the result. This is why Torah is important to the personal relationship we have with Yahweh. The sending of a Messiah did not do away with Torah, it did away with the Law—the spiritual consequences. The Law being a recompense or remediation, as in a penalty. Yahshua fulfilling Torah allows us to know and understand the instruction given by Yahweh to live a righteous path. In Torah, one lives a life peacefully with Yahweh first, then peacefully toward others, with ourselves coming last. This is completely different than all other religions.

Why? How? Well, *Torah* (**H8451**) is instruction, and this instruction shows us or teaches us where the mark is. It is the throwing of a finger to point us in the direction to walk or live. Also, the direction we are to take in our life. Most Christians believe that Torah is done away, because they believe that Torah is Law. This misunderstanding gives the impression that Yahshua did away with the Torah which was given at the beginning.

Upon further study, we will find that the commandments had been made known by Yahweh from the time of Adam and Eve and Abraham, Genesis 2:1-3, 26:5. When the commandments were given in Exodus 20, the Israelites were far removed from their patriarchs' recognition of Yahweh and Yahweh's ways. The Egyptian culture had dominated their lives for 400 years.

A reiteration of instruction from their God, their redeemer, was necessary for societal, cultural, and religious realignment. Most importantly, if we enter a covenant with Yahweh, this is our code of conduct. Torah is the standard for living our lives within a covenant with Yahweh. The Law that was fulfilled by Yahshua is the recompense when we fall out of Torah, however this was fulfilled by his atonement, thus we have the blood of the Lamb. Hence, the scripture grace for grace.

In **Proverbs 6:23**, we read, **"For this command is a lamp, this teaching (Torah) is a light, and correc-**

tion and instruction (Torah) are the way to life."
With this in mind, what do we measure against when we
miss the mark? That would be Torah!

As we discovered earlier, the root of Torah (**H8451**) is
yarah (**H3384**) instruct, as in to point the way one is to walk
in life. When we get off track, we do not beat each other or
ourselves up. We measure the error against the correct mark
and try again. We repent, which is to turn one's mind or
head, to re-aim so we will hit the mark. In this way, we get
back onto the right path to walk in life. There is the path of
righteousness!

Here in John 1, the supreme being, our creator, is about
to have his word or promise manifested in a human. By his
Holy Spirit, we can also receive Yahweh's Holy Spirit to have
the power to become children of Yahweh. Who are the children? Those who follow the Torah as a light and obey his
commandments as guideposts.

Now, keep in mind, this is a fluid message, meaning this
message is a timeline leading to a summation of events
regarding the Word being made flesh. We are almost there!
Our Messiah, who walked perfectly on this earth, makes it
attainable for us to perform Torah, and he is going to enable
us in this endeavor while also providing the way for repentance when we fail. This is why the blood of our Messiah
Yahshua is vital – so there is no enmity between Yahweh
and man.

In **Hebrews 2:17**, we read, **"For this reason he had
to be made like them, *fully human in every way*, in
order that he might become a merciful and faithful
high priest in service to God, and that he might**

make atonement for the sins of the people." Also, in **1 Timothy 2:5**, we read, **"For there is one God and one Mediator between God and men,** *the Man* **Messiah Yahshua."**

This allows us to be free of penalty under the law which required the sacrificial system. Yahshua's blood, when accepted, makes amends for the times we miss the mark and allows for repentance, so we can try to hit the mark again being covered by his blood.

If Yahweh had been Yahshua, this would not count for three reasons:

1. Yahweh cannot be tempted.

2. Divinity and flesh cannot coexist in one being.

3. A true God cannot be sacrificed for human sin because a God cannot die.

But as many as received him, to them gave the power to become the sons of Yahweh, **even to them that believe on his name:** *John 1:12*

to those believing	on	his	name.
πιστεύουσιν	εἰς	αὐτοῦ	ὄνομα

G4100 pisteuo – From G4102; to have faith (in upon or with respect to a person or thing) that is credit; by implication to entrust (especially one's spiritual well-being to Messiah):- believe (-r) commit (to trust) put in trust with.

G4102 pistis - (from 3982/peithō, "persuade, be persuaded") – properly, persuasion (be persuaded, come to trust); faith. Can only come from Yahweh.

G1519 eis – A primary preposition; to or into (indicating the point reached or entered) of purpose (result etc)- properly, into (unto) – literally, "motion into which" implying penetration ("unto," "union") to a particular purpose or result, to or into (indicating the point reached or entered, of place, time, purpose, result). Usage: into, in, unto, to, upon, towards, for, among.

G846 autos - From the particle au (perhaps akin to G109 through the idea of a baffling wind; backward; (1) self (emphatic) (2) he, she, it (used for the third person pronoun) (3) the same. Usage: he, she, it, they, them, same. In itself it signifies nothing more than again, applied to what has either been previously mentioned or, when the whole discourse is looked at, must necessarily be supplied. Also, see

G848 hautou- a contraction for G1438; self.

G1438 heautou him -self, alone

G3686 onoma - From a presumed derivative of the base of G1097 (compare G3685); a name (l or F) (authority character); - called (+sur -) name (-d).

G1097 ginosko - A prolonged form of a primary verb; to know (absolutely) in a great variety of applications and with many implications (as shown at left with others not thus clearly expressed): - allow, be aware (of), feel (have) known (-ledge), perceive, be resolved, can speak, be sure, understand.

G3685 oninemi - as in notoriety.

This verse is interesting because of the contrast between the beginning and the ending of this same verse. Based on a simple reading, it appears receiving and believing are two different avenues to becoming the sons of God.

However, the original Greek does not have the word *even*. This was added by the English translators. What this verse actually says is that to those who are becoming believe Yahweh is who he says he is and gave this Word at the beginning of time. They are becoming the sons of Yahweh. It is clearly up to these people, and that is the power. So often we do not realize the power which our Father has given us!

Look at the Greek: *pisteuo* (**G4100**) to have faith upon. So, if you choose to receive Yahweh's Holy Spirit, you will allow yourself to be persuaded to see and understand what is going on, and this can only come from Yahweh.

Eis (**G1519**) to or into. Along with *autos* (**G846**) pronoun and here speaking of Yahweh, his Holy Spirit. Name is *onoma* (**G3686**) character, frame, reputation. The derivative of this Greek word is *ginosko* (**G1097**) and this means to know absolutely.

In Hebrew, the word "name" is very interesting, as the breath of a man is what gives man his character. Names are not an identifier but are what that person will become in his life. The name describes the character. What is Yahweh's character? Faithful, Righteous, Rock, and if we truly believe the Holy Spirit is Yahweh—which he is, then we know Galatians 5:17 sums it up perfectly: "But the fruit of the Spirit is love, joy, peace, longsuffering, gentleness, goodness, faithfulness, meekness, and self-control."

Another verse which reveals the character of Yahweh is

Numbers 14:18: "Yahweh is slow to anger and abounding in steadfast love, forgiving iniquity and transgression, but he will by no means clear the guilty, visiting the iniquity of the fathers on the children, to the third and the fourth generation." (See also Psalm 54:4, Hebrews 13:6).

A rendering of this verse could look like: **But** (also) **as many as** (whosoever) **received** (actively lay hold of to take) **him** (a baffling wind, Holy Spirit) **to them** (they) **gave he** (were given) **power** (rights, privilege, authority) **to become** (to become, changed) **the children** (children, not of penalty) **of Yahweh** (Yahweh).

When one receives the power to see and understand anything, then we have an understanding of what that topic is and what its relation is to you. Of course, there is always a baseline, and being the inquisitive beings we are, relationships grow as we grow, and more is always learned.

His name gives us authority since this is character. Because we believe this, we are given that power. The belief that Yahweh spoke it and it is now coming to pass is paramount to who and what the Messiah is for us and how we can accept that as a reality. Yahweh said it, so it is true.

Just imagine if we visited history in 3 B.C.E to experience the cultures, the crossroads, the technologies, Judaism, and the Roman Empire. Perhaps what we experience today amongst all this modern tragedy and despair in our world was also the same thing experienced by people in 3 B.C.E.

This should cause a nagging question in everyone's mind who believes, or anyone for that matter, who might consider all this as crazy coincidence. That a Hebrew Bedouin believed and recorded this ancient prophecy that has surely come to pass. Clearly, the religious right did not understand it correctly and neither did the governments or peoples of that time either. Cultural fads come and go all the time, much like war and peace. It really is an interesting thought to sit back and meditate on times from history and compare them to ours today. The only thing we have is hope at the end of it, and true hope only comes from one source. The Logos which is the light, the promise, the word of Yahweh. And that is all that matters, His Authority (**H3068 יהוה** Yahweh).

Which were born, not of blood, *nor of the will of the flesh, nor of the will of man, but of Yahweh.* ***John 1:13***

Which — οἳ

G3739 hoi – Probably a primary word (or perhaps a form of the article G3588); the relative (sometime demonstrative) pronoun who which what that: - one (an the) other some that which who (-m-se) See also G3757.

G3757 hou- Genitive case of G3739 as adverb; at which place that is where: - where (-in) whither (soever).

G3588 ho - The masculine feminine (second) and neuter (third) forms in all their inflections; the definite article -he.

were born — ἐγεννήθησαν

G1080 gennao - From a variation of G1085; to procreate (properly of the father but by extension of the mother); figuratively to regenerate: - bear, beget, be born, bring forth, conceive, be delivered of, gender, make, spring.

G1085 genos – From G1096; kin (abstractly or concretely literally or figuratively individually or collectively): - born country (-man), diversity, generation kind (-red), nation, offspring, stock.

G1096 ergento or ginomai – properly, to emerge, become, transitioning from one point (realm, condition) to another; means "to become, and signifies a change of condition, state or place. means to come into being/manifestation implying motion, movement, or growth" (at 2 Pet 1:4) Thus, it is used for God's actions as emerging from eternity and becoming (showing themselves) in time (physical space)

not — οὐκ

G3756 ou - A primary word; the absolutely negative (compare G3361) adverb; no or not: - +long, nay, neither, never, no (X man), none.

G3361 me - a primary particle of qualified negation.

of — ἐξ

G1537 ek – (a preposition, written eks before a vowel) – properly, "out from and to" (the outcome); out from within. ek ("out of") is one of the most under-translated (and therefore mis-translated) Greek propositions – often being confined to the meaning "by." (ek) has a two-layered meaning ("out from and to") which makes it out-come oriented (out of the depths of the source and extending to its impact on the object).

blood — αἱμάτων

G129 aima - Of uncertain derivation; blood, literally (of men or animals), figuratively (the juice (the juice of grapes), or specifically (the atoning blood of Christ); by implication bloodshed, also kindred: - blood.

Which were born, not of blood, **nor of the will of the flesh,** *nor of the will of man, but of Yahweh.* **John 1:13**

nor
οὐδὲ

G3761 oude – From G3756 and G1161; not, however, that is, neither, nor, not even: - neither (indeed), never, no (more nor not), nor (yet) (also even them) not (even so much as) + nothing so much as.

G3756 ou – A primary word; the absolutely negative (compare G3361) adverb; no or not: - +long nay neither never no (X man) none.

G1161 dé - A primary particle (adversative or continuative); but, and, etc. -- also, and, but, moreover, now (often unexpressed in English), (a conjunction) – moreover, indeed now, on top of this, next...

of
ἐξ

G1537 ek – (a preposition, written eks before a vowel) – properly, "out from and to" (the outcome); out from within. ek ("out of") is one of the most under-translated (and therefore mis-translated) Greek propositions – often being confined to the meaning "by." (ek) has a two-layered meaning ("out from and to") which makes it out-come oriented (out of the depths of the source and extending to its impact on the object).

the will
θελήματος

G2307 thelema – (from G2309 /theló, "to desire, wish") – properly, a desire (wish), often referring to God's "preferred-will", i.e. His "best-offer" to people which can be accepted or rejected. [Note the -ma suffix, focusing on the result hoped for with the particular desire (wish). (theléma) is nearly always used of God, referring to His preferred-will. Occasionally it is used of man (cf. Lk 23:25; Jn 1:13.)

G2309 thelo - (a primitive verb, NAS dictionary) – to desire (wish, will), wanting what is best (optimal) because someone is ready and willing to act. ("to desire, wish") is commonly used of the Lord extending His "best-offer" to the believer – wanting (desiring) to birth His persuasion (faith) in them which also empowers, manifests His presence. [Note the close connection between faith (4102 /pistis, "God's in birthed persuasion") and this root

of the flesh,
σαρκὸς

G4561 sarx - Probably from a base of G4563; properly, flesh ("carnal"), merely of human origin or empowerment. sarks ("flesh") is not always evil in Scripture.

G4563 saroo – From a derivative of sairo (to brush off; akin to G4951) meaning a broom, to sweep: - sweep.

G4951 suro - to trail – drag, draw, hale. Probably akin to haireomai G138.

G138 haireomai - (a primitive verb, always in the Greek middle voice) – properly, lay hold of by a personal choice. [The Greek middle voice emphasizes the self-interest of the one preferring (deciding) to grasp or take.]

Which were born, not of blood, nor of the will of the flesh, **nor of the will of man,** *but of Yahweh.John 1:13*

nor

οὐδὲ

G3761 oude - From G3756 and G1161; not, however, that is, neither, nor, not even: - neither (indeed), never, no, (more nor not) nor (yet) (also even them) not (even so much as) + nothing so much as.

G3756 ou – A primary word; the absolutely negative (compare G3361) adverb; no or not: - +long nay, neither, never, no (X man), none.

G1161 dé - A primary particle (adversative or continuative); but, and, etc. -- also, and, but, moreover, now, (often unexpressed in English), (a conjunction) – moreover, indeed now, on top of this, next . . .

of

ἐξ

G1537 ek – (a preposition, written eks before a vowel) – properly, "out from and to" (the outcome); out from within. ek ("out of") is one of the most under- translated (and therefore mis-translated) Greek propositions – often being confined to the meaning "by." (ek) has a two-layered meaning ("out from and to") which makes it out-come oriented (out of the depths of the source and extending to its impact on the object).

the will

θελήματος

G2307 thelema – (from G2309 /theló, "to desire, wish") – properly, a desire (wish), often referring to God's "preferred-will," i.e. His "best-offer" to people which can be accepted or rejected. [Note the -ma suffix, focusing on the result hoped for with the particular desire (wish). thelēma) is nearly always used of God, referring to His preferred-will. Occasionally it is used of man (cf. Lk 23:25; Jn 1:13.]

G2309 theló - (a primitive verb, NAS dictionary) – to desire (wish, will), wanting what is best (optimal) because someone is ready and willing to act. ("to desire, wish") is commonly used of the Lord extending His "best-offer" to the believer – wanting (desiring) to birth His persuasion (faith) in them which also empowers, manifests His presence. [Note the close connection between faith (4102 /pistis, "God's in birthed persuasion") and this root

man,

ἀνδρὸς

G435 aner – A primary word (compare G444); a man (properly as an individual male): - fellow, husband, man, sir.

G444 anthropos – From G435 and countenance; from G3700); man faced that is a human being.

G3700 optanomai – The first (middle voice) to gaze that with eyes wide open as at something remarkable.

Which were born, not of blood, nor of the will of the flesh, nor of the will of man, **but**
of Yahweh. *John 1:13*

but

ἀλλ'

G235 alla – Neuter plural of G243; properly other things that is (adverbially) contrariwise (in many relations): - and, but, even, howbeit, indeed, nay, nevertheless, no, notwithstanding, save, therefore, yea, yet.

G243 allos – A primary word; else that is different (in many applications): - more one (another) (an-some an-) other (-s -wise).

of

ἐκ

G1537 ek - (a preposition, written eks before a vowel) – properly, "out from and to" (the outcome), out from within. ek ("out of") is one of the most under-translated (and therefore mis-translated) Greek prepositions – often being confined to the meaning "by." (ek) has a two-layered meaning ("out from and to") which makes it out-come oriented (out of the depths of the source and extending to its impact on the object).

Yahweh

Θεοῦ

2316 theós (of unknown origin) – properly, God, the Creator and owner of all things (Jn 1:3; Gen 1 - 3).

BLOOD, FLESH, AND WILL

I kept these lines of text together in a different way from past verses because, in order to understand it, this verse needs to be read as a whole.

What John describes in the verse as a whole, combined with each piece of the verse as we see with the commas, forms one of the most important foundations of Christianity and Judaism. Yahweh seeks, offers, visits, and secures relationships with every single human being if we allow each step to move forward as individual human beings.

This verse is often read quickly, causing it to be misunderstood, and this verse can become confusing. Confusing because, at this point, one could easily believe John is speaking of Yahshua. One could also confuse the words chosen in English, extrapolating perhaps that this is some sort of predestination doctrine. Predestination, in this case, meaning "only a select few are called," instead of realizing the door is open to all which is the predestined: *that all should be saved*.

Now, let's look at the first part of this verse where *hoi* (**G3739**) is being used as a demonstrative pronoun, describing those same people who received and believed in verse twelve. This word is neuter in gender, as this is about men and women.

Gennao (**G1080**) is a very important word choice, as John is telling us these people were not born of a specific kin or country, nation, or stock. These people were from all over the known world, not just Israel. This is crucial because,

Scripturally, this creates hope in and of itself. The idea that Yahweh has a remnant shows us that while he is a loving Elohim, he does visit us yet lets us control our own affairs (1 Kings 19:18, Zephaniah 2:7-10, Romans 9:27-28, Acts 15:15-17).

This word, with its related variations and root, describes that this was not a specific breeding, such as highborn, which allowed us to partake in Yahweh's divine plan. These people made the choice. *Ou* (**G3756**) tells us that this word, translated 'not,' is to be understood as an absolute negative, as in no way, not possible. The preposition *ek* (**G1537**) as in "of," and this word is used in two ways "out from" and "to," due to the close nature of the English word "by." Hence, this use of *ek* is from origin. Blood, *aima* (**G129**) the blood of men and animals as we understand. This blood used here is speaking of common man blood, not high born. Simply put, anyone who wanted to receive and believe what the creator was doing.

Here, we can see that *oude* (**G3761**) is used with both *ou* (**G3756**) and *de* (**G1161**) as roots forming an absolute negative as a particle yet in a continuative mode. So, as we were reading at the beginning of the text, this word agrees with this line in continuation, not as *ou* (**G3756**). We see *ek* (**G1537**) as a point of origin from the will, *thelema* (**G2307**) to desire or wish for what is best.

In Christianity we hear a lot of discussion concerning the will—i.e., choosing our direction and then going after our choice. That can be anything from getting a raise, doing better at a job, skill, or seeing that girl in high school and marrying her. Where there is a will, there is a way, as the famous saying goes. The *ma* suffix, focusing on the result hoped for with the particular desire.

This word *thelema* (**G2307**) is almost always used of God which refers to his preferred will. As Strong's noted and continues to note, this word is occasionally used of man. With that, this Greek word shows us again that coupled with flesh, *sarx* (**G4561**) flesh as opposed to the spirit. So, by choice, the pleasure being the will of the flesh in Greek thinking, and then in Hebrew thought, it is desire or delight.

Here, we see again that this is not brought about by fleshly desire, as we know from scripture that our flesh seeks pleasure, but almost a Godly desire. To marry and have children is for the best. To practice hedonism in any form or level is just simply fleshly self-centered pleasures. That is the Limbic brain. The prefrontal cortex is our governor designed to help us put our brain in order and submission. Now the prefrontal cortex in our brain has far more connectivity, and it is much larger than that of any other animal on the planet. This is what separates us from all other biological life on the planet. Yahweh gave us a limbic brain for a reason—to find food, to procreate, and to seek shelter or protection. These are crucial to all elements of the animal kingdom. When we use only our limbic brain, the flesh takes over, thus a choice is made. These choices make up our life's walk, and we can choose to include Yahweh in that walk or not. Either way, Yahweh's will shall be accomplished. To be led by Yahweh's Holy Spirit takes maturity and is a journey. The prefrontal cortex speaks to the conscience and so does Yahweh's Holy Spirit. The Limbic brain does not and is a protection mechanism when we encounter danger or trauma. All of this is said to say man's flesh will do what it will do as we are given personhood. We cannot thwart the plans of Yahweh, and He will offer salvation to anyone who will accept it, regardless of our bloodline.

That word *sarx* (**G4561**) in its definition can also be the meat of an animal or by extension the body. This is also why special attention was given to us when Yahweh made us in his likeness; thus, we have the motor skills to teach our brains to remain in control of our intellect and emotional systems. It is not the knowledge that we will die that marks the difference from other life. Every facet of our brain and body wants us to live. It is the fact we, as a species, look to what is beyond death which makes us different. All life propagates itself through the next generation.[2] Therefore, the will of the flesh did not in any way, either physically or morally, drive Yahweh to offer his Logos which at this point is his Holy Spirit for what is to come.

In this section of text, we have already covered the first three Greek words which are *nor of the will*. These three words mean it's absolutely not from a point of origin or with a desire, as it is not necessarily man's desire to do what is best. This part of the text is also in agreement with the first part of the text and furthers the prior explanation. That is that the will of man does not dictate the option of receiving or that the believing had anything to do with Yahweh's intention. This was strictly Yahweh seeking a relationship with his creation and that the whole of humanity was predestined to obtain everlasting life—not a chosen few from that creation. Remember, though, offering and accepting are two different actions entirely.

Looking at *aner* (**G435**) a man, as an individual. This word come from *anthropos* (**G444**) from **G435** and countenance; from **G3700**); man-faced, that is a human being. *Optanomai* (**G3700**) The first (middle voice) to gaze at with eyes wide open as at something remarkable. Stemming from an intellectual sense, that is the will of man, is now implying that the likeness of Yahweh in man has somehow been recognized and is in awe seeking this relationship.

When we study out this word *optanomai*, there are several tenses used in conjunction with this word. To gaze, voluntary observation, mechanical, passive or casual vision, earnest but more continued inspection, and a watching from a distance. What John is telling us is that, in this time period, man was going about his business, even if one believed or was religious, but the intellect of man in these senses were not bringing about Yahweh's Holy Spirit for receiving or believing. In other words, mankind was scurrying about like ants, and this was strictly an act of Yahweh in his deep desire for mankind.

Most importantly, we need to understand that the last piece of this text articulates that the words chosen throughout this passage is not the Greek/English mindset of "by." The English and Greek mindset is "of," as in a point of origin. Again, John uses this word *ek* to show all of this power, and Yahweh's Holy Spirit comes from the Father (not Yahshua), and that the Word (Logos) was about to make his appearance in our world as the plan of Yahweh unfolded – His Logos. The ability to accept this power and choose to be a child of Yahweh, at this time period, was earth-shattering.

This also changes Catholicism and Protestantism

doctrines, as most believe this power did not come until the book of Acts, and this just is not true.

Yahshua our Messiah said, "I will send you a comforter" John 16:7. We can now see Yahweh's Holy Spirit was here on this earth prior to Yahshua, visiting back and forth, John 1:11 *erchomai* (**G2604**). The Holy Spirit filled Yahshua at the baptism scene (John 1:32, Isaiah 11) *meno* (**G3306)** to stay. "And John bare record, saying, I saw the Spirit descending from heaven like a dove, and it abode (*meno*) upon him." Where was Yahweh's Holy Spirit? Abiding with Yahshua, empowering him to do what needed to be done. Not causing Yahshua to behave like a robot; no, in scripture, we see several times where Yahshua continuously accepted the role and chose the role of Messiah. Once Yahshua fulfills his role, that is to be hung on a cross, resurrected, then ascend to Heaven, afterward, he will send Yahweh's Holy Spirit with power!

What is comforter? *Parakletos* (**G3875**) an intercessor consoler, and that is the vehicle for this Power.

We can easily see how this idea of a Trinity is widely accepted in society—then and now. Most people, when reading this in the Bible, will conclude that Yahweh and His Holy Spirit and Yahshua are one together or three in one.

However, we must keep in mind this is extremely blasphemous, as Yahweh and His Holy Spirit are one and the same. Yahweh's Holy Spirit is how Yahweh visits us on this earth, as Yahweh's natural form would cause death. The spirit of Yahweh (Isaiah 11:2) *is* Yahweh.

Here is a concept which has been lost to time and that is that Yahweh is omnipresent.[3] The understanding Yahweh is altogether everywhere all the time has unfortunately been altered since 300 A.D. with the onslaught of a trinity doctrine.

Claiming Yahshua was preexistent or pre-incarnate is very dangerous for three reasons:

1. Yahweh cannot be tempted.

2. Divinity and Flesh cannot coexist in one being.

3. A true God cannot be sacrificed for human sin because a God cannot die.

Why is this so important?

We must understand the concept of the sacrificial system in the Bible and how this affects us as his children. Reviewing Adam and Eve's fall, we see disobedience had occurred. They violated a direct command from the Father: "Do not eat from the tree at the center of the garden" (Genesis 2:17). The end result was the sacrifice of an animal to make coverings for them, so they were no longer naked (Genesis 3:21).

A basic level of understanding, or the first level of understanding of this scripture, is within what is called a PaRDeS. Coming from Jewish rabbis, the acronym is as follows. In this simple line of Biblical text, the P'shat (P) is simply the moment our eyes are open and now we see we are naked – cover yourself. In disobedience, we see our shame. This is the first understanding you will see when reading this text. The Remez (R) goes a little deeper and shows us disobedience has consequences and blood must atone for our sin. The Drash (D) being the hidden understanding within the text and reveals the chain of events which is now leading toward the fulfillment of the plan, which is the Word or Promise (Logos). The Sod (S), which is the deepest level of understanding, and in this case, the Logos, revealed taking John's timeline along with the Genesis story of Adam and Eve reveals the Logos coming into action. It also informs how the sacrificial system came into being, how the Torah affects us, and how the Messiah's blood fulfilled Law and did not do away with the Law but fulfilled!. Torah was not done away with! It will be with us until all has been fulfilled and that is not yet.By willingly giving up his life for us in Torah so we may perform Torah consistently with Messiah's intercessory assistance. He covers us in our shame and disobedience, and Yahshua will ultimately become our sacrifice by willingly giving up his life to reconcile us with Yahweh. That is a mouthful and the reason why there is a lot of strife between Christianity and Judaism. This strife is also present within Christendom.

Let's take a look at that thought. How did the Messiah's blood fulfill Torah? When I share this thought, I am in no way doing away with Torah. Inconceivable! Torah is the standard, it is the kingdom way of living, and the way we should treat Yahweh, others, and ourselves (Deuteronomy 6:5, Matthew 22:39, 1 Corinthians 6:19-20).

The Messiah is not God, as we only have one God – Yahweh. Yahshua, as a human, had to walk out Torah in order to become the Messiah. This is what I meant by fulfilling Torah. Throughout his life on earth, he completed all the requirements. He was sinless, Torah-driven, willingly laid down his life, resurrected and ascended to make intercession. This is how He has fulfilled Torah for us, so that we who believe can repent and come back to Torah when we fail. (Isaiah 53, Titus 2:11-12, Galatians 5:18, 1 Timothy 2:3-6).

Now, when I say, "did away with the law," we need to understand parlance.[4] Parlance is a manner or mode of speech (idiom). In Hebrew, law would be *dawt* (**H1881**) דָּת a precept or law. A law is the remediation or recompense for breaking a command, rule, ordinance, or precept. This is exactly what Adam and Eve did in the garden and brought about the necessity of the sacrificial system. However, the Messiah, who willingly gave up his life, did away with the animal blood and covered us with his shed blood.

Adam (**H120**) אָדָם man-faced, man who has a *neshamah* (**H5397**) נְשָׁמָה a puff of wind, angry or vital, divine intellect or an animal. A *nephesh* (**H5315**) נֶפֶשׁ now makes man a living soul that is properly a breathing creature that is animal or vitality. Because this man is now alive and breathing, we know he has a *ruach* (**H7307**) רוּחַ wind; resembles breath, i.e. a sensible (or even violent) exhalation.

I share this knowledge with you because you must understand that we, without Yahweh, are just animals. This will upset many right-wing Christians, and I make no apologies, as it is a concept within the Scriptures. When we accept the atonement of Yahweh and follow through on his instruction on how to remediate the sin committed by missing the mark, then we can repent and come back to Torah. Now we can see why an animal was chosen first, why there was a plan for the Messiah, and why that plan made the blood so precious. When we are in Yahweh and receive and accept His Holy Spirit, we need the Messiah's blood to give us an equal footing. This means human blood—not animal and not Divine blood—is the only way we can be made whole and claim being children of Yahweh. This is how verse thirteen reveals the importance of verse twelve!

Romans 8 sums this up best:

"There is therefore now no condemnation to them which are in Messiah Yahshua, who walk not after the flesh, but after the Spirit. For the law of the Spirit of life in Messiah Yahshua hath made me free from the law of sin and death. For what the law could not do, in that it was weak through the flesh, Yahweh sending his own Son in the likeness of sinful flesh, and for sin, condemned sin in the flesh: That the righteousness of the Torah might be fulfilled in us, who walk not after the flesh, but after the Spirit. For they that are after the flesh do mind the things of the flesh; but they that are after the Spirit the things of the Spirit. For to be carnally minded is death; but to be spiritually minded is life and peace. Because the carnal mind is enmity against Yahweh: for it is not subject to the Torah of Yahweh, neither indeed can be. So, then they that are in the flesh cannot please Yahweh. But ye are not in the flesh, but in the Spirit, if so be that the Spirit of Yahweh dwell in you. Now if any man has not the Spirit of Messiah, he is none of his. And if Messiah be in you, the body is dead because of sin; but the Spirit is life because of righteousness. But if the Spirit of him that raised up Yahshua from the dead dwell in you, he that raised up Messiah from the dead shall also quicken your mortal bodies by his Spirit that

dwelleth in you. Therefore, brethren, we are debtors, not to the flesh, to live after the flesh. For if ye live after the flesh, ye shall die: but if ye through the Spirit do mortify the deeds of the body, ye shall live. For as many as are led by the Spirit of Yahweh, they are the sons of Yahweh. For ye have not received the spirit of bondage again to fear; but ye have received the Spirit of adoption, whereby we cry, Abba, Father. The Spirit itself bears witness with our spirit, that we are the children of Yahweh: And if children, then heirs; heirs of Yahweh, and joint-heirs with Messiah if so be that we suffer with him, that we may be also glorified together. For I reckon that the sufferings of this present time are not worthy to be compared with the glory which shall be revealed in us. For the earnest expectation of the creature waits for the manifestation of the sons of Yahweh. For the creature was made subject to vanity, not willingly, but by reason of him who hath subjected the same in hope, Because the creature itself also shall be delivered from the bondage of corruption into the glorious liberty of the children of Yahweh. For we know that the whole creation groans and travails in pain together until now. And not only they, but ourselves also, which have the first fruits of the Spirit, even we ourselves groan within ourselves, waiting for the adoption, to wit, the redemption of our body. For we are saved by hope: but hope that is seen is not hope: for what a man sees, why doth he yet hope for? But if we hope for that we see not, then do we with patience wait for it. Likewise, the Spirit also helps our infirmities: for we know not what we should pray for as we ought: but the Spirit itself makes intercession for us with groanings which cannot be uttered. And he that searches the hearts knows what is the mind of the Spirit, because he makes intercession for the saints according to the will of Yahweh. And we know that all things work together for good to them that love Yahweh, to them who are the called according to his purpose. For whom he did foreknow, he also did predestinate to be conformed to the image of his Son, that he might be the firstborn among many brethren. Moreover, whom he did predestinate, them he also called: and whom he called, them he also justified: and whom he justified, them he also glorified. What shall we then say to these things? If Yahweh be for us, who can be against us? He that spared not his own Son, but delivered him up for us all, how shall he not with him also freely give us all things? Who shall lay anything to the charge of Yahweh's elect? It is Yahweh that justifies. Who is he that condemns? It is Messiah that died, yea rather, that is risen again, who is even at the right hand of Yahweh, who also makes intercession for us. Who shall separate us from the love of Messiah? shall tribulation, or distress, or persecution, or famine, or nakedness, or peril, or sword? As it is written, for thy sake we are killed all the day long; we are accounted as sheep for the slaughter. Nay, in all these things we are more than conquerors through him that loved us. For I am persuaded, that neither death, nor life, nor angels, nor principalities, nor powers, nor things present, nor things to come, nor height, nor depth, nor any other creature, shall be able to separate us from the love of Yahweh, which is in Messiah Yahshua our Master."

And the Word was made flesh and dwelt among us, *and we*

beheld the glory, the glory as of the only begotten of the Father, full of grace and truth.

John 1:14

And
Kai

G2532 kai - and (also), very often, moreover, even, indeed (the context determines the exact sense).

the Word
Λόγος

G3056 Logos something said (including the thought); by implication, a topic (subject of discourse), also reasoning (the mental faculty) or motive; by extension, a computation; specially, (with the article in John)

was made
ἐγένετο

G1096 ergento – properly, to emerge, become, transitioning from one point (realm, condition) to another. means "to become, and signifies a change of condition, state or place. means to come into being/manifestation implying motion, movement, or growth" (at 2 Pet 1:4). Thus, it is used for God's actions as emerging from eternity and becoming (showing themselves) in time (physical space).

flesh,
σάρξ

G4561 sarx – Probably from a base of G4563; properly, flesh ("carnal"), merely of human origin or empowerment. sarks ("flesh") is not always evil in Scripture.

G4563 saroo – From a derivative of sairo (to brush off; akin to G4951) meaning a broom, to sweep: - sweep.

And	dwelt	among	us,
Kai	ἐσκήνωσεν	ἐν	ἡμῖν

G2532 kai - and (also), very often, moreover, even, indeed (the context determines the exact sense).

G4637 eskenosen - - properly, to pitch or live in a tent, "denoting much more than the mere general notion of dwelling"

G1722 en – properly, in (inside, within); (figuratively) "in the realm (sphere) of," as in the condition (state) in which something operates from the inside (within).

G2254 hemin – Dative plural of G1473: to (or for with by) us:- our (for) us we.

G1473 ego – A primary pronoun of the first person I (only expressed when emphatic):- I me.

BECOMING THE WORD

This is the verse we have long waited for! *Finally.*

However, we need to really think about this one, my friend. Yes, the prophecy came true. Yes, Mary had the child who would be called the Messiah. Yes, baby Yahshua is in a manger wrapped in swaddling clothes. We need to keep what was promised in the Light in proper context. What was said in the Word of Yahweh and how this would work up to completion. Yahweh said, "Let there be Light," and that light was hope and that hope is a promise and that promise is a Messiah. This hope would be a process, and the process was a long one.

All of life goes through stages, and all of life has to struggle to get to an endpoint or the fulfillment of who, what, where, how, and why they are. Baby Yahshua did not just come from the birth canal to be the Messiah in the manger, as this negates all the prophets and Torah. This would, by all accounts, negate Yahweh's Word.

Let's review the Greek word *Logos* (**G3056**) λόγος a word, being the expression of a thought; a saying. In Strong's Lexicon, the second sentence of the definition states this well: is preeminently used of Christ (Jn 1:1), expressing the thoughts of the Father through the Spirit. This is an actual fact, and this is truth, as this is an expression of the Messiah by the Father through His Holy Spirit. It is just an expression and not the creation of the Messiah. As we have discussed in several instances in this book, the true faith is revealed in this description; specifically, the Father, Yahweh, is speaking through His Holy Spirit who is hovering above the waters.

The scriptures tell us that Yahshua was able to conquer sin. He was able to keep his flesh obedient, and his spirit in control. Isaiah 53:1-12 and Philippians 2:6-8 talk about his struggles as a youth to adult. 1 John 2:2 and Romans 3:25 discuss propitiation whereby Yahshua's overcoming of a sinful nature reconciled us to Yahweh once he died on that cross. There are plenty of scriptures to see where Yahshua defeated and conquered sin: Hebrews 1:1-14, 2:17, 9:14, Matthew 20:28.

The only way Yahshua could have been a perfect blameless sacrifice was to be able to overcome sin. Not as a god, as this would negate our salvation, but as a brother, in human flesh, to become that spotless lamb of Yahweh. Yahshua had to walk this out just like we do, and because he walked the walk, then we are justified. He had to accept this role at multiple points in His life, those highlight points being the temple at 12 years old, his baptism, the wilderness, each and every miracle, the trial, the cross, the resurrection, and so on. These things fulfilled all scripture, thus making Yahshua the Lamb of Yahweh. This does not take away from the announcement, the virgin birth, or the prophecy of this babe whatsoever, as Yahshua was the child who would become the Messiah.

We can see that, yes, the Logos has been made flesh. That child in the manger is the chosen one to be called the Messiah. Can he fulfill this role, will he accept the challenge?

Yahweh never demands anything from us; we have free choice to live how we want (Matthew 26:36-46, Luke 22:39-

46). A lot of Christian denominations will tell us or instruct us with a stern warning that the Old Testament is filled with demands and laws that we are required to take part in—*or else*! This simply is not true.

Yahweh gives us a choice, and we can live our life as we wish. However, because of this fallen world (declension), we are subject to missing the mark (sin). These shortcomings will allow for death to be in paths. With Yahweh, we are given a path, and yes, we will fall short or veer off course from time to time.

Yet, we are allowed to keep practicing by the blood of the Messiah, the blood which filled the gulf between us and Yahweh. The Torah of the Old Testament is part of a marriage contract whereby we live according to ways which set us apart from living in our own construct. If we want eternal life through the Messiah, accepting the blood he shed and following Yahweh's (God's) Torah is how we live. As Messiah is Torah, then there is a standard of living we must adhere to, and this standard of living is being set apart (holy). This standard of living actually becomes a joy because the life we lead will be rewarding and blessed by our Father in heaven, the brothers and sisters we respect, and the way in which we treat ourselves.

And (indeed) **the Word** (the thought uttered) **was made** (become, from word to flesh) **flesh** (merely human) **and** (indeed) **dwelt** (not only live in a tent but with us as well) **among** (inside, in the sphere of) **us** (you and me).

And the Word was made flesh and dwelt among us, **and we beheld the glory, the glory as of the only begotten from the Father,** *full of grace and truth.* **John 1:14**

and	we beheld	his	glory,
Καὶ	ἐθεασάμεθα	αὐτοῦ	δόξαν,

G2532 kai - and (also), very often, moreover, even, indeed (the context determines the exact sense).

G2300 etheasametha - (from tháomai, "to gaze at a spectacle") – properly, gaze on (contemplate) as a spectator; to observe intently, especially to interpret something (grasp its significance); to see (concentrate on) so as to significantly impact (influence) the viewer. Compare G3700.

G3700 optanomai – The first (middle voice) to gaze that with eyes wide open as at something remarkable.

G846 autou - From the particle au (perhaps akin to G109 through the idea of a baffling wind; backward; (1) self (emphatic) (2) he, she, it (used for the third person pronoun) (3) the same. Usage: he, she, it, they, them, same. In itself it signifies nothing more than again, applied to what has either been previously mentioned or, when the whole discourse is looked at, must necessarily be supplied. Also, see

G848 hautou - a contraction for G1438; self, alone

G1438 heautou him -self, alone

G1391 doxan – From the base of G1380; glory (as very apparent) in a wide application (I. of F objectively or subjectively); - dignity glory (-ious) honour praise worship.

G1380 dokeo – A prolonged form of a primary verb doko properly, suppose (what "seems to be"), forming an opinion (a personal judgment, estimate). ("suppose") directly reflects the personal perspective (values) of the person making the subjective judgment call, i.e., showing what they esteem (or not) as an individual.

the glory, δόξαν	as ὡς	of the only begotten μονογενοῦς	from παρὰ	The Father, Πατρός

G1391 doxan – From the base of G1380; glory (as very apparent) in a wide application (l. of F objectively or subjectively) – dignity, glory(-ious), honour, praise, worship.

G1380 dokeo – A prolonged form of a primary verb doko properly, suppose (what "seems to be"), forming an opinion (a personal judgment, estimate). ("suppose") directly reflects the personal perspective (values) of the person making the subjective judgment call, i.e., showing what they esteem (or not) as an individual.

G5613 hos Probably adverb of comparative from hos; which how, i.e. In that manner (very variously used, as follows) -- about, after (that), (according) as (it had been, it were), as soon (as), even as (like), for, how (greatly), like (as, unto), since, so (that), that, to wit, unto, when(-soever), while, X with all speed.

G3439 monogenes - From G3441 and G1096; only born that is sole: - only (begotten child).

G3441 monos – Probably from G3306; remaining that is sole or single; by implication mere: - alone only by themselves.

G3306 meno – A primary verb; to stay (in a given place state relation or expectancy): - abide, continue, dwell, endure, be present, remain, stand, tarry (for X) thine own.

G1096 ergento or ginomai – properly, to emerge, become, transitioning from one point (realm, condition) to another, means "to become, and signifies a change of condition, state or place. means to come into being/manifestation implying motion, movement, or growth" (at 2 Pet 1:4). Thus, it is used for God's actions as emerging from eternity and becoming (showing themselves) in time (physical space).

G3844 para – with the genitive; and as in Greek prose writings always with the genitive of a person, to denote that a thing proceeds from. the side or the vicinity of one, or from one's sphere of power, or from one's wealth or store. From, beside (l. or F).

G3962 pater- Apparently a primary word; a father (l. or F near or more remote): - father, parent.

I truly believe that verse fourteen is a verse which encompasses Yahshua's life, especially from his childhood to his baptism scene. I say this because this baby, this toddler, and this teenager, as he became a young adult, must have garnered respect and favor with his people and his peers.

The word chosen here in the Greek, *doxan* (**G1391**) means glory, dignity, or honor. The root word *dokeo* (**G1380**) means forming an opinion of the personal perspective. So, Yahshua was being seen with astonishment, even though he was not necessarily handsome, as Isaiah stated. People were amazed at his skillset, knowledge, and disposition.

This must have revealed the kind of glory of Yahweh which can only be begotten of the father. This also begs the question of our little word friend *autou* (**G846**). Why is this not Yahweh's Holy Spirit any longer? Because the context of the pronoun has changed.

The focus has now shifted from Yahweh's Holy Spirit to the Word, and the Word has now become flesh. Yahweh's Holy Spirit cannot be flesh, as that would be Yahweh (in the flesh). We know divinity and flesh cannot have two natures at any one time. So, the focus is now on this promised Word who has become flesh: namely, Yahshua. That is why the pronoun changed from referring to Yahweh's Holy Spirit to referring to Yahshua.

What happened at the moment the Logos was uttered from Yahweh? A brilliant, bright Light burst forth and spread throughout the universe and settled throughout the universe becoming first light. A light which is there continually.

Have you ever noticed when we see images from space,

they always seem to have a light in the contrast? This is not added for definition, and it is not the light reflected from a nearby star. Of course, we can see the light reflected from the star near the celestial bodies, though we can also see in between the stars and in between the planets. As a child, I always thought when I wanted to be an astronaut that it would be pitch black between the stars. Planets cast no light of their own, and space is the void without light, right? Not so!

Now we see space is quite lit up, if you will, and that does not only come from all the stars and reflective galaxies. This light is the first light. It is the physical representation of the hope uttered in the beginning for all of Yahweh's creation: He has a plan.

First light is a glory of Yahweh. It is His majesty proclaimed by the heavens! The baby Yahshua was laid in the manger for all of creation to witness the glory of the father which was on that child. Why? Because this event was Yahweh's word fulfilled, and this meant that because that promise was kept and fulfilled, there could be nothing but glory on him as only begotten of the father. Do you see it? Not an automatic Messiah card whereby baby Yahshua is the Messiah and has no say in the matter whatsoever. I say this because some in Christendom believe that the baby Yahshua was able to forgive sins, do miracles, and function fully as the Messiah right then. Friends, this is similar to idol worship, making Yahshua an object of worship, where Yahweh is the only one true God, and equating anything to Yahweh is a no-no in our Christian faith. When we give glory to another entity, especially as a god, we violate the first, second, and third commandments.

Glory is defined as (a): praise, honor, or distinction extended by common consent (b) a height of prosperity or achievement (c) a state of great gratification or exaltation (d) great beauty and splendor and, (e) a ring or spot of light.[5] Even though all five definitions apply, I did use definition number three. Why? It applies to the context of this passage, and it is the only one that fits logically and scripturally.

This word glory (*doxan* and *dokeo*) is contextually sound, as it refers to the people being astonished that Yahweh's word has finally come to pass, and they are excited, and this is a moment in human history to praise and give adulation, and worship to Yahweh.

Please understand, brothers and sisters, I am not taking away from this baby who will be my king soon and who is my savior, my joy, and my salvation! Far from it, and I am, in no way, disrespecting Yahshua as a baby, toddler, boy, teenager, and young man.

I would rather die than diminish my savior. Begging the question, where did my hope go from me? I must follow the rules of our faith and not equate Yahshua with Yahweh since this would be wrong and subjects me to fire and to be destroyed.

Exodus 20:3-4: "You shall have no other gods before me. You shall not make for yourself an image in the form of anything in heaven above or on the earth beneath or in the waters below," and 1 Timothy 2:5: "For there is one God and one medi-

ator between God and mankind, the *man* Christ Jesus."[6]
___

At every turn Yahshua tells us that all things are through the father. Not once did Yahshua equate himself with Yahweh. "I came from the bosom of my father" is the closest statement he gave which came close. In this line, the meaning is the Father's glory is manifested in the Word made flesh.

In this small line of text within verse fourteen, John also reveals that we are on a timeline still. We are not one and done. This baby must grow into the Messiah's role and show that He is Yahweh's salvation! Just like our salvation is a walk, an exodus from the world which we work out with much fear and trembling (Philippians 2:13), we also copy our Master's walk to be made like him when the day of our reward comes nigh.

In this chapter, we have seen the English and Greek definitions of glory, so let's take a look at the Hebrew definition of glory. Glory, *kabod* (**H3519**) כָּבוֹד someone or something that is heavy in weight, wealth, abundance, importance, or respect. Honor—to consider something as heavy in the sense of respect. In the Hebraic mindset, we can definitely apply glory to this baby because he is something of importance and weight. The weight contains the alteration and implication that this male will have on human history and the great importance of the Word being fulfilled in this male child.

And (indeed) **we beheld** (to gaze remarkably) **his** (self, baffling wind) **glory** (esteem), **the glory** (esteem) **as** (which) **of the only begotten** (born to emerge) **from** (of the vicinity) **the Father** (Yahweh).

And the Word was made flesh and dwelt among us, and we beheld the glory, the glory as of the only begotten of the Father, **full of grace and truth.** *John 1:14*

full
πλήρης

G4134 pleres - From G4130; replete, or covered over; by analogy, complete -- full.

G4130 pletho - A prolonged form of a primary pleo (which appears only as an alternate in certain tenses and in the reduplicated form pimplemi) to "fill" (literally or figuratively (imbue, influence, supply)); specially, to fulfil (time) -- accomplish, full (...come), furnish.

of grace
Χάριτος

G5485 charitos - From G5463; graciousness (as gratifying), of manner or act (abstract or concrete; literal, figurative or spiritual; especially the divine influence upon the heart, and its reflection in the life; including gratitude) -- acceptable, benefit, favour, gift, grace (- ious), joy, liberality, pleasure, thank (-s, - worthy).

G5463 chairo - A primary verb; to be "cheer"ful, i.e., Calmly happy or well-off; impersonally, especially as salutation (on meeting or parting), be well -- farewell, be glad, God speed, greeting, hail, joy (- fully), rejoice.

and
Καὶ

G2532 kai - and (also), very often, moreover, even, indeed (the context determines the exact sense).

truth.
ἀληθείας

G225 aletheia - From G227; truth:- true X truly truth verity.

G227 alethes -- From G1 (as a negative particle) and G2990; true (as not concealing):- true truly truth.

G2990 lanthano -- Prolonged form of a primary verb which is only used as an alternative in certain tenses; to lie hid, be hid, be ignorant of unawares; in order (or so) that not.

GRACE AND TRUTH

In the last part of this text, we see an important piece of information which is often overlooked. Who is it describing? Not the Father, as He is described by the glory. While punctuation was not always used in common Greek, we do have examples of partial biblical texts that do contain punctuation. There were times when paper and ink were too expensive so punctuation was left out to save space. It is often taught or declared that there were no commas in the original manuscripts and this is just not true.[7] The commas play an important role here, showing us that the Word (Promise, Light) is now flesh, full of grace and truth.

Who is full of grace and truth? The Word! And the word was just made into flesh. So, here, we are able to see the timeline within this text alone.

This is not just a one-time event as 1) the word was made flesh, and 2) that word dwelt among us. Not that this happened multiple time in history but seeing this event played out in Yahweh's prophetic calendar and hundreds of generations desiring to see this marvelous promise unfold. This reveals the Logos that Yahweh gave us and is a spectacular display of us being made in His likeness. This is an extremely important concept to understand, and theologically, it is equally as important since this Messiah, this prophetic word, is now here and living amongst us. This was hoped of by Adam, Abraham, Jacob, and the Prophets! This is the redemption plan in a physical form! The Bedouin shepherds knew, the angels knew, and then we have the

Magi, who also knew, coming from afar a couple of years later.

The understanding of Torah and the prophets surely made the priesthood aware of this significant event coming soon. There were prophecies, there were words, and we must believe that Yahweh was speaking to this generation of Yahshua's birth.

Look at John the Baptist who was to be priest in the lineage of his father, yet he chose to be a prophet. He chose to give all of that up as soon as he was convinced the Messiah was here and was about to become High Priest, taking the scepter and the breastplate to a whole new level. John knew the priesthood was about to be put on hold. In verse fifteen, this becomes clear and then abundantly clear from verse nineteen.

Now imagine being the priests of the temple. These guys had it made, so they received the choicest of offerings and they ate thereof. They also rightly received the tithings, and they also controlled what appears to be a money exchanging/offering stock yards within the temple grounds. This is a money-making system and also keeps the poor, poor! Was the rich man actually a Levite?

Did Yahshua just decide one day to get angry at this? Or was this a recurring day-in, day-out transactional business not regarding Yahweh whatsoever? It appears Yahshua saw this happening with no regard for the sacredness of the temple and the holiness thereof. Additionally, the poor were being taken advantage of and manipulated. Yahweh abhors when the strong prey on the weak, and Yahshua knew this.

By this point, Yahshua was growing into his messiahship

a little more every day and being infilled by Yahweh's Holy Spirit as time continued. He knew who and what he was to become, and he knew the High Priest was as an intercessor for man to Yahweh and then King. The priests saw their time coming to an end. Yahshua's arrival as a carpenter—who preached serving and choosing to be last (instead of first)—jeopardized them. The threat of Rome and the Greek cultural influence on religion and philosophy was also taking a toll on Judaism.

By observation, one could say Yahweh had selected the utmost in perfect timing for the Messiah to be on the Earth. Of course, it is true! Would Yahweh choose anything other than the perfect timing?

One area that we all hate to lose in is in our money; these priests were no different. It is so engrained in our minds that mammon makes the way for us and our families. Wars are fought over trade; people are killed over money squabbles, and this is nothing new.

This system set up by the priesthood in Yahshua's time was not one to honor Yahweh, but to create a revenue source under the guise of pleasing Yahweh to the masses. The priesthood wouldn't come to a stop just because some guy from Nazareth is supposedly the Messiah. Don't think so!

Now we should also look at the definition of grace. This word is always given multiple meanings and is the most overused word in churches today with no clear under-standing of the concept, and it leaves millions of people perplexed every week.

Grace, in English, is a whole lot of examples. However, what we are looking for is not a generic meaning that is now acceptable by cultures due to the cultural shift of the church or government or academia. We want and need to know and understand how Yahweh is using this word in His word!

So, we should start with the Hebrew. Grace in Hebrew is *chen* (**H2580**) חֵן kindness, favor; and this idea comes from *chenan* (**H2603**) חָנַן to bend or stoop in kindness to an inferior. In the ancient Hebrew script, we see the *heth* ח as a wall and the *nun* ן as a sprouting seed. The concept is a continuing wall. This concrete idea or picture is representative of the nomadic tents which were placed in a circle when camp was set up. The concept here is that one can find favor or beauty or kindness, even refuge or mercy and salvation. The idea also here is that when we are part of a family, we can find refuge and rest in the camp to try and do better when we find ourselves outside the safety of the camp.[8] Now, when we view this in light of dwelt among us, we do not see a get-out-of-jail-free card, but we see the ability to do better and work on our shortcomings.

In the Greek, *charitos* (**G5485**) is acceptable, benefit, joy, gratitude, favor, and this come from *chairo* (**G5463**) cheerful, calmly happy, as in well off. In English, we see grace defined as: unmerited divine assistance given to humans for their regeneration or sanctification, a virtue coming from God, a state of sanctification enjoyed through divine assistance. APPROVAL, FAVOR, archaic: MERCY, PARDON.[9] Our Messiah was not a grumpy, unthankful child, by any means. He was happy, well-off, calm, and thankful. When we experience grace in the fullest or we impart grace to another, there is a sense of well-being that is very grateful, to the point of being joyous. Full of grace!

When we look to the definition of truth in the Hebrew, we see *emeth* (**H571**) אֱמֶת stability, trustworthiness. Contracted from *aman* (**H539**) אָמַן which is to support, firm, trust. In the Ancient Hebrew script, we see a picture of an oxen head, water, seed, and a mark this pictograph is telling us: truth, what is firm.[10]

When we look at the ancient Hebrew pictograph, we see Yahweh (oxen head) throughout the chaos (waters) keep the truth (seed) marked (cross). The truth comes from the source, not the other way around, as most of academia will tell you now. That source comes from Yahweh, and it can always be found, even in the bleakest of times and culminated at the cross.

In the Greek, we see truth as *aletheia* (**G225**) true, truth, verity, which is a true principle or belief, especially one of fundamental importance. This word comes from *alethes* (**G227**) which is open truth, and its counterpart *lanthano* (**G2990**) which is hidden truth. This is really interesting, as it appears John was showing in Greek that this word made flesh would have truth both open and hidden revealed. Truth in English is (1): the body of real things, events, and facts: ACTUALITY, (2): the state of being the case: FACT, (3) often capitalized: a transcendent fundamental or spiritual reality. The property (as of a statement) of being in accord with fact or reality, fidelity to an original or to a standard, sincerity in action, character, and utterance.[11]

This child was born with grace and truth. This was a gift he carried into a boyhood and then as a young man and onward into his earthly ministry. This was the Word made flesh.

Full (filled to completion) **of grace** (joyful acceptance) **and** (moreover) **truth** (fundamental truth both open and hidden).

This is good news, and it makes the gospels so much clearer. Our salvation becomes that much sweeter and more believable. When was the last time someone explained to you or you were actually taught how Jesus was in heaven with Yahweh and then went into Mary's womb to be born a baby? Most likely, you have not or were not ever.

You were told, just like I was, and believed it! Why?

Three reason we went over in an earlier chapter.

1) because our family tradition tells us so.

2) because our pastor or a pastor told us so.

3) based on our construct before we met Yahshua dictates how we read the scriptures.

There is only one God (Elohim) and that is Yahweh.

And there is only one mediator between God and man, and that is Yahshua the Messiah—a man born as a human who fulfilled every aspect of human life perfectly before Yahweh, thus being qualified to be the Messiah.

CHAPTER 7
THE SPIRIT OF THE MESSIAH
THE JOHN 1:1 FACTOR

John bare witness of him, and cried, saying, this was he of whom I spake, he that cometh after me is preferred before me: for he was before me.*John 1:15*

John	bare witness	of	him	and	cried,	saying,
Ἰωάννης	μαρτυρεῖ	περὶ	αὐτοῦ	καὶ	κέκραγεν	λέγων
2491 Ioánnēs Of Hebrew origin H3110 Ioannes (that is Iochanan the name John).	**G3140 martureo** – From G3144; to be a witness that is testify (literally or figuratively): - charge give [evidence] bear record, have, obtain, of good honest report, be well, reported of, testify, give, have testimony (be, bear, give, obtain) witness. **G3144 martus** – a witness (literally [judicially] or Figuratively [generally]): by analogy a martyr: - martyr, record, witness.	**4012 peri** – From the base of G4008; properly (used for the superlative of G4009); through (all over) that is around; concerning, of, pertaining to, for sake. **G4008 peran** – apparently the accusative case of an obsolete derivation of peiro (to pierce); through (as adverb or preposition) that is across: - beyond farther (other) side over.	**G846 autou** (1) self (emphatic) (2) he, she, it (used for the third person pronoun) (3) the same. Usage: he, she, it, they, them, same, in itself, same. in exact sense).	**2532 kai** (the most common NT conjunction, used over 9,000 times) (as a raven) or – and (also), very often, moreover, even, indeed (the context determines the	**G2896 krazo** - A primary verb; properly to croak scream that is (generally) to call aloud (shriek exclaim intreat): - cry (out).	**G3004 lego** – primary verb properly to lay forth (relate in words) say, speak, call or tell.

(perhaps akin to G109 through the idea of a baffling wind.)

John bare witness of him, and cried, saying, **this was he of whom I spake,** *he that cometh after me is preferred before me: for he was before me.* **John 1:15**

This
Οὗτος

G3778 houtos – From the article G3588 and G846; the, he (she, it) that is, this, or that (often with the article repeated); - he

G3588 ho - The masculine (feminine (second) and neuter (third) forms in all their inflections; the definite article -he.

G846 autou - In itself it signifies nothing more than again, applied to what has either been previously mentioned or, when the whole discourse is looked at, must necessarily be supplied. From the particle au (perhaps akin to G109 through the idea of a baffling wind.

G109 aer - From aemi (to breathe unconsciously, i.e., Respire; by analogy, to blow); "air" (as naturally circumambient) – air.

was he
ἦν

G2258 ane—Imperfect of G1510; I (thou) was (wast or were); - agree be have the relative (sometime charge of hold was were.

G1510 eimi - (the basic Greek verb which expresses being, i.e., "to be") – am, is, 1510 (eimi), and its counterparts, (properly) convey "straight-forward" being (existence, i.e., without explicit limits).

of whom
ὅν

G3739 hos – Probably a primary word (or perhaps a form of the article G3588); the relative (sometime demonstrative) pronoun who which what that: - one who which what that: - one (an the) other some that which who (-m-se) See also G3757.

G3588 ho - The masculine feminine (second) and neuter (third) forms in all their inflections; the definite article -he.

G3757 hou- Genitive case of G3739 as adverb; at which place that is where:- where (-in) whither ((soever)).

I spake
εἶπον

G2036 epo – ἔπω – Primary verb (used only in the definite past tense the other being borrowed from G2046 G4483 and G5346); to speak or say (by word or writing):- answer, bid bring, word, call command, grant, say, (on) speak, tell. Compare G3004.

G3004 lego – primary verb properly to lay forth (relate in words) say, speak, call or tell.

THE APPEARANCE

In this verse, we can now see that the timeline is complete for the Messiah's appearance on this Earth. The next phase is about to begin.

Here, we see John the Baptist giving an account, which is to bear witness (**G3140** *martureo*) to testify or bear record. John was literally giving a record of who, what, when, where, and why this man Jesus was here.

Now we have Yahweh's declaration of who John the Baptist was in John 1:6-8. Yet, can we find historical evidence of the Baptist from a man's account? Of course, we have Matthew, Mark, Luke, and John giving an account of whether the Baptist even existed and whom he was. Even if we take these accounts out of the canon and only look at them as actual historical documents, we see the need for more historical documentation, as these apostles are still biased toward Yahweh and apostles of the Messiah.

Flavius Josephus was a Jew who grew up to be a general in the Israeli forces and fought against the Roman forces in the Roman-Jewish War (66-70 AD) and was then captured by Roman forces. After this, Josephus dedicated the rest of his life to recording not only the war but all of the history of the Jews. According to Book 18 Chapter 5 of the Antiquities of the Jews[1], we see that John the Baptist was a popular preacher and that quite a few Jews thought he might lead an uprising to overthrow the Roman government. This coincides with the gospel account where John the immerser calls out the marriage of a Herod to a new wife and the sudden divorce of his previous wife. This is a clear violation of Jewish law, not to mention morally and ethically wrong in the Roman culture.

So, we have the perfect excuse to kill John the dipper to stop a potential uprising and to silence the newly formed blemish on the king's throne. This blemish could cause a huge uprising! Islam also testifies to this baptizer in the Quran (Quran, sura 19 (Maryam), verse 7) and is regarded in the Quran as a prophet.[2]

This is remarkable, as most of us have been taught that Islamic thought, ideas, and scriptures are an enemy to Christianity. Once again, however, we find ourselves at a crossroads where faith plays a major role in oneself deciding whether they will believe or not.

We must also address the "him" in the text as well. *Autou* (**G846**) is not speaking of Yahweh's Holy Spirit again but of whom verse fourteen was describing. Now we see that the pronoun previously mentioned is "the word made flesh" and not Yahweh's Holy Spirit as before.

This is important, as we have uncovered that the baffling wind (**G846**) is Yahweh's Holy Spirit, so why has it now changed? Because Yahweh's Holy Spirit breathes life into us.

The moment two zygotes come together and a heartbeat occurs can only happen by the breath of Yahweh, and we know Yahweh's Holy Spirit is Yahweh. We all have a piece of Yahweh in us from conception throughout our life. We have puffiness, light, and breath.

When we, as humans, reject the idea of a God (Yahweh), we reject Yahweh's Holy Spirit, and this is dangerous. This "him" is Yahshua, and John is recognizing and calling out loudly, shown by the use of *krazo* (**G2896**) to croak, scream, to call aloud. The sole purpose of John the Baptizer is to declare the remission of sins, show the path, and prepare the way of Yahweh.

What is the way of Yahweh? The messiah – Logos! How do you prepare? Immerse your bodies completely as a cleansing ritual.

As I discussed before in a previous chapter, this was not a new idea in the Old Testament. A ritual bath was required in many aspects of both Judaism and Islam. When we take a bath (**H4723** *mikveh* מִקְוֶה) from qavah; something waited for, i.e., Confidence (objective or subjective); also, a collection, i.e. (of water) a pond, or (of men and horses) a caravan or drove—abiding, gathering together, hope, linen yarn, plenty (of water), pool. This collection of water is used as a pool to cleanse oneself – to repent. This repentance is (**H5162** *nacham* נָחַם) repent, sigh and then (**H7725** *shub* שׁוּב) to return, turn back, and this is what was so remarkable about John. A priest by all rights, in the wilderness at the River Jordan, declaring hope for the people of Israel. He proclaimed that the Messiah is coming, even at the door, and to repent and be immersed as to receive him! This was an exciting topic in those days, as Rome had an iron grip, while Greek culture dominated and overpowered the Hebrew culture. In those days, Judaism was at a decline due to the Greco-Roman influence and the political policies of the time stifling the Judaic way of life and vying for governance of Israel's people. Here, we have this man preaching the Messiah, and to the Romans, this became a powder keg awaiting ignition.

John's immersion had great impact on the times and really meant something huge to those who were a resident of the area. This is why baptism is an integral part of Yahshua's sayings in all of his ministry, as it lined up with Torah, and Torah was still alive at that time and today. Simply put, this part is a reiteration of the first part of this text. This also clues us into which "he" the immerser speaks of.

Ane (**G2258**) is telling us that this was or were, while *eimi* (**G1510**) reveals yes, this is alive and present or exists. The word *epo* (**G2036**), which is to speak or say, is compared with *lego* (**G3004**) and reveals that the Baptist is leaving no room for error in his words.

This is also revealed in the author's choice of Greek words, as every word lines up to show that the Messiah is about to be revealed, and this revelation is imminent. We must remember John knows who the Messiah is, yet no one else knows at this point except for John, Mary, and Joseph, Anna, some shepherds, the Magi; a very small group of people. This was John's sole purpose in life as a priest and prophet: to reveal and declare the Messianic age. He was sent to reveal that Yahshua was the long-awaited logos from Yahweh.

When we break down this first part of the verse, it looks like: **John** (Iohannes) **bare witness** (testified or gave record) **of** (concerning) **him** (Yahshua, a baffling wind) **and cried** (moreover scream aloud) **saying** (to lay forth), **this** (this) **was he** (wast or were, exists, am) **of whom** (which) **I spake** (spoke of or had laid forth).

John bare witness of him, and cried, saying, this was he of whom I spake, **he that cometh after me is preferred before me:** *for he was before me.*

John 1:15

He that cometh ἀλλ'	after ὀπίσω	me μου	is preferred γέγονεν	before me ἔμπροσθέν
G2064 erchomai – Middle voice of a primary verb (used only in the present and imperfect tenses, the others being supplied by kindred [middle voice] eleuthomai (el-yoo'-thom-ahee), or [active] eltho (el'-tho), which do not otherwise occur) to come. to come. Of persons: to come from one place to another, and used both of persons arriving and of those returning, to appear, make one's appearance, come before the public. Metaphor: to come into being, arise, come forth, show itself, find place or influence. be established, become known, to come (fall) into or unto to go, to follow one.	**G3694 opiso** – From the same as G3693 with enclitic of direction; to the back that is aback (as adverb or preposition of time or place; or as noun): - after (that is aback (+get) behind (+ward) - after back (-ward) behind. follow. **G3693 opisthen** – From opis (regard; from G3700) with enclitic of source; from the rear (as a secure aspect) that is at the back [adverb and preposition of place or time]: - after, - hardly, backside, behind. **G3700 optanomai** – The first (middle voice) to gaze that the first person I (only expressed when emphatic): - I, me. ****INTERLINEAR**** **G1473 ego** – A primary pronoun of the first person I (only expressed when emphatic): - I, me.	**G3450 mou** – The simpler form of G1700; of me: - I, me, mine (own), my. **G1700 emou** – A prolonged form of G3449, of me: -me, mine, my. **G3449 mochthos** – From the base of G3425; toil that is (by implication) sadness: - painfulness travail. **G3425 mogis** – Adverb from a primary word mogos (toil); with difficulty: - hardly.	**G1096 ergento or ginomai** – properly, to emerge, become, transitioning from one point (realm, condition) to another. means "to become, and signifies a change of condition, state or place. means to come into being/manifestation implying motion, movement, or growth" (at 2 Pet 1:4). Thus, it is used for God's actions as emerging from eternity and becoming (showing themselves) in time (physical space).	**G1715 emprosthen** – From G1722 and G4314; in front of (in place [L or F] or time): - against at before (in presence sight) of. **G1722 en** – properly, in (inside, within); (figuratively) "in the realm (sphere) of," as in the condition (state) in which something operates from the inside (within). **G4314 prós** (a preposition) – properly, motion towards to "interface with" (literally, moving toward a goal or destination).

John bare witness of him, and cried, saying, this was he of whom I spake, he that cometh after me is preferred before me: **for he was before me**. *John 1:15*

for

ὅτι

G3754 hoti – Neuter of G3748 as conjugation; demonstrative that (sometimes redundant); causatively because: - as concerning that, as though, because (that), for (that), how (that), (in), that, though, why.

he was

ἦν

G2258 ane – Imperfect of G1510; I (thou) was (wast or were): - agree, be, have charge of, hold, was, were.

G1510 eimi (the basic Greek verb which expresses being, i.e., "to be") – am, is, 1510 (eimi), and its counterparts, (properly) convey "straight-forward" being (existence, i.e., without explicit limits).

G4253 pro – A primary preposition; "fore", i.e. In front of, prior (figuratively, superior) to -- above, ago, before, or ever. In the comparative, it retains the same significations: - above, ago, before, or ever. In compounds it retains the same significance.

before

πρῶτός

G4413 protos – Contracted superlative of G4253; foremost (in time place order of importance): - before beginning best chief (-est) first (of all) former.

me.

μου

G3450 mou – The simpler form of G1700; of me: - I me mine (own) my.

G1700 emou – A prolonged form of G3449, of me: -me mine my.

G3449 mochthos – From the base of G3425; toil that is (by implication) sadness: - painfulness travail.

G3425 mogis – Adverb from a primary word mogos (toil); with difficulty: - hardly.

INTERLINEAR

G1473 ego – A primary pronoun of the first person I (only expressed when emphatic): - I me.

ABOVE, BEFORE, AND PREFERRED

In this second part of the text, we have several issues which have allowed for strange doctrines or arguments. The first thing we need to tackle is the idea that John had a ministry of his own. This is false and built upon the premise that John had followers since his birth and declares Yahshua usurped John's role or took his teachings from John. The Mandaeans believe this to be the case and that Yahshua is not the Messiah.[3]

John had a ministry which was to prepare the way of Yahweh, to prepare the way in which Yahweh's salvation was to come. See John 1:6-8. In this verse, John describes the Baptist's role very clearly, and it seems to me that people get confused despite the commas being laid out well in the Greek. This confusion most likely came from some manuscripts containing punctuation and some that did not. Yet in the English, depending on which translation you read, the commas have been taken out and a colon inserted near the end of the text. Yahshua came after John, both in birth and ministry. This was purposely done, as John would announce the Messiah and show people how to make ready the paths Isaiah 40:3, thus resembling Elijah, which is why Jews and the Messianic faiths still celebrate this in the Passover Seder.

"He that cometh after me," there is the first comma, and this punctuation mark (,) in English, this comma, indicates a pause between parts of a sentence. It is also used to separate items in a list and to mark the place of thousands in a large numeral. This is the same in Greek. "Is preferred before me," means Yahshua is preferred or *ginomai* (**1096**) I come into being, am born, become, come about, happen. This refers to Yahweh's actions from the beginning and showing themselves in time. In other words, Yahshua, who was prophesied as the Logos, is more important than John the Baptist, thus, Yahshua is preferred. John knew this and was perfectly fine with their respective roles. John is expressing that he is not worthy and is only here to lead the way to Yahweh's salvation.

Yahshua is now beginning to move into his ministry role and is about to be immersed by John the Baptist. Many people find this strange and ask why would God incarnate need to be baptized if he is God? Herein lies the issue people do not understand. To wit: Yahshua is not God incarnate. He is a man who is to be the Messiah, and he will be the Messiah when all things are completed. What is to be completed? The walking of Torah, the ministry, the teaching, the baptism, the death, the burial, and the resurrection.

If Yahshua as a man does not perform and fulfill all things, then we are hopeless.

If Yahshua is a God, then we are hopeless, as a God cannot die, nor coexist with flesh, and a God cannot be tempted by evil.

When we understand Yahshua is a man and had to walk out Torah perfectly to be our Messiah, this means he had to obey his Father as well.

Who sent John? Did John have instructions? And what were they?

Since we know John was sent by Yahweh to clear a path and prepare the highway to declare the Logos, that promise of old. Then Yahshua, being a man, had to be obedient to the father and be baptized. Not because he had sin but because it is a form of worship because obedience is worship.

We seem to have forgotten this truth in this generation: "But be ye doers of the word, and not hearers only, deceiving your own selves." James 1:22. The Messiah must fulfill all things in order to be the Messiah, and we are instructed to be imitators of Yahweh set apart and like our Messiah, be obedient and walk in love as he did. Ephesians 5:1 clearly tells us to imitate Yahweh, and verse two expresses to model Yahshua to accomplish this goal or mindset. This a mouthful!

The last section of this text in the Greek is not a list made by a colon but by a comma. This is important because the colon is as a list directing us to believe that it is the equivalent of this idea: introduce clauses or phrases that serve to describe, amplify, or restate what precedes them. However, the comma here in the Greek tells us this is the third part of a list: "for he was before me." The colon in the English translation is sharing with us a phrase that describes, amplifies, and restates what preceded in the text.

My friends, this is not a smoking gun for Yahshua being in Heaven with Yahweh before the earth or even at the point of Light. This is simply stating that the promise of this man who will become the Messiah is here and was before the thought of me. It is this simple. If we pull anything else into it, we are creating a new doctrine from thin air.

Hoti (**G3754**) is for, as though, because. *Ane* (**G2258**) is telling us that this was or were, while *eimi* (**G1510**) is revealing that yes, this is alive and present or exists. *Protos* (**G4413**) is foremost in time, place, order of importance, and *pro* (**G4253**) is in front of, prior (figuratively superior). This also helps to understand and verify the scripture that the Messiah was slain from the foundation of the world Revelation 13:8. <u>Not slain twice but the Logos being prophesied.</u>

So, both the Greek and English have this grammatically correct. In English only, as our language is one that has a lot of words to describe every little thing, can this be taken to mean something else.

This drives home my point that we must study Scriptures in their entirety to understand what is being told or shared with us. Not making the Word to no avail but to show that relationship requires understanding as to what is being said. Yahweh knows we definitely need more of this.

When we break down this whole verse, we see: **John** (Iohannes) **bare witness** (testified or gave record) **of** (concerning) **him** (Yahshua, a baffling wind) **and cried** (moreover scream aloud) **saying** (to lay forth), **this** (this) **was he** (wast or were, exists, am) **of whom** (which) **I spake** (spoke of or had laid forth), **he that cometh** (he that comes before the public) **after** (from the rear) **me** (me, John), **is preferred** (Yahweh's actions from the beginning and showing themselves in time) **before me** (in front of me): **for** (for, as though, because) **he was** (wast or were, exists, am) **before** (foremost in time, place order of importance) **me** (me, John).

And of his fulness we all have received, and grace for grace. **John 1:16**

And καί

G2532 kai – and (also), very often, moreover, even, indeed (the context determines the exact sense).

of ἐκ

G1537 ek – (a preposition, written eks before a vowel) – properly, "out from and to" (the outcome); out from within. ek ("out of") is one of the most under-translated (and therefore mis-translated) Greek prepositions – often being confined to the meaning "by." (ek) has a two-layered meaning ("out from and to") which makes it out-come oriented (out of the depths of the source and extending to its impact on the object).

his αὐτοῦ

G846 autou · (1) From G847; self (emphatic) (2) he, she, it (used for the third person pronoun) (3) the same. Usage: he, she, they, them, same. In itself it signifies nothing more than performance.

fullness πληρώματος

G4138 pleroma · From G4137; repletion or completion, i.e. (subjectively) what fills (as contents, supplement, copiousness, multitude) or (objectively) what is filled (as container, performance, period): – which is put in to fill up, piece that filled up, fulfilling, full, fullness.

G4134, pleres · From G4134; to make replete, i.e. (literally) to cram (a net), level up (a hollow), or (figuratively) to furnish (or imbue, diffuse, influence), satisfy, execute (an office), finish (a period or task), verify (or coincide with a prediction), etc.: – accomplish, X after, (be) complete, end, expire, fill (up), fulfil, (be, make) full (come), fully preach, perfect, supply

we ἡμεῖς

G2249 hemeis – Nomitive plural of G1473, we (only used when emphatic): – us we (ourselves).

G1473 ego – A primary pronoun of the first person I ("I") means), X daily, + ever, every (one, way), as many as, + no (-thing), X thoroughly, whatsoever, whole, whosoever.

INTERLINEAR

G1473 ego – A primary pronoun of the first person I (only expressed when emphatic): – I, me.

all πάντες

G3956 pas – every, all manner of, including all the forms of declension; apparently a primary word; all, any, every, the whole – properly, to lay hold by aggressively (actively) accepting what is available (offered), lambanō ("accept with initiative") emphasizes the volition (assertiveness) of the

have received ἐλάβομεν

G2983 lambano · (from the primitive root, lab-, meaning "actively lay hold of see NAS dictionary) – properly, to lay hold by aggressively (actively) accepting what is available (offered), lambanō ("accept with initiative") emphasizes the volition (assertiveness) of the

INFILLING AND THE GIFTS

In verse sixteen, we are still speaking of Yahshua when we define our pronoun "his" again. This is important, as we must keep our pronouns in place, or else we can get way off course.

This verse is very well worded, as you can read and comprehend the first part of the text. In the Septuagint, this ancient text reads, "and out of the filling of him." This intends to convey that the Holy Spirit is in the filling of Yahshua we have received.

For some, this seems too basic to understand. The reason I emphasize this point is because at this juncture, we see the filling of Yahweh's Holy Spirit begins within Yahshua. If we are reading this and have been told that evidence of the receiving of Yahweh's Holy Spirit is tongues and yet you did not receive the gift of tongues, be not dismayed.

Forgive that pastor or lay member of the church who said this and come back home to Yahshua and let him guide you. Please recognize that Yahweh's Holy Spirit was filled in you already. The gifts of Yahweh are vast, and tongues are just one aspect of these gifts.

So many people have been hurt by this one sole error, creating self-doubt and division. This does not come from Yahweh's Holy Spirit, as that is what the adversary does – kill, steal, and destroy. Killing your faith, stealing your joy, and destroying the hope which was made available to you just by receiving the Messiah's good work and the good news of it.

It looks as though we can see another aspect of what Yahshua meant when he said "blasphemy of Yahweh's Holy Spirit." Brothers and sisters, it is right there in the text, in the Greek and in the English!

This sets the standard for those of us who have become the sons of Yahweh to receive Yahweh's Holy Spirit as it is described in verse twelve: "But as many as received him, to them gave he the power to become the sons of God, even to them that believe on his name." To believe in Messiah, this man Yahshua, is what will allow you to receive Yahweh's Holy Spirit.

If you are a son of Yahweh, you have full rights to the kingdom.

If you are a daughter of Yahweh, then you have full rights to the kingdom.

Why? Well, when we believe in Yahshua's work and what he did for us: walking a Torah-led life, living sin-free, fulfilling every aspect of Messiahship to become Messiah, including the walk, the talk, the trail, the death, the resurrection and the accension, and at that point we receive *lambano* (**G2983**) to take, literally or figuratively. Not in a violent or forceful way such as *aihreomai* (**G138**), but to choose and to let it wash over oneself.

Who is the Holy Spirit? Yahweh is! And when we choose to believe, He will fill us, making each of us a son or daughter of Yahweh.

The angels were also called the sons of Yahweh; those angels actually received Yahweh's Holy Spirit and spoke to mankind on behalf of the Father in order to give a message or direction Ex.3:2-6, Gen 16:7, Judges 2:1-2, Acts 12:7, Gen

21:17. These sons of Yahweh were filled by Yahweh's Holy Spirit in that form to deliver that message.

The idea, thought, or teaching that this was Yahshua is a doctrine of demons, as Yahshua was not in existence at this time but in thought only. The idea that Yahshua was an angel or acted as an angel is a Gnostic teaching. Had Yahshua been or infilled any one of these angels, it would have been strange doctrine in both Judaism and early Christianity.

Folks, the bottom line is: Yahweh is the only God in the known universe and the only God outside the universe of time. Yahweh's Holy Spirit is Yahweh and not a second person of a trio!

Yahshua is our mediator and soon to be king, not a God. He is our savior and due all the love, loyalty, and respect we can give the one who laid his life down for us. To accept anything else shows that one does not understand their own faith, God, or the Word which He gave us. This is blasphemy and a product of the Roman Catholic Church.

Looking at the word "fullness," *pleroma* (**G4138**) is repletion or completion that is what fills or what is filled. Repletion is defined as filled or well-supplied with something. This word *pleroma* comes from *pleroo* (**G4137**) to be replete, that is to cram, level up, and furnish. This word choice by John is not describing a personal favor by Yahweh. When Peter stated, "Yahweh is no respecter of men" Acts 10:33-34, and Paul in Romans 2:11-16, they understood this well and not in a negative light but a positive light that is all-inclusive; the invitation is open to all!

All three of these witnesses show that Yahweh is not slack

in his promises. This "fullness" reveals the mercy of Yahweh by the filling of our human need by Yahweh's Holy Spirit in the person of Yahshua, which is Yahweh's power and provision. This is important because one cannot arbitrarily become the Messiah. This is why people in Christianity believe Yahshua was God in the flesh, and here lies the crux of the matter!

The Logos is fulfilled by this human man who set his life apart for Yahweh's plan and for us his brothers and sisters. Thus, the Word is fulfilled, crammed full with full measure. This Yahshua is the man at hand, and Yahweh's Holy Spirit confirms this. Now he being Yahshua, needs to complete the messianic role, Matt 24:34 – *genea* (**G1074**) which is age nation or race – all-inclusive and open for all, Matt 5:18. Not Law, as this would mean the Messiah's work would not count. Not one jot or tittle will fall away from the Torah! Torah = Light = Yahshua. He must be fulfilled – all things! Luke 4:21, Matt 5:17, Luke 22:37, Matt 26:56, John 18:19, Mark 1:15, Luke 24:44, Luke 18:31, Luke 24:49. All these scriptures across all four gospel accounts come from our savior's mouth.

And of his fulness we all have received, **and grace for grace.** *John 1:16*

and
καὶ

G2532 kai – and (also), very often, moreover, even, indeed (the context determines the exact sense).

grace
Χάριν

G5485 charis - From G5463; graciousness (as gratifying), of manner or act (abstract or concrete; literal, figurative or spiritual; especially the divine influence upon the heart, and its reflection in the life; including gratitude): -- acceptable, benefit, favour, gift, grace (- ious), joy, liberality, pleasure, thank (-s, -worthy).

G5463 chairo - A primary verb; to be "cheer" ful, i.e., Calmly happy or well-off, impersonally, especially as salutation (on meeting or parting), be well -- farewell, be glad, God speed, greeting, hail, joy (- fully), rejoice

for
ἀντὶ

G473 anti - A primary particle; opposite, i.e. Instead, or because of (rarely in addition to): -- for, in the room of. Often used in composition to denote contrast, requital, substitution, correspondence, etc.

grace.
Χάριτος

G5485 charis - From G5463; graciousness (as gratifying), of manner or act (abstract or concrete; literal, figurative or spiritual; especially the divine influence upon the heart, and its reflection in the life; including gratitude): -- acceptable, benefit, favour, gift, grace (- ious), joy, liberality, pleasure, thank (-s, -worthy).

G5463 chairo - A primary verb; to be "cheer" ful, i.e., Calmly happy or well-off, impersonally, especially as salutation (on meeting or parting), be well -- farewell, be glad, God speed, greeting, hail, joy (- fully), rejoice

GRACE

Now grace, for some reason, is so often misunderstood. It is almost like we are somehow back in the fourteenth century in front of a king, queen, or duke giving homage. We really must go back to the Hebrew to understand what is being conveyed when the translated word grace occurs in scripture; after all, this did originate from the Hebrew.

(**H2583** חָנָה) (khaw-naw) to decline, bend down, encamp. Properly, to incline; by implication, to decline (of the slanting rays of evening); specifically, to pitch a tent; gen. To encamp (for abode or siege) – abide (in tents), camp, dwell, encamp, grow to an end, lie, pitch (tent), rest in tent. The basic understanding of this word in Hebrew is to bend the knee to kneel.

When we read the phrase "and grace for grace" this is telling us that we not only had grace by Yahweh bending the knee and fulfilling his Logos (word) to mankind with the hope of the Messiah coming into existence, but also implying that the Messiah was crammed full of this free gift of salvation to give freely to anyone who wants to accept it. Now, this does not mean a get-out-of-jail-free card! We just learned in the previous section that not one jot or tittle will fall away from the Torah till all things be fulfilled!

(**H2603** חָנַן) (khaw-nan) A primitive root, properly, to bend or stoop in kindness to an inferior; to favor, bestow; causatively to implore. These are the giving of gifts, as in the gifts of Yahweh's Holy Spirit when we become the sons of

Yahweh or that Messiah came bearing the gift of salvation, freedom, and life.

What does the Aaronic blessing say? May Yahweh bless you and keep you, may Yahweh make his face to shine upon you and be gracious unto you: Yahweh lift up his countenance upon you and give you peace. Numbers 6:24-26. Let's examine the words in this blessing.

Bless is to kneel or stoop, and a related Hebrew word is to bring a gift to us. The word *keep* is to put a hedge of protection around us as in thistles to keep enemies out. The word *face* in Hebrew is always written in a plural form, as we all have different faces of our being. That being said, this is a gift that our wholeness of being may be kept and met with Yahweh's whole being. *Light* is (**H215 אוֹר**) (or) a verb in this passage to shine or give light. This is used so that order is brought and reveals what is in the darkness. *Gracious* is in verb form as well and is meant for protection to be in the camp, or in our case, in the assembly or church where we are protected. *Grant* basically means to set down in a fixed or arranged place. *Peace* is used to make whole or complete, as in to give restitution if we have wronged someone or caused deficit to someone. Typically, we see this word in English as the absence of war, which is not wrong, but it loses flavor of the Hebrew intent.[4] These are gifts, and in understanding this passage from John 1:16—which, by the way, is a completely Hebraic thought, not a Greek one—we see the direct correlation of what is meant by gift for gift; the Messiah encompasses all of these concrete ideas. Though, this shows us some astounding things, such as kindness for gift, gift for gift, favor for gift, gratitude for gift, liberty for gift, mercy for gift, and it goes on and on. The implication of this is wonderful news. That our God would keep us in His mind through the ages and actually deliver on a promise where all the other gods fell short. Truly amazing.

We must examine one more point to this phrase in verse sixteen of John 1. The verb "received" is something which must be discussed, as it is noteworthy. This verb is in the Aorist tense and means an unqualified past tense of a verb without reference to duration or completion of the action. If you will remember, we discussed this verb form and its aspect on verbs in Chapter Five. Aorist tense states that an action has happened and is past tense and simple. There is no time frame involved and the action has happened with no extra information about continuing or completing the action.

This is so noteworthy because it shows an attribute of our Elohim. This action has not ceased, as there is not directive to cease. Until when? Until all things are fulfilled by the Messiah!

He spoke a word and gave a promise, and His mercy endures forever. Yahweh knows we are incapable of perfection. This is why He gave the Messiah Yahshua to us, so that we can, through Yahshua's conquering, be taken up to be made like our master Yahshua (Philippians 3:20-21, 1 Corinthians 15:51-53.

We will be changed and clothed in garments that do not spoil. No more death, no more rape, no more slavery of any sort. This line of text shows again that all people, all humanity are allowed to take part in this gifting by Yahweh.

A breakdown of this verse could be seen as: **And** (moreover) **of** (concerning) **his** (Yahshua, a baffling wind) **fulness** (what is filled completely and furnished) **we** (we) **all** (all manner of including all forms of declension) **have received** (actively to lay hold of aggressively what is available), **and** (moreover) **grace** (by divine influence upon the heart, cheer and gift) **for** (because of, rarely in addition to) **grace** (by divine influence upon the heart, cheer and gift).

For the law was given through Moshe, but grace and truth came through Yahshua Messiah. *John 1:17*

For	the law	was given	through	Moshe,
ὅτι	νόμος	ἐδόθη	διὰ	Μωϋσέως

G3754 hóti – Neuter of G3748 as conjugation; demonstrative that (sometimes redundant); causatively because: - as, concerning, that, as though because (that), for (that), how, (that), (in) that, though, why.

G3748 hóstis, hétis, hóti – From G3739 and G5100; which some that is any; also (definitely) which same: - X and (they) (such) as (they) that in, that they, what (-soever), whereas ye, (they) which, who (-soever). Compare G3754

G3739 hós – Probably a primary word (or perhaps a form of the article G3588); the relative (sometime demonstrative) pronoun who, which, what, that: - one, (an the) other, some, that, which, who, (-m-se) See also G3757.

G3757 hoú – Genitive case of G3739 as adverb; at which place that is where: - where (-in) whither (soever).

G3551 nomos – is used of: a) the Law (Scripture), with emphasis on the first five books of Scripture; or b) any system of religious thinking (theology), especially when nomos occurs without the Greek definite article

G1325 didomi – A prolonged form of a primary verb (which is used as an alternate in most of the tenses); to give (used in a very wide application properly or by implication [or F; greatly modified by the connection]): - adventure, bestow, bring forth, commit, deliver (up), give, grant, hinder, make, minister, number, offer, have power, put, receive, set, show, smite (+with the hand), strike (+with the palm of the hand), suffer, take, utter, yield.

G1223 dia – a primary preposition denoting the channel of an act; through.

G3475 Mouses – Moses, a leader of Israel.

PARLANCE AND THE LAW

In the prior verse (sixteen), we saw grace for grace which can also be liberty as a gift. Now this is an interesting concept because I am not speaking of liberty as we typically use the word in Western English. In Western English, it means Liberty as in the state of not being held prisoner nor enslaved. However, there are three definitions to this word, but I am focusing on this first entry and the second example as it applies to this line of scripture. The other entries do as well; yet this one encapsulates the Messiah and Yahweh's benevolence toward mankind in a profound way.

We must again look at sin for what it truly is, and that is, sin is synonymous with one's missing of the mark. This missing of the mark can lead to all kinds of consequences.

When we form unhealthy habits, we continually miss the mark and then we receive the wages of sin. That wage is death, and this death is not just a spiritual death. These habits can lead to an early physical grave or a lifetime of pain and melancholy. This is why we must get back up and aim better. This mentality is in the spirit of the text at hand. Thus, the law was given and placed within the Torah to give people of the faith a way of recompense, as there was no Messiah. Blood was required for justification, and animals did not just give this up freely.

Interestingly, however, the Messiah did. He was willing to lay down his life for his friends' well-being.

In this first part of this verse, I am thrilled to see John use correct terminology in two ways. The first way is that Moshe did not give the Torah, as the Torah was established long before Moshe. Secondly, John is dealing strictly with the recompense or remediation of sin to get back into the camp with Yahweh. John knew and understood the prophecy and was given special insight to relay exactly that. John recognized that this was the Logos from Genesis, and this logos was now flesh on this earth to fulfill the Law.

So, since this fulfillment or liberty has been given to us as a gift, does this give us a freedom to sin? Certainly not! It is the freedom or liberty to repent and come back to Torah when we fail or fall short.

Instead of slaughtering an innocent animal for the blood sacrifice, this man, Yahshua, carried this to a whole new level. He meant to make us aware of the nature of the sin and where we missed the mark in Torah and then to try again. Thus, this understanding in Hebraic terms, shines a light on the error even more since we now have the liberty to work on sin in our lives. Freedom to enjoy Torah in its fullness to where we are not bound up in the recompense.

When we acknowledge that the Jews were setting the stage, we understand it is tremendous and quite literally earth-altering. Allow me to elaborate.

We really need to focus on the fact that the Israelites were tasked with giving the Light (Torah) to the world for they were chosen at Mount Sinai to do so. The Light is Torah (see Proverbs 6:23), and the law was given as a remediation, redemption, reconciliation, or recompense when the Torah was broken. Hence these words in Matthew 5:17-18: "Think not that I am come to destroy the law, or the prophets: I am not come to destroy, but to fulfil. For verily I say unto you, till heaven and earth pass, one jot or one tittle shall in no wise pass from the law, till all be fulfilled."

Some might accuse me of changing Scripture. However, I would implore all believers to follow the logic I am presenting straight from the words of our Messiah. If the Messiah said the text exactly as this was translated, then the statement cancels itself out. Simply put, If Yahshua was come to fulfill the Torah (Torah being the same thing as Law) then in the next sentence he says till heaven and earth pass away, not one jot or tittle shall in no way pass from the Torah till all things be fulfilled! This makes no sense and is a complete contradiction of what Messiah is saying. The Catholic Church's stance dictated that the Jews and all things Jewish were old and done away with and that Torah was the Law. The proper translation would be "Think not that I am come to destroy the law, or the prophets: I am not come to destroy, but to fulfil. For verily I say unto you, till heaven and earth pass, one jot or one tittle shall in no wise pass from the Torah, till all be fulfilled."

On one hand, Yahshua says I did not come to destroy but fulfill the Law and the Prophets, and then he says not one jot or tittle will fall away from the Law. Friends, this is parlance (a particular way of speaking or using words, especially a way common to those with a particular job or interest and manner or mode of speech: IDIOM.[5]

For a lack of a Greek word, therefore no direct translation, the word chosen is *nomou* (**G3551**) - to parcel out especially food or grazing to animals; law though the prescriptive usage; generally (regulation) specifically (of Moses [including the volume]; also, of the Gospel) or figuratively (a principle): law. In today's world the definition of principle has become synonymous with law, thereby continuing the idiom instead of just understanding principle to be a rule of conduct. This comes from Webster's Dictionary 1913.[6] A principle should be understood as a standard by most current and older definitions. This can be seen in both ways, those being: "Yes, I do see Torah as a standard (principled) way of living," and "Your honor, I do understand that the law stipulates the standard (principle) correction for my action is a fine." The particular sense(s) of *nómos* (**G3551**) is determined by the context. The context with both of the definitions stands as law, not Torah, thus the context of the word law in verse eighteen should have been transliterated as Torah.

Here is why. In **Matthew 5:18**, it says, **"For verily I say unto you, till heaven and earth pass, one jot or one tittle shall in no wise pass from the Torah, till all be fulfilled."** A jot is actually the Hebrew letter *yod*, and it is represented in the Paleo Hebrew as the hand of Yahweh. The iota in Greek is the equivalent letter. The tittle are the little marks which distinguish letters of the Hebrew alphabet. These are called horns, and in the Greek are called *keraia* (**G2762**) properly, a little "horn," i.e., "a little hook, an apostrophe" on letters of the alphabet, distinguishing them from other like-letters, or a "separation stroke" between letters.

When we look at Moshe, the subject of our current text, something interesting also comes into view. Have you ever noticed the sculpture of Moshe with horns?[7] The little horns are there because of Exodus 34:30: "And when Aaron and all the children of Israel saw Moses, behold, the skin of his face shone; and they were afraid to come nigh him."

Here is the actual translation of this scripture: "And Aaron and all the sons of Israel saw Moshe and behold his skin of his face had horns, and they were afraid to come near him."

The word here is (**H7160** *qaran* קָרַן) have horns, shine. This leads us to the noun form of the word (**H7161** קֶרֶן) - From qaran; a horn (as projecting); by implication, a flask, cornet; by resemblance. An elephant's tooth (i.e., Ivory), a corner (of the altar), a peak (of a mountain), a ray (of light); figuratively, power -- X hill, horn.

Now this might bother some of us, but please remember this was an authority, as in a crown placed on his head. Just like the majestic stag in the field with its set of horns. Moshe was made as God (Elohim) to Pharaoh Exodus 7:1, and Moshe was given a scepter Exodus 4:1-4.

So, by the time we get to and are living next to Mount Sinai, Moshe has grown horns and has a scepter. Why, this man was Israel's messiah at this juncture in time. Moshe was a foreshadow of Yahshua the one true Messiah. The horns represent the mantle of authority, and the scepter is the power. Now, let's return to the scripture at hand; the *yod* is the hand of Yahweh, and the horns are his majesty or crown.

———

In summation, Moshe was a man who was commissioned by Yahweh to deliver the Israelites from slavery and then condi-

 tion them to live and act in their own set of rules (Torah) given by Yahweh to them as a marriage contract. The Torah being the principled way in which to live one's life. The law was the penalty required when the principle was not met, in order to stay in the assembly. The same thing is happening right now under Yahshua as Messiah, showing us how to live by Torah for the kingdom which is coming. The Torah was established and taught at the very beginning with Adam and Eve.

Moshe did not give the Torah, he reiterated the Torah to a people who had been in servitude and far removed from Abraham, Isaac, and Jacob. Moshe gave the law as the scripture says to show one the way to get back to the camp or assembly when sin occurs – The blood atonement. What about the garden atonement and Abraham's sacrifices? Were those ever listed out as in-depth and encompassing for an individual, group, or society as what Moshe gave? When we equate Torah and Law, we are doing ourselves a great injustice and perpetuating this misnomer which creates division, strife, and schism to the point of Blasphemy of the Holy Spirit without even realizing we are doing just that.

For the law was given through Moshe, **but grace and truth came through Yahshua Messiah.** *John 1:17*

but grace	and	truth	came	through	Messiah	Yahshua
χάρις	καὶ	ἀλήθεια	ἐγένετο	διά	Χριστοῦ	Ἰησοῦ

but grace — χάρις

G5485 charis - From G5463; graciousness (as gratifying), of manner or act (abstract or concrete; literal, figurative or spiritual; especially the divine influence upon the heart, and its reflection in the life; including gratitude): -- acceptable, benefit, favour, gift, grace (-ious), joy, liberality, pleasure, thank (-s, -worthy).

G5463 chairo - A primary verb; to be "cheer" ful, i.e., Calmly happy or well-off; impersonally, especially as salutation (on meeting or parting), be well -- farewell, be glad, God speed, greeting, hail, joy (-fully), rejoice.

and — καὶ

2532 kai - (the most common NT - conjunction, used over 9,000 times) -- and (also), very often, moreover, even, indeed (the context determines the exact sense).

truth — ἀλήθεια

G2225 aletheia - From G2227; truth: -- true X truly, truth, verity.

G227 alethes - From G1 (as a negative particle) and G2990; true (as not concealing): -- true, truly, truth

G1 alfah - Of Hebrew origin; figurative only; the first.

came — ἐγένετο

G1096 ergento or ginomai - properly, to emerge, become, transitioning from one point (realm, condition) to another; means "to become, and signifies a change of condition, state or place, means to come into being/manifestati on implying motion.

G2990 lanthano --Prolonged form of a primary verb which is only used as an alternative in certain tenses; to lie hid, be hid, be ignorant of unawares, in time (physical space).

growth" (at 2 Pet 1:4). Thus, it is used for God's actions as (showing themselves) in order (or so) that not.

through — διά

G1223 dia - a primary preposition properly, "the channel of an act; through.

G5547 Xristós - (from 55480) denoting the Anointed One," the Christ (Hebrew, "Messiah").

G5548 xrió - to anoint by rubbing or pouring olive oil on someone to represent the flow (empowering) of the Holy Spirit. Anointing (literally) involved rubbing olive oil on the head, etc. especially to present someone as divinely- authorized (appointed by God) to serve as prophet, priest or king.

Messiah — Χριστοῦ

Yahshua — Ἰησοῦ

G2424 Iesous - Greek transliteration of Yahshua meaning "Yahweh saves" (or "Yahweh is salvation").

Being calmly happy or well off would be a great way to spend the rest of our lives. Having a gift which keeps on giving every day would be great as well. This is the point of the second part of verse seventeen which leads with the word grace.

We discussed grace in great length earlier in this chapter, so I won't add needless words on this page to describe the same thing. However, when coupled with the word truth, a guarantee is put on the offer of grace.

The word *alethes* (**G227**) is true, as in not concealed or hidden away truth to be discovered. This word is directly from *alfah* (**G1**) which is from Hebrew origin, aleph which is first, as in the first truth. The first thing spoken by Yahweh for our environment was "let there be light" (see chapter 1). This is a truth as it comes from the source, and that source has the origination point – of Yahweh. Due to declension, the truth was spoken concerning the Messiah, and we know this because the word states just that, and if we believe the Word is truth, then there is our truth. When we look at *lanthano* (**G2990**) to lie hid, be ignorant of meaning even if there is ignorance or unawareness of the truth, the truth is still the truth. This grace and truth emerged (**G1096** *ergento*) to emerge through *dia* (**G1223**) the channel of an act. What was the channel? Yahshua Messiah!

Seeing that Moses came to give the Law and Yahshua came to give grace, another verse comes into play. This verse is Matthew 22:42-45: "What do we think about the Christ? Whose son, is He?" "David's," they answered. Jesus said to them, "How then does David in the Spirit call Him 'Lord'? For he says: 'The Lord said to my Lord, "Sit at My right hand until I put Your enemies under Your feet.'" So, if David calls Him 'Lord,' how can He be David's son?"

This scripture refers to Psalm 110:1 (A Psalm of David). "The LORD said unto my Lord, sit thou at my right hand, until I make thine enemies thy footstool." This is quite simple when the false doctrine of pre-existence is removed.

In the Psalm, it is showing us by the use of all caps LORD is *yod hey vav hey* יהוה, and this is Yahweh's name in Hebrew. Now the next Lord is capital L, and this refers to master or another name for Messiah. In Matthew, we see Yahshua initiating the question after he was just tempted by the questioning concerning the greatest commandment. Yahshua asks about the Psalm, and the Pharisees answer correctly. The second question, though, Yahshua specifically uses the words "in spirit" and then drops the bomb "how then can he be his son?"

This is not a clue or a validation of pre-existence, as that would equate Yahshua with Yahweh, and the Messiah himself never did that. This is getting the Pharisees to recognize the promise, the miracle, and the fact that the Messiah will be lifted up to be seated next to Yahweh till the Messiah's enemies are made his footstool. This is a prophetic view and nothing else except the attempt to get the Pharisees to see that they have a spirit of anti-Messiah about them.

The grace is the gift, and the truth is the accomplished action, as it reveals truth from Yahweh's Holy Spirit which is Yahweh. That accomplishment is the fruition of the Messiah on earth or that is the Word made flesh. This grace and truth came directly from Yahweh's Holy Spirit through Yahshua.

The Messiah laid down his life in several ways for us, and this is just one way that he did.

There are several examples where Yahweh is working through Yahshua, and Yahshua confirms this – such as: John 10:38, Matt 12:28, John 7:16-19, John 9:3 and then also attested to by the apostles in Acts 2:22, Luke 9:42, Ephesians 1:19-21. Does this diminish Yahshua? Not at all.

Even the apostles and modern-day men and women perform miracles wrought by Yahweh. However, only one was perfect: Yahshua. Once again, we have confirmed that John is writing a timeline of events leading up to the Messiah on Earth. Even though John has mentioned some points in prior verses not on the timeline, we can see that he is staying true to his style, revealing just who this man is and that he is one of us.

Breaking verse seventeen down, we read: **For** (Because) **the law** (reconciliation, redemption) **was given** (given) **through** (channel of an act) **Moshe** (Moses) **but grace** (the gift given cheerfully) **and** (moreover) **truth** (truth absolute as to not conceal whether ignorant or unawares) **came** (to cause to be) **through** (the channel of an act) **Yahshua Messiah**.

No one has seen Yahweh at any time; the only begotten Son, which is in the bosom of the Father, he hath declared him. *John 1:18*

No one	hath seen	Yahweh	at any time;	the only begotten	Son
οὐδεὶς	ἑώρακεν	Θεὸν	πώποτε	μονογενὴς	υἱός

G3762 oudeis - Including feminine oudemia (oo-dem-ee'-ah), and neuter ouden (oo-den') from oude and heis; not even one (man, woman or thing), i.e. None, nobody, nothing; -- any (man), aught, man, neither any (thing), never (man), no (man), none (+ of these things), not (any, at all, -thing), nought.

G3708 horáō – properly, see, often with metaphorical meaning: "to see with the mind" (i.e., spiritually see), i.e., perceive (with inward spiritual perception).

G2316 theós - (of unknown origin) – properly, God, the Creator and owner of all things (Jn 1:3; Gen 1 - 3).

G4455 popote - From po and pote; at any time, i.e. (with negative particle) at no time - at any time, + never (...to any man), + yet, never themselves.

G3439 monogenes – From G3441 and G1096; only born that is sole: - only (begotten child).

G3441 monos – Probably from G3306; remaining that is sole or single; by implication mere: - alone only by themselves.

G1096 ergento or gínomai – properly, to emerge, become, transitioning from one point (realm, condition) to another; means "to become, and signifies a change of condition, state or place. means to come into being/manifestation implying motion, movement, or growth" (at 2 Pet 1:4). Thus, it is used for God's actions as emerging from eternity and becoming (showing themselves) in time (physical space).

G3306 meno – A primary verb; to stay (in a given place, state, relation, or expectancy): – abide, continue, dwell, endure, be present, remain, stand, tarry (for) X thine own.

G5207 huios Apparently a primary word; a "son" (sometimes of animals), used very widely of immediate, remote or figuratively, kinship -- child, foal, son.

SEEN, DISCERNED, OR PERCEIVED?

In this verse, we see the foundation of thought which the Roman Catholic Church and the Nicene council initiated, where they justify and then later incorporate the doctrine of the Trinity. Then, in subsequent church history, the beginnings of the pre-existence theory occur, using this scripture to provide proof that Yahweh in the Old Testament was actually Yahshua.

Instead of rehashing everything I mentioned in chapters one through four, I will begin with the Greek word *oudeis* (**G3762**) not even one man, woman, or thing. Within the definition of this word, we find that the *ou* is an absolute negative and, in all persons, both masculine and feminine, and this is the case as well. No man or woman has ever seen Yahweh is a pretty big statement, especially after we have read the Old Testament and *seen* this play out in what seems to be at least one hundred times. Did we see it? Or was it discerned from the text presented?

These are huge questions with implications for you, me, and future generations. I emphasized the word *seen* above with italics and underlining to give an example of what I mean.

In English, when we see or have seen some things while reading, we use our mind's eye. Sometimes, we are reading a book and using our imagination without any facts other than what we are reading through the lens of our own personal context.

Now I am not saying that the Bible is not fact or is not

based on fact—no, not at all! In the example above, you and I, when we read the book of Genesis, have witnessed nothing in person nor have we seen anything except for words on a page. As we read, we comprehend in our mind what this scene looked like.

In English, we read quickly as native English-speaking people. We are accustomed to our language and sometimes take understanding expressions for granted. However, sometimes, in translations, words and phrases are presented from other languages (translations) and the best words are chosen for us. The issue is that some of these words chosen to represent that other language or culture are not always put in the best light to be _seen_ for what they are or they it mean! No pun intended.

Seen is one such word. This is also where I believe an agenda can easily come into play without revealing any overtly nefarious actions. That may seem like I'm speaking of a conspiracy in a place where none exists, but is it?

The Greek word chosen for "hath seen" is _harao_ (**G3708**) to stare at, that is to discern clearly (physically or mentally), to attend to: by Hebraism to experience; passively to appear: behold, perceive, see, take heed. Now, why am I arguing against this word _seen_ if that is what the definition says it is?

The definition which is often selected in this case by Strong's team, and this team made their decision based on accepted Christian doctrine of the trinity, that no man hath seen the father. This is why a vast number of Christians and theologians will tell us that it had to be Jesus back in the book of Genesis, because no man has seen the father!

I believe that Abraham did see the father, that is

Yahweh's Holy Spirit! I believe Sarah did as well when she brought out the cakes and maybe even when she peered out of one of the corners of the tent, giggling at the idea of her and Abraham having productive, enjoyable fun again in their older age. However, the point is that I am not arguing that you and I or Abraham saw anything, I am simply arguing that the word chosen is incorrect in context with the text of the verse. The correct word should have been "discerned" or even "hath attended to." Perhaps *perceived* might be the best choice, as that makes much more sense than seen. Maybe they chose what they did for ease of reading, likely doctrinal acceptance, and the least controversial choice amongst the denominations. Why did they do this?

When we look at John 6:46, we see the same translation issue happening. Here, a translated word has deep spiritual implications upon people of faith, causing an error in faith and equating Yahshua with Yahweh—something our beloved Messiah never alluded to or said. John 6:46 reads: "Not that any man hath seen the Father, save he which is of God, he hath seen the Father." Can you see the father? Why, yes, we can, and this came from Yahshua's mouth.

Change the word choice: "Not that any man hath discerned the Father, save he which is of God, he hath discerned the Father." Let's try: "Not that any man hath attended to the Father, save he which is of God, he hath attended to the Father." One more time with John 1:18: "No one hath discerned Yahweh at any time; the only begotten Son," and once more, "No one hath attended to Yahweh at any time; the only begotten Son."

Let us try one application using the next word, perceived.

"Not that any man hath perceived the Father, save he which is of God, he hath perceived the Father." This examination of the translated words may come across as very technical or a matter of semantics, maybe even seem like hair-splitting. Perhaps, however, when we equate Yahshua with Yahweh will every hair of our head be accounted for in the judgment? Blasphemy or anything akin to blasphemy is a dangerous game, friend.

The next words in the text are "at any time" and is *popote* (**G4455**) any time and with a negative particle at no time, at any time, never. This word comes from an infinite adverb and that means *pote* (**G4215**) at some time ever, in the old time, in time past, once or when.

Now, when chasing the etymology of this word, one could begin to see the verse unfolding with the word *seen* and that word being acceptable as I used the word in the example in the above paragraph. When we take the whole verse, most people read this as "No man has seen Yahweh except Yahshua who is from the bosom of Yahweh," or something close to this train of translation.

The main point here is that the word *seen* is the word which jumps out and sticks in our minds, causing the whole message to be tweaked in a way which does not convey what John was saying. What is being said is "No one has discerned Yahweh at any time in history (except in Spirit), save Yahshua who is from the bosom of his Father, and will show you Yahweh as you have never seen him before!" Drop the mic! That is good news and goes with the gospel like never before—well, at least since the second century AD.

Next, we have *monogenes* (**G3439**) from **G3441** and

G1096; only born that is sole: only. *Monos* (**G3441**) sole or single. Here is where this translation gets more interesting. This word *monos* comes from *meno* (**G3306**) which is to stay (in a given place, state, relation, or expectancy) and *ginomai* (**G1096**) to cause to be, that is to become.

This word choice for the translated term "the only begotten" is phenomenal, as this is telling us that because of Yahshua's surrender to Yahweh for us, Yahweh stays with Yahshua, Yahweh stays in this state with Yahshua, Yahweh is in a relation with Yahshua, Yahweh has an expectancy of Yahshua and that he is the only one to have such a state of existence.

This tells us that Yahshua was a man and was infilled by Yahweh's Holy Spirit. Yahshua paved the way for us! Luke 2:40, Luke 4:1, John 5:19, John 3:34, Luke 10:21, Luke 3:22, Matthew 12:28.

No one has seen Yahweh at any time; the only begotten Son, **which is in the bosom of the Father, he hath declared him.** *John 1:18*

which	is	in	the bosom	of the Father	he hath declared	him (Yahweh)
καὶ	ὤν	εἰς	ᾖν	Πατρός	ἐκεῖνος	Θεόν

G3588 ho - The masculine feminine (second) and neuter (third) forms in all their inflections; the definite article -he

G5607 ousa - Including the feminine ousa (oo'-sah); and the neuter on (on) present participle of eimi; being -- be, come, have.

G1519 eis – A primary preposition; to or into (indicating the point reached or entered) of place time or (figuratively) purpose (result etc)– properly, into (unto) – literally, "motion into which" implying penetration ("unto," "union") to a particular purpose or result, to or into (indicating the point reached or entered, of place, time, purpose, result). Usage: into, in, unto, to, upon, towards, for, among.

G2589 kolpos - properly, the upper part of the chest where a garment naturally folded to form a "pocket" – (result etc)– properly, called the "bosom," the position synonymous with intimacy (union).

G3962 pater - Apparently a primary word; a father (L or F G3778; near or more remote) - father parent.

G1563 ekei – Of uncertain affinity; there; by extension thither; - there, thither; - there, thither (-ward) (to) yonder (place), alone.

G3778 houtos – From the article G3588 and G846; the, he (she, it) that is, this, or that (often with the article repeated); - he

G1565 ekeinos - From G1563; that one or (neuter)

G2316 theós - (of unknown origin) – properly, God, the Creator and owner of all things (Jn 1:3; Gen 1 - 3).

G3588 ho - The masculine feminine (second) and neuter (third) forms in all their inflections; the definite article -he.

G846 autou - From the particle au (perhaps akin to G109) through the idea of a baffling wind.

The second part of this verse is a mouthful and should underline our faith and doctrine, not based upon a body of men or even a body of believers, but by the body itself whom is the Messiah. That sounds great and all, but let's really stop and look at this text.

Ho (**G3588**), which is the definite article, would be the only begotten Son, in the present tense, not the past tense. *Ousa* (**G5607**) – in (indicating the point reached or entered) "pressed into the father." *Kolpos* (**G2589**) – upper part of the chest at the pocket, synonymous with intimacy or union.

Yahshua when he first gave up his life—as in gave up sex, marriage, children, career, whatever things were destined for him by the choices he would end up making—gave his life over to Yahweh for us. This created that **G3439** experience we just learned about and that solely selected him for a union with Yahshua being filled with Yahweh's Holy Spirit. This allowed an intimacy where Yahshua pressed into Yahweh, and Yahshua could do nothing unless the father was doing it because he chose this way completely! John 10:30, John 17:11, John 14:10, Matthew 11:27. Yahshua set the course for all relationships with the Father past, present, and future. John 6:44, John 14:6, 1 Timothy, 2:5, Romans 5:2, Hebrews 9.

For our friends who do not believe that Yahshua is the Messiah, we need to concentrate right here. *Pater* (**G3962**) is the Greek word for father. This father spoken of here is the same father in context with the rest of the chapter. This father is in the beginning of the chapter starting in verse one and is the Greek word *theos* (**G2316**) – a deity, especially the supreme divinity, meaning Yahweh or in Hebrew: *"yod hey vav hey."*

Most Jews and Christians today, at this juncture in human history, believe Yahweh has form and that his nature is similar to our own. This is impossible because we cannot even begin to understand Yahweh's form, as it is pure, pure energy, all-consuming, and his spirit—yes, he has a spirit—called the Holy Spirit. Yahweh's Holy Spirit is not a person, it is not a separate deity, it is Yahweh, as is every other part of Him.

In short review, the pronoun chosen by John is used to show that Yahweh's Holy Spirit is participating, moving, and interacting with humankind – his creation. This is seen from verse three to verse five. Picking up again in verse seven through fourteen, we can see him now declared as a father, a parent. I share this now so we can keep our pronouns in line, as that is the key to understanding what Yahweh is accomplishing here in this text in John. This makes it personal for you and me. Thus, creating relationship between ourselves and the father who is Yahweh.

In verse fourteen, we see that this word made flesh is now fulfilled. This man Yahshua, who was publicly declared by John the Baptist, appears in recorded history in several accounts. Yahshua is also mentioned in public record by a couple of noteworthy Israeli/Roman citizens, who by no means declared an affinity or public declaration of faith toward this man Yahshua. They had no religious interest in this Yahshua at all. Over three hundred eyewitnesses who knew Yahshua personally, twelve from his closest circle, also went on to die horrid deaths for their public declaration of faith in Yahshua; yet they, in no way, declared him Yahweh or equal to Yahweh. People of countries and territories witnessed this man perform miracles and preach the Torah for everlasting life. Subsequently, the religious leaders of the time, those being the Sanhedrin, Herod, the governor of both Judaism and the political realm of Israel, snuff out the existence of this man Yahshua at all costs.

Zoroastrianism and Islam both claim that this man Yahshua was a miracle birth, yet relegate Yahshua only to the status of a prophet. All evidence from Moshe to the prophets to religious leaders to political leaders report this man, Yahshua, as doing these wonderous things.

Who else in history has gone this path? Please tell me by emailing me using the email in the back matter. I have read many accounts, pored over historical figures, and no one man has walked the prophecies and the actions of this man Yahshua. I implore all believers to think on the evidence presented here and ask Yahweh's Holy Spirit to show you who this man Yahshua was and is. Yahweh is merciful to answer our seeking.

This verse, after unfolding the Greek, has really grown on me, allowing what I feel is a glimpse into the relationship between Yahweh and Yahshua, that is the relationship between Father and son. The translated verse is: "No one has seen Yahweh at any time; the only begotten Son, which is in the bosom of the Father, he hath declared him."

The Septuagint version is this: "God not yet one has seen as when the only generated son the one being into the bosom of the father that one unfolds." Remember, this version is translated directly from the Greek.

The English translation is given, so that the sentence makes sense in the English and cleans this up for us as readers of English. The Greek direct translation sounds very choppy when we read the verse directly from the Greek Septuagint.

As I have described above, the common belief, held currently, is that Yahshua is God. This translation into English by James and others clearly says that as well. However, the Septuagint does not. A breakdown of this verse would reveal: Yahweh, the Supreme being of unknown origin no one perceived at any time only begotten (of) the supreme being the existing unto the bosom of the father that declares or unfolds the way.

Yahweh pledged a savior to/for mankind. What do we all do when we make a pledge? We cover our heart. Where is our heart? In our bosom. Get it?

If we will remember, in a previous chapter, we discussed the Greek word *en* (**G1510**) which means to exist or I AM.

What did Yahweh tell Moshe to tell the tribes when they asked, "Who sent you?"

"Tell them I AM sent me."

Who is I AM? I AM made the pledge for a deliverer. For the children of Israel, it was Moshe and even Moshe told them, "there was one to come that will come from amongst you"—not from heaven. Deuteronomy 18:15

We often seem to get hung up on this phrase I AM. Why would Yahshua use the phrase to talk about himself when it was clearly Yahweh? This verse also tells us explicitly that Yahshua came from a pledge of Yahweh's being, not that he's been standing alongside him throughout time. This is why the Messiah knows, perceives, and discerns the father. Additionally, this is why Yahshua says I AM, because he (Yahshua) now exists!

Yahshua is that wondrous pledge or promise fulfilled for mankind.

CHAPTER 8
SUMMATION
THE JOHN 1:1 FACTOR

BREAKDOWN OF EACH VERSE

Writing this book has been a very exciting journey, and honestly, I did not know if I would dead-end or agree with my conclusions or go back to how I used to believe. The journey has opened the door to more truth about our Savior and our Elohim and the differences between them. Now that I have come to the final chapter, I find myself certain, without a shadow of doubt, that Yahweh is my God, and Yahshua is my brother who is currently my High Priest and soon to be King. In conclusion, I want to share the breakdown of each verse and what Yahweh's Holy Spirit has shown me along the way.

———

In Chapter One, we discovered that the timeline amongst biblical and secular scholars, archeologists, and linguists concerning human history and the biblical records indeed line up, and this changes human history in a huge way. Keep in mind, we only touched the surface, so please go and study these topics, as you will be amazed. I encourage you to do so. Remember, though, take one thing at a time, so you can compartmentalize your findings and not overwhelm yourself.

We also found the Ancient Hebrew and the impact this had on the surrounding cultures. We also touched on the many semitic languages of Levant and Canaan and how closely related they actually are. We also made a case for why we believe John truly did write the Gospel of John. We also displayed the different usages of the word "word" in Hebrew and Greek and the importance of the differences and the selections used within John's gospel. We realized Logos is actually a Greek word for a thought that is uttered. With this understanding we can see the Light created, and it is, in this case, with ample evidence, the phrase or divine command: "Let there be Light." We also discovered the true Biblical meaning of Light: that Light is Torah. We examined the impact mankind has had on Christianity over the last 1800 years and how this impact has changed the religion to include manmade doctrines instead of relying only on sound biblical teachings.

Consider these questions:

. . .

1. Could the Ancient Hebrew have been the original form of writing until the dispersion in Babel mentioned in the Bible?

2. Can a man or woman become motivated through a passion of a subject and be inspired with guidance by the Holy Spirit?

3. Did Yahshua actually equate himself with Yahweh?

4. Is it possible to shake off 1800 years of education and realize that Yahweh is God and has no form that we can comprehend and is the Holy Spirit that reveals himself to you?

———

Within Chapter Two, we again confirmed the Greek definition of Logos. We were able, through Biblical definitions, to confirm that Light is Torah. Then we realized that the Word is still the Torah at this point in Scripture. Moreover, all three of these are a promise or a pledge from Yahweh. This promise was with Yahweh in the beginning, and He was this promise, meaning He is as good as his word. We also learned Yahweh is outside of time and is not of form. The form Yahweh chooses to express himself to humans is in the form of his Holy Spirit. This chapter also revealed a lost, yet age-old, truth that Yahweh is omniscient, omnipresent, and omnipotent. We also saw how translations from Greek to English can be difficult, even with simple words like "was" and "am." We dove in headlong into the choices and meanings of the word "word" for a clear understanding of the text. We uncovered the different religions and belief systems through human history concerning a virgin birth and realized there were none. We also took a look at how likeness and image are truly depicted.

Some questions believers of Yahshua should ask themselves:

1. Why would there be Torah prior to Genesis 1:1?

2. Does Torah reveal darkness?

3. Does Torah reveal the Way?

4. Do humans need Torah as believers?

———

Chapter Three helped us to discover an element of Hebrew poetry - which is a doubling down of a statement. Verse two emphasizes and reveals that this is a very important statement being made. We became aware of the Septuagint,

Interlinear, and King James Version, and their historical respective roles in translations. We began to really focus on the pronouns to ensure we were following John in whom John was speaking of, and we showed that Yahshua is not yet mentioned in these verses. We discussed the Greek and Roman influence on a changing Israel and the world at large. We also realized in a huge way that a "god" cannot die, thus, showing us that if a god died for us then our salvation is bunk. We verified again that Yahweh is one, not three persons in one. We came to the realization that the Holy Spirit, who is Yahweh, created the creation and mankind, not Yahshua. We kept in line with our pronouns, realizing that "him" in verse three is not Yahshua but Yahweh's Holy Spirit. We began to see that declension is real, and Yahweh —who is omnipresent—knew this would happen concerning his creation. We perceived that we are all given life by Yahweh's Holy Spirit and that this life is our light in our eyes and the puffiness of our flesh. It also became apparent that John is giving us a timeline that runs concurrently with Genesis. We also saw that darkness will constantly try and eagerly take the light because it cannot comprehend the light.

Some important questions to consider:

1. When you read scripture, do you try and read several chapters at a time or one chapter and study each verse relating the context throughout?

. . .

2. Have you ever considered that a god cannot die?

3. Can you see how the two trees in the Garden of Eden were strategically placed there as a blessing for mankind?

4. How has Yahweh been omnipresent, omniscient, and omnipotent in your life? (Can you realize how the darkness eagerly tries to steal your light?)

———

John the Baptist was finally introduced in Chapter Four, and we saw how Yahweh *sent* John the Baptist, as well as Yahshua. We soon discovered, though, that neither Yahshua nor John the Baptist was in heaven before all of this as well. Instead, we learned that give, given, or gave is actually the best understanding of the word *sent* as translated. However, sent in its true understanding is useful as well.

We saw that Yahweh delivers on appointed times under His direction and prophetic watch. We were shown that John the Baptist was a Levite and in line for the office of a priest because he was a firstborn. We also saw the absolute importance of a fully submerged baptism and where this idea originated. This chapter also showed verse seven's true colors, meaning that a Hebrew wrote it, as the concepts are Hebraic in nature. Revelation occurred when we also saw in verse seven, again, that the Light (Light = Torah = Word) is the promise of a messiah, but the messiah himself is neither preexistent nor pre-incarnate. We encountered the fact that Yahweh's Holy Spirit, who is Yahweh, is our comforter. We learned living in the way of Torah is walking in our Messiah's footsteps. We became aware that Yahshua at this time was fulfilling the requirements to become that Messiah for us. We came to understand that Yahshua is not "The Angel of the Lord" as once thought. We also discovered that the Holy Spirit, who is Yahweh, is the "Angel of the Lord." Also realizing the belief that if Yahshua were Yahweh and that Yahweh cannot be around sin, then Yahshua could not come to Earth and that would also negate preexistence. Yahweh's Holy Spirit has shown throughout the Biblical timeline He can be around sin. This is important because we see the indwelling and fulness of Yahweh's Holy Spirit in Yahshua later in this chapter. We also saw Hebraic poetry again, with verse seven and eight doubling down on this important point. We discovered Logos was not flesh but a set-in-course action of Yahweh. We also discovered how important Torah is in our life.

1. Have you considered that your words are seeds?

2. Have you been taught that Yahweh cannot come to this earth because of sin?

3. Have you ever thought about who woos mankind to the Messiah?

4. Have you considered that injustices being heard in the world are actually humanity's instilled hope of the Messiah?

———

Chapter Five shows that the Holy Spirit, who is Yahweh, is in the world and goes back and forth to see if his creation recognizes him. We realized that verse ten is not speaking of Yahshua but of Yahweh. This verse also verifies Yahweh created heaven and the earth. We recognized again that Yahweh in the form of the Holy Spirit can move amongst men on this earth.

We were able to really drill into the word "appear" and see the different ways in which this word has been used to verify that this was not Yahshua spoken of here besides the pronoun used to show just that. We came to see that reading the scriptures in large portions or reading too fast is like we're reading a Sunday newspaper, and scripture is not designed for that. We began to touch on the famous "I Am" statements and learned that they mean the Messiah was thought of before all of this happened or else none of this could have happened at the appointed time. We came to realize that Yahweh's Holy Spirit filled Yahshua and when Yahshua is equated with Yahweh we encourage a spirit of anti-messiah. We found an amazing gem where the English word "by" is causative, yet "through" is an end result. The *dia* is a channel through which an act comes to be. We see where the act of abortion is against the Holy Spirit because of the creation process. We also found that the seed of Satan theory is a false theory, as everyone in this world ever born has the option to be saved, and verse eleven is another dose of Hebrew poetry doubling down the prior statement. Both Jews, Gentiles, and creation did not recognize the creator.

1. Have you taken the time to look at all the different belief systems within Christianity alone?

2. Do you believe that creation was affected by mankind's fall?

3. Do you believe Yahshua replaced Yahweh as God?

4. Have you ever considered where all of these doctrinal beliefs come from?

————

The clarity really began to build in Chapter Six where we found the Holy Spirit is again moving and stirring up people who are anticipating the Messiah. The Greek word *lambano* dispels any idea that there was a dead period where Yahweh did not interact with mankind. We discovered that because we receive him – the Holy Spirit, who is Yahweh—and aggressively take hold of Yahweh, we are given power. This power is important in that it is a right and privilege to be a son of Yahweh. We also found that Torah is the standard of living in covenant with Yahweh and that breaking Torah is missing the mark (sin). We see that verse twelve reveals the walk of salvation upon believing on the name of Yahweh. We came to a realization that Yahweh cannot be seen because death will occur; yet if we believe that Yahshua is Yahweh, how could the disciples and people of his day live? We discovered verse thirteen explicitly tells us that blood/heritage, flesh/pleasure, or heritage/procreation does not and will not dictate who can receive Yahweh's Holy Spirit, who is Yahweh, and this is strictly determined by Yahweh alone. We also realized that this verifies that all are predestined to come into the opportunity for a relationship with the Logos, the Promise, and this opportunity is not limited to a select few. We also found three rules of divinity: 1) God cannot be tempted, 2) Divinity and Flesh cannot coexist, 3) A God cannot die. These three rules negate the doctrine of preexistence or that Yahweh and Yahshua are the same. We saw where the Logos was made flesh and the process of becoming Messiah is at hand. We saw the glory of Yahweh's first light which is the Logos manifested. We discovered that Yahshua showed us how we can walk in Yahweh's glory and power. We came to a Hebraic under-standing of the word grace as a gift, not grace as perpetual leniency, and that truth comes from the source and that source is Yahweh.

1. Did you know that when you accepted Yahshua as your savior you were given power as a privilege to put sin away or conquer it?

. . .

2. Did you know that sin is actually missing the mark?

3. Did you know that Torah was taught to Adam and Eve in the garden?

4. Are you on a first-name basis with the Creator of this universe and his son the Messiah?

———

Chapter Seven disclosed several interesting points, chiefly being that the pronoun in the Greek is now changed and refers to Yahshua. We see that the Messiah's appearance on the Earth has come to pass and that the timeline has moved forward. We see an interesting and often confused point that "before me" indicates Yahshua was alive or in existence before John the Baptist, however, "before me" is the thought of Logos as the foundation and "preferred" is above me as in his function or mission is greater than mine.

We saw that Yahweh's Holy Spirit filled Yahshua to the brim. We realized that there are many gifts from Yahweh, not only a few as previously preached. We verified that the word "receive" is to take aggressively. We also saw that the Word or Logos is fulfilled and with a full measure! It was revealed in verse sixteen that these gifts are not the result of personal favor but the outcome of obedience, as in worship.

The Hebrew understanding reiterated that the word grace is gift, and it is the gift that keeps on giving.

We learned that John the Baptist is an actual historical figure as described in the Bible. We also learned we all have a piece of Yahweh in us from birth. The Law was given to Moses and by Moses, acting as a messiah by Yahweh. Grace was given through Yahshua by Yahweh. This grace being given was Yahshua fulfilling the Law—not Torah, the Law. The gift (grace) is to walk according to Torah and repentance. We discovered that the Greek word choice *dia* is again used to reveal that this came via Yahweh's Holy Spirit through Yahshua.

We also discovered that no one has ever discerned the Father. The only man who has discerned the Father is the man Yahshua. This historical man of record is the only one given of the Father. We also reviewed how a pledge or a promise in quite a few cultures through the ages required that a hand was placed over their heart (the bosom) and that is where Yahshua was always. In Yahweh's heart as a Logos, to the patriarchs as a Promise, to the Israelites as a hope, to us as a mediator, intercessor, and High Priest—always residing in the heart of the Father.

1. Did you know that this same Yahshua is listed in the Talmud?

2. Have you considered obedience as a form of worship?

. . .

3. Do you truly know your faith?

4. Do you believe that Yahshua is the Messiah prophesied?

HIGHLIGHT OF EACH VERSE

Within each verse, I also looked for the highlight of that verse. Now, of course, the following is my personal opinion based on all the research of each Greek word in these verses we have studied.

Here are the results:

Verse 1: Logos

Verse 2: same

Verse 3: created

Verse 4: light

Verse 5: shined

Verse 6: John

Verse 7: witness

Verse 8: light

292 THE JOHN 1:1 FACTOR

Verse 9: enlightens

Verse 10: within

Verse 11: received

Verse 12: authority

Verse 13 Yahweh

Verse 14: glory

Verse 15: preferred

Verse 16: fullness

Verse 17: gift

Verse 18: bosom

When we create a sentence out of these chosen words, I was rather astonished at what derived:

The logos is the same that created the light that shined. John bore witness of that light, that enlightens within those who received authority of Yahweh. His glory is preferred for fullness of gift from Yahweh's bosom.

. . .

This is the exact story John describes, and it lines up perfectly for who the logos is and what the logos will do for us. This simple exercise is quite revealing as, once again, we see Yahweh is the creator, not Yahshua, and Yahshua came into existence somewhere around 3B.C.E. Yahshua is the only man in human history to have thrown aside his own identity and willingly chose a path which, if accepted, would lead him to eternal life. I challenge anyone to find another man such as this.

This first chapter of John is for you and me. Once again, the Messiah—that is the man Yahshua—laid down his life for us completely and certainly fulfilled all things so we can have everlasting life with our dad!

NEW TESTAMENT EXAMPLES OF YAHSHUA NOT BEING YAHWEH (NOT BEING IN HEAVEN PRIOR TO HIS BIRTH) AND THE TRINITY

In this section, I would like to point out the scriptures most often used to prove Yahshua is God or was with God in heaven before creation or, as some say, even created at creation. There are scriptures in the New Testament, when read quickly or not studied out word by word, can certainly appear to claim one of the prior three ideas. Unfortunately, this is most likely due to the translator's error, the translator smoothing out the translated text through eisegesis for easier reading, the lack of understanding one's personal study, or by hearing of someone else's questionable teaching.

A common example of the latter instance would be someone starting in John 1:1with the word Logos, and because they know the book of Revelation, they jump ahead and teach the Logos in Revelation 19:13 is Yahshua as the word and then jump back into John 1:1 to claim Yahshua exists from the beginning. The issue here is that the timeline cannot support this claim. Though, it sure does look that way when we know the whole Bible and have been to Bible college.

The next example of this instance would be an individual well-acquainted with the Word of Yahweh and reading John 1:1. They come to the conclusion by reading these verses and hearing a tele-preacher teach that the Logos is Yahshua.

Now having heard from their preacher about the trinity, they automatically read the scripture and say, "Wow, this is the Father, the Son, and the Holy Ghost." Sally tells Joe, and Joe tells three people while Sally tells five more. All of a sudden, we have a new doctrine made by joining two teachings, and certainly, that must make a truth. When, in fact, it does not, since the trinity is not described anywhere in the Bible. Not understanding the timeline laid out by scripture is actually a tragedy.

These two instances could have been averted by fifteen minutes of reading to highlight those "gotcha words." I call them gotcha words as they tend to grab your attention and can make a huge impact on your belief system. These words are a signal to research more in depth. Some might even say these words are little flags in which Yahweh's Holy Spirit is trying to show something! After highlighting those words, we follow through with fifteen more minutes used to look up word definitions and examples of their usage in other scriptures. When this is completed, we will begin to see where translators took abstract Greek words to try to convey a concrete Hebrew idea and present it smoothly in scripture for your easy-reading pleasure.

Another common example is instances where an individual comes into relationship with Yahshua and begins to explore scripture with excitement and fervor. As instructed, this person starts reading in the New Testament since this is where they can find their savior Yahshua speaking, walking, and living. The new Christian reads on and sees all the examples of the Father, the Son, and the Holy Ghost. In English, we can easily determine these are three distinct beings by the word choices given in the English tongue.

However, most people find Christianity's claims of one God, as in monotheism – a one-God religion. This typically comes a little later in their walk, as the individual reading is experiencing a huge amount of culture, wisdom, and love. This is overwhelming to a large degree, as most people experience our current world as a mean, tough, and a highly competitive plane of existence. As more truths and ideologies are exposed through continued reading of scripture, a huge amount of culture goes unrecognized, and we unintentionally and subconsciously place our culture into the text.

This creates issues with how we comprehend the text and come to understand the applications thereof. Here, most readers find a spiritual community of like-minded believers.

Typically, but not always at this point in the journey, a newfound Christian begins to ask questions. There are times when one of the very first questions or discussions or fact-finding missions is: what about this three-person godhead the Word keeps talking about?

Scriptures never once use the actual word *godhead*, and this was used by translators in place of the true word *deity*. This is a result of the beliefs of the translators commissioned to translate the good book. Some subsequent translations utilized Strong's lexicon, where the godhead was doctrine believed to be based on truth. This definition of deity was rendered *godhead*, and that is why it is in our Bibles today (see Colossians 2:9).

The ramifications are huge, as this alters the text and varying doctrines of Christianity, resulting in ripples of slight doctrinal issues throughout the movement, hence the reason for so many denominations within Christendom.

Now, let's return to the new believer who is confused and slightly frustrated, as there appears to be no solid answer within this strange concept of a trinity. Enter pastor, theologian, or seminary graduate who expresses that this is what is called the Trinity. One in three, three in One = the godhead!

Now more questions arise; questions such as "where is this spoken about in the Bible?" "Why did Yahshua not speak about this?" and more. Our new Christian is now taught Jesus is God, and that God has blatantly expressed this throughout scripture where we see all three members of the godhead present as once such as Matthew 3:16-17. And if we do not believe Jesus is God, our salvation is in question, so the conjecture goes. Oh my! The first lie to enter Christianity has been reproduced once again, and our young Christian goes along with the teaching without challenging it.

Please note: these examples are not meant to attack anyone's study time! Most of us have never been taught how to study, even when we are told to read our Bibles. Okay, we read it, now what? These examples are used to show us how the process typically works in a believer's life. We do not have to be a Greek or Hebrew scholar in order to study Yahweh's Word. However, a little time and small chunks of scripture can reveal a multitude of information.

Let's take Ephesians 6:17: "Take the helmet of salvation and the sword of the Spirit, which is the word of God." Wait, I thought Yahshua was the Word!? Yahshua *is* the word. After he fulfills all things in his Messiahship, he will fully embody the Word! The Word of Yahweh as in he is the Bible? No, he is the Promise, the Light, the fulfillment of Torah! He is what John was speaking of in his Gospel.

Also, he is what John recorded in Revelation 3:14: "And to the angel of the church in Laodicea write: 'The words of the Amen, the faithful and true witness, the beginning of God's creation." This verse is showing us who Yahshua is. He is the fulfillment (amen), he is the faithful, he is the one selected to complete the mission to one hundred percent. He is the true witness—as in he is the one who represented Logos, the Promise filled. He is the Light and the beginning of Yahweh's creation—which is that he is the first *thought* in creation, the thought of provision for us.

Now let's read in Revelation 19:11: "Then I saw heaven opened, and behold, a white horse! The one sitting on it is called Faithful and True, and in righteousness he judges and makes war."

We can confirm that, yes, this is Yahshua John is speaking of and that Yahshua is Faithful and True. He is the one who accepted and completed His mission from Yahweh and remained true to every detail which Yahweh laid out so he could be that Logos for us!

TIPS FOR FUTURE BIBLE STUDY

When we find and study scripture, it's best to have at least some understanding of the Old Testament. Most people skip the books of Leviticus, Numbers, Deuteronomy, and most of the prophets. Christianity terms some of the prophets as minor prophets based on the original size of their scroll. However, these prophets have a smaller scroll because they are succinct and right on prophetic point. Read those to understand the timeline of events. Stop seeking television preachers on YouTube or teachers on networks who have no idea what they are talking about because their method of study is lacking. Vet them, not ignoring them, but knowing scripture so that you are not led away to a conclusion that has a piece of truth and yet is scripturally off as a whole. This new habit of study and reflection will take time, and that is okay. Don't give up.

In your reading, become intimate with Yahweh's Holy Spirit. When you do this, He will take you on a journey, not simply a dictatorial school of learning but of understanding. Now, take a scripture which has intrigued you, especially those verses which seem to have abstract words or ideas.

Look up the scripture in Biblehub.com or E-sword, and then study each word in Hebrew or Greek respectively. If the abstract word seems odd, first look at that word in a lexicon and discover if it points you to a Hebrew word which it has been derived from. You may have to find and read reference scripture or look at the different scriptures this word is found in different texts and then compare the uses.

Once you have found the word, use both a dictionary and a Bible dictionary and possibly an encyclopedia to study the culture in which the word originated. This extra step in studying will give you an awesome perspective into the culture and different ways the word has been used in different cultures. Please remember to not to close off your mind and limit yourself to using a biblical dictionary. Utilize both secular and biblical documents to gain your cultural perspective because you will find the mood and attitude of that time period very helpful.

A great resource to use in this process is Jeff Benner's Ancient Hebrew Research Center.[1] The wealth of knowledge he has worked so hard on is truly a treasure. The most important part to this whole process is knowing your Old Testament scriptures. This is where our belief system came from, so we must know and understand the source, otherwise just reading the New Testament will eschew sound biblical teaching, thus creating strange doctrines. Do you remember what Messiah said in Matthew 9:17? Most biblical scholars will ignore this passage, or they will use it to show the delineation of the Old and New Testaments. "Nor do they put new wine into old wineskins, or else the wineskins break, the wine is spilled, and the wineskins are ruined. But they put new wine into new wineskins, and both are preserved." Always read the whole chapter after you find the target scripture. The days of using one scripture as a little cutesy saying to make yourself feel better about your issue are waning quickly.

We must remember that taking Old and New Testament concepts into one understanding is not strange new wine. The New Testament is a reiteration of the Old Testament, and the two are the same wine completely. We have been taught that the New Testament has replaced or superseded the Old Testament, and this is flat wrong. Yahshua *fulfilled* all things of the Old Testament, paving a way for the Jew who believed and the Gentile to be a part of the kingdom and walk in Torah. Thus, the Gentile can be grafted into the commonwealth of Israel. The foundational scriptures of the Old Testament, chiefly Torah, and then the Prophets give root or pillars if you will to *fulfill* the New Testament role that the Messiah *filled*. This was not new wine; this was aged wine and was just as refreshing as the aged wine from before. The only difference being that you and I can drink of it freely and not worry about the wine bag's seams coming apart. Now, if we only understand the New Testament and then come up with new ideas or doctrines that do not line up with the Old Testament foundation, the whole thing comes apart, hence wars, inquisitions, church splits, and schism! This should give you enough to get started, and honestly, start in Genesis, as this is the most important book in the whole of the Bible to understand who and what we are in the Messiah.

WAS YAHSHUA IN HEAVEN BEFORE HIS BIRTH?

Let us start with **Galatians 4: 4-5: "But when the fullness of time had come, God <u>sent</u> forth his Son, born of woman, born under the law, to redeem those who were under the law, so that we might receive adoption as sons."**

Here, we see the word sent, and this word is often used as Yahshua was in heaven and sent to earth to accomplish a mission. Why would Yahshua come from Heaven as a grown deity to begin life as a baby, grow up, and then accomplish the mission when he had already been in heaven? If he existed before, this would have been from whence Yahweh sent him. This is not biblical nor logical, and this has nothing to do with Paul saying Yahweh confounds the wise with the ways of Yahweh. The word "sent" is **G1821** *exapostelló,* to send out from among and set apart for a mission. As we can see, this does not indicate coming down from heaven, this means set apart from his people to complete a task or mission to be accomplished.

When the *fullness* of time had come, he was born of a woman under the Law. So, (*to redeem those who were under the law, so that we might receive adoption as sons*) there is the setting apart – to *fulfill* the Law, so we, both Jew and Gentile, can be adopted into the kingdom (see John 1:16-18). This understanding is scriptural and prophetic *filling* and logically sound on all three points. The word "fullness," **G4138** *pleroma,* is important, as it conveys repletion or completion—not necessarily in terms of a specific timeline but brought into fullness when Yahweh was ready. It means to fill up fully or cram at repletion. When Yahweh gave Yahshua his mission, it was perfect timing which finds credence in the scriptures John 2:4 and Mark 10:35-40. Remember: Yahshua did nothing unless his father told him to accomplish it (John 5:19). In this example, we see that at the right moment Yahweh gave his son Yahshua the mission to be set apart from his brethren.

Hebrew 2: 6-8 is commonly misunderstood as Yahshua being "made a little lower than the angels," but it is speaking directly to the creation and then backed with the phrase "for whom are all things and by whom are all things." It is mankind who was made a little lower than the angels, and this is confirmed in Psalm 8:4-6.

Then we also see in Hebrews 2:9 that Yahshua was made a little lower than the angels and in continuation of this chapter of Hebrews 2 confirms that Yahshua is a man. Because of that, Yahshua, as a man, by Yahweh's grace _might_ taste death for everyone. Hebrews 2:10 also backs this up because Yahweh is the creator, and He ordered all things for the sole purpose of us having a Messiah, thus giving us a way to be in fellowship with Yahweh! This chapter confirms and stands in line with John 1:1-18 completely, which is stating the exact same things. Once again, we find scripture showing us that Yahshua was not in heaven before his birth - what is commonly referred to as preexistence.

Colossians 1:15-16 is another scripture that is often used to defend the preexistence of Yahshua. The two verses state: **"The Son is the image of the invisible God, the firstborn over all creation. For in him all things were created: things in heaven and on earth, visible**

and invisible, whether thrones or powers or rulers or authorities; all things have been created through him and for him." To understand these two verses, we must first understand our faith. As I expressed in Chapter One and Chapter Two, the promise or Word which Yahweh gave is the express image of Himself. An Image is our character, not simply a copy of our ten fingers and ten toes. Moreover, the breath which makes us unique is our likeness.

Here, firstborn is simply the first thought brought about in order for this realm to function. When Yahweh said, "Let there be light," Torah existed. Then it formed and separated itself, exposing the darkness (John 1). The sole function and purpose for this world is to redeem mankind, and for that to happen, a foundation must be established. To reiterate quickly – The Torah (Light) being created, mankind placed in dominance over the creation, the two trees placed in the garden along with Yahweh's omnipotence. These moments in Yahweh's timeline are purposed for mankind and the foundation for a Messiah to redeem what Yahweh knew would fall. That foundation from the beginning of our story is Yahshua, but not the physical, existing body of Yahshua since the Messiah is human as we have read in Hebrews 2 and in Colossians 1.

The next line tells us that "in him all things were created." This concept is confirmed by the Greek word "in" **G1722** *en* and is used as a preposition not a verb. In continuing our study, we see that this word is among or in the realm of, as in the condition in which something operated from the inside. Within this context, we can see that all things were created with the mindset or end result of the

Messiah. That is what this means, simply put. He was not embodied or a created, physical divinity standing beside Yahweh creating the heaven and the earth.

The next argument is that he created the heaven and the earth in verse sixteen. Well, let's examine this more. "heaven" **G3772** *ouranos* means air, heaven, sky; by extension, heaven (as the abode of God); by implication, happiness, power, eternity; specially, the Gospel (Christianity)—air, heaven(-ly), sky. This is from the root word **G3735** *oros* (through the idea of elevation) as in to rise, a mountain or hilltop. This specific word is used in the sense of the vaulted expanse of the sky with all the things visible in it; generally, as opposed to the earth, Hebrews 1:10; 2 Peter 3:5, 10, 12.[2] This area which is defined by this word choice is the atmosphere which surrounds the earth, the mountaintops area. This is not the abode of Yahweh because His abode is outside of time and outside of this universe. This does not mean Yahshua was born or manifested or existed where Yahweh dwells, this simply means he was the first thought though. Remember, a Logos is a thought uttered. When we create something, it is always sparked by a thought!

The next word we must remember to keep in understanding is that tricky little English word "by," **G1722** *en,* and I will argue till my last breath on this plane this word should be translated "through." Now this seems very technical, yet look what this has done to Christianity as a whole. For English speakers/readers this word implies ownership and, in this understanding, will cause one to lean toward Yahshua doing the creating instead of realizing the need for a Messiah. The word *through* accomplishes this perfectly, both doctrinally and logically. Why for him? Keep steady with our pronouns and we see that him is Yahshua in these verses of Colossians 1:14-20. In Colossians 1:16 we read "and for him" Yahshua will be our king and we will rule and reign with him!

Finally, all things were subjected to the Messiah and placed under his authority directly from Yahweh. Yahshua was given the inheritance of Yahweh to rule and maintain humanity, and this is coming soon upon his return. Right now, Yahshua is our High Priest and soon coming King. Yahweh is the *Melech Ha Olam* - King of the Universe. Does this diminish Yahshua? Not at all. Does this negate the respect, admiration, and loyalty due to him? Not at all! It magnifies it. This was a man who gave up everything to be our savior. This gives me hope that I can be a good man, can walk out Torah, can treat others right, have a close relationship with the Father, and be accepted by my Father. That this Yahshua is much more than just some man walking down the street!

The next scripture I would like to address is **John 17:5**: **"And now, Father, glorify me in your presence with the glory I had with you before the world began."** Here, Yahshua is speaking to Yahweh as though Yahshua is another entity. This is a case where we see it proves once again that Yahweh and Yahshua are not one person but two distinct beings. What is this glory Yahshua is speaking of? This is the Light or Logos, the Light that is the Light of men. This is the Light promised to mankind, and it revealed the darkness that could not overtake the light. Keeping in lock-step with Scripture, that being Genesis 1:3, Proverbs 6:23,

Psalm 119:105, and John 1:5 we find an equation that is most spectacular: Promise = Word = Light = Torah. My friends, this is an extremely important understanding so we may retain our faith in Yahweh. The Light was the glory of Yahweh, and Yahweh waited for the right moment to bestow that glory and to fulfill the most important promise He ever made! See Hebrews 1:1-5, James 1:17, John 1:9.

"I had with you before the world was" which is simple. Who is the Light? In the beginning, the light is the promise of a Messiah. That was Yahweh's glory, and He gave a crown of glory to that man Yahshua – Hebrew 2:9. This scripture is a crowning event, literally, as Yahshua is about to go to his death for mankind, willingly giving up his life for his brothers and sisters. When he is led to slaughter for our sins, Yahshua completes another step in becoming the Messiah and fulfilling Messiahship. That is Yahweh's glory given to Yahshua as he is fulfilling the promise, which is the Light, which is also Yahweh's glory.

TRINITY?

The most famous scripture used to defend the Trinitarian belief and to firm up the notion that Yahshua is Yahweh is **Colossians 2:9. "For in him (Yahshua) dwells all the fullness of the Godhead bodily."**

The most common reaction here is that Yahweh and the Holy Spirit are *in* Yahshua! Those who subscribe to the Trinity use this to say the trinity is verified! This thought is then backed up by the word godhead used later in the verse.

However, the big issue here is that the word godhead

does not exist in the scriptures. In the original languages, it does not appear at all. Zilch! The word here is deity, and there is a difference.

When Strong created his lexicon, he put a theological slant in the definitions which pertained to God, Jesus, and the Holy Spirit. The most notable theological slant is the trinitarian doctrine. The word deity is **G2320** *theotes* which is defined in the Greek as divinity and has a root of **G2316** *Theos* which is the supreme Divinity, God, godly; of uncertain affinity; a deity, especially (with ho) the supreme Divinity; figuratively, a magistrate; by Hebraism, very -- X exceeding, God, god(-ly, -ward) = YAHWEH.

This causes a huge issue because the word godhead has come to mean the triune God, and this is not a scriptural doctrine. This is a doctrine built upon a translation made by a fallible man. The word godhead is a modern word used to signify Yahweh but as a triune God and that is sacrilege. As it states in Deuteronomy 6:4: "Hear O Israel the Elohim Yahweh is ONE."

Yahshua taught this same *Echad* (One) teaching as well, and this word "godhead" is not used in Acts 17:29 (divine) **G2304** nor in Romans 1:20 (divinity) **G2305**. These two words in these two examples are the same word describing the fact that Yahweh is divine. Yet Strong's has input godhead into the definition to be understood as though Yahshua is deity as well. This would be okay if the word godhead was simply a definition only including the father or supreme deity Yahweh. Adding in the triune aspect creates a devastating issue in the history of the church, and the last

1700 years really set this notion in stone—making it doctrine.

Simply put, John 1:16 is echoed by Colossians 2:9 whereby Yahweh's Holy Spirit is crammed into Yahshua, dwelling in Yahshua completely. The divine dwells in Yahshua completely. So, because I abide in Yahshua and he abides in me, that makes us the same entity? Also, does this make you and me divine? This is the reason Yahshua could look into a person's eyes and see things in their lives. He was tuned into Yahweh's Holy Spirit uniquely, as he was crammed full of it, and it dwelt (tabernacled) with Yahshua overflowingly. Then, why can we not do the same thing if we are full of Yahweh's Holy Spirit? We are not the Messiah! Yet, we can have gifts.

In Luke 3:22, we see the awesome scene where Yahshua is baptized. This is another common scripture used to shore up the doctrine of the trinity. As I have mentioned before, the Holy Spirit is Yahweh's spirit. In this passage, Yahshua is in the water and a dove in bodily form represents this Spirit of Yahweh, descending upon Yahshua. Yahweh cannot be seen, only heard. Yahweh is all in all, and He is beyond our ability to see him, and if we did, we would be consumed by his power. This is why He is called Elohim in Hebrew because He is power, and that power is all-consuming, not because He is plural!

You see, this event is Yahweh (Yahweh's spirit) descending in the bodily form of a dove onto Yahshua, and Yahshua accepting his first task of Messiahship. This is the infilling of Yahweh's Holy Spirit. Where did the dove go? He remained upon him – John 1:32. It appeared to John first as a sign to John to announce Yahweh's Messiah. See John 1:33-34, Luke 3:21-22, Mark 1:9-10, Matt 3:16-17. Only Yahshua and John saw this as these four accounts proclaim. This was given in detail four times so we can see that the Word was made manifest and continues to be made manifest to fulfill the scriptures of John the Baptist. There are only two separate and distinct entities in these settings, and these are Yahweh's Holy Spirit and Yahshua—one divine being and one fleshly being.

Another scripture used commonly to establish a doctrine of the trinity or duality is **1 Corinthians 8:6**, stating, **"Yet for us there is but one God, the Father, from whom all things came and for whom we live; and there is but one Lord, Jesus Christ, through whom all things came and through whom we live."**

I wrestled with even mentioning this scripture because Yahweh's Holy Spirit is not mentioned in this verse to complete or make a trinity. The scripture plainly states that we have ONE God – the Father, and we know that is Yahweh. If we notice, in describing our Messiah, it says correctly "through whom all things came." This is actually the best translation of the word *through* used as a preposition, proving that this idea is one where all things were made through Yahshua for the purpose of Yahshua who is the end result! There is no proof for a trinitarian or duality doctrine here.

Acts 20:28 declares: **"Keep watch over yourselves and all the flock of which the Holy Spirit has made you overseers. Be shepherds of the church of God, which he bought with his own blood."** This scripture is also used to show a trinity and indicate Yahweh and Yahshua are the same. However, this scripture must be taken in context once we see that the direct object is Yahshua, not "the church of God." The Church of God is the church which is shepherded by the overseers who Yahweh's Holy Spirit put into place as He infilled them to do such a task by the result of Yahshua's resurrection. The blood mentioned here is not the church of God's blood or Yahweh's blood, as He has no blood because Yahweh is not flesh. See Numbers 23:19. The blood is the blood from the individual spoken about in verses 19, 21, 24, and this is the blood of Yahshua the Messiah.

1 John 5:7 is often used to establish a trinity belief. In verse seven the verb "bear witness," and some argue that the word "are" is the main verb here as well, and I will not disagree. The three that are bearing witness is the idea we are looking for. Yahweh bears witness to this, Yahweh's Holy Spirit bears witness to this, and Yahshua, the Messiah bears witness to this. This does not make them one except in agreement; thus, of one mind not multiple Gods or one godhead. Verse seven also confirms the fact that the Word is Logos made manifest. Yahweh's Word is established, and Yahshua fulfilled that which will not change ever. Yahweh's Word is everlasting. In this scripture, Yahshua has already ascended and is at the right hand of Yahweh; thus, he is still fulfilling that role of Messiah for us at that time. So, the Word is what? The Logos – Promise made flesh!

The point is that there is agreement coming from above, and agreement coming from the Earth, and this is proof positive that the Messiah is witnessed by Yahweh, and this is not confirmation of a trinitarian doctrine.

For example, if we are of one mind since we are all believers, do we not also all have individual bodies and remain separate? Yes, and that is all it is. It is proof of being in agreement. Yahweh is in Yahshua because he is the image of Yahweh, and he has one goal: mankind's redemption.

IS YAHSHUA THE YAHWEH OF THE NEW TESTAMENT?

In this section, I have a desire to say please see the previous examples, since I have already come to terms with the idea these are all basically tied to the trinity doctrine. The first scripture we should look at in this section is Philippians 2:6. This verse can be confusing, as "the form of God" and "equal with God" is basically staring us down. We should begin with the whole scripture: "Who, being in the form of God, thought it not robbery to be equal with God."

It appears self-explanatory until we peel back the English, and we look at the original Greek text. In the Greek, Philippians 2:6 actually reads: "Who in a form of Yahweh already belonging not to seizing existing equally with Yahweh." This is rough for English speakers, and it's hard to flesh out. This is why the translators "fixed" the text; however, they did not fix it properly.

The word for form is **G3444** *morphḗ* – properly, form (outward expression) that embodies essential (inner) substance so that the form is in complete harmony with the inner essence.

This word comes from **G3313** *meros* – part, share. From an obsolete but more primary form of *meiromai* (to get as a section or allotment); a division or share (literally or figuratively, in a wide application). This in no way has to do with Yahshua being Yahweh or being the same as Yahweh. This does tell us that Yahshua was filled completely with Yahweh's Holy Spirit and was part of, or had a share of, Yahweh in him.

The next word we need to define is "robbery" **G725** *harpagmos* – to seize, especially by an open display of force. The correct translation is: "not seizing existing equal with Yahweh." We can see where the translator used common doctrine or belief systems to "smooth out" the scriptures for our ease and reading pleasure of this scripture. The correct rendering appears to be: "Who in a form (a part or share) of Yahweh, already belonging (Logos) not to seize on existing equally with Yahweh."

What a great verse! It confirms John's first chapter, shows the agreement between Paul and John, and clears up that the Logos was a promise from our beginnings, being a part of Yahweh (thought uttered at the foundation of our world). A Messiah was the foundation for all humankind's realm (creation). That's why Paul states in Colossians 1:15 that he was firstborn (chief) over all creation. He was not created first, but he was the basis for everything; otherwise, there would be nothing. This is why verse 16 of Colossians 1 reads, "For in him all things were created: things in heaven and on earth, visible and invisible, whether thrones or powers or rulers or authorities; all things have been created through him and for him." Not that Yahshua was created before all else, but because in the order of all things, the Logos came first, which is the Promise of a Messiah and all was created through him and for him by the time he comes to be in existence.

But wait, there is more! The word "equal" **G2470** *isos* – equality; having the same (similar) level or value; equivalent, equal in substance or quality (J. Thayer).

Well, hang on a minute! So, this verse is not speaking of Yahweh and Yahshua being equal as in *equality*, it is saying that Yahweh and Yahshua His son are equal in *substance* or *quality*. Hmmm. Both love me, both want me, and both gave something up for me. Yahweh gave His son charge over me and my brethren, and Yahweh and Yahshua both want me to follow Torah. They are of equal substance and quality so that our well-being is taken care of completely.

Thus, substance means being the very image of his substance, i.e., of God's invisible essence or being, the manifestation of God Himself.[3] Did Yahweh manifest himself in Yahshua? Yes, he did! Completely, to the point of overflowing. Does this mean that Yahshua and Yahweh are the same or part of the trinity or the duality doctrine? No, not at all. What this does mean is that our daddy loved us so much, He gave himself fully to the man who chose to walk Torah perfectly to save us from declension.

Let's take a look at Hebrews 12:2, and we can see Yahshua is actually sitting at the right hand of Yahweh. If Yahshua is sitting at the right hand of Yahweh, how can he *be* Yahweh? It may seem rather trivial at first glance. Perhaps it seems almost as though we are on the same page, and perhaps it seems this is all just a matter of semantics. Know that I would love to agree with you, and at one point in my journey, we would have agreed.

However, the Word in both New and Old Testaments tell us there is ONE God. It's clearly stated. Not as a triune deity, as that would be polytheistic. To count anyone else as a God breaks a commandment, and if we break a commandment then we do not love Him. See 1 John 5:2-3, John 14:15, Deuteronomy 11:13-14.

Hebrews 1:1 also confirms there is not a trinity or duality, but that Yahweh is a separate being as, again, Yahshua sits at his right hand. We should also note that the word "worlds" actually means ages. John 14:7-11 also testifies to the fact that Yahshua and Yahweh are separate beings—one Divine and the other flesh. Although, these verses are often used to support a trinity or duality doctrine, they are far from proof or support.

To say "I am *in* the Father" or "I am the Father" are two entirely different statements altogether. Yahweh will not cause confusion nor allow His word to come back empty. Being filled completely with Yahweh does not mean the same as being Yahweh, it means being in Yahweh and of one <u>accord</u>.

OLD TESTAMENT EXAMPLES OF YAHSHUA NOT BEING YAHWEH

One of the things I first learned as I came into the Hebrew Roots sect of Christianity is the idea of the Aleph-Tav. The Aleph is the first letter and Tav is the last letter in the Hebrew alphabet, corresponding with the Greek's Alpha (first letter) and Omega (last letter), as well as English's A and Z. I was taught that in the Masoretic text anytime you see an Aleph-Tav, then Yahshua is right there in the text. Whether he is literally in the text as an Angel or as Yahweh or as a foreshadowing. Of course, foreshadowing is either prophetic or shows up in the story text, revealing the similarity between the future Messiah and some aspect of that Bible story. We can see foreshadowing in many places in the Old Testament. However, we do not need an Aleph-Tav to show us the way.

The Aleph Tav, in most cases, does not even appear in the text to dictate the idea or thought of a foreshadowed Messiah. When we, as humans, have an experience, we are created to have an imprinted emotional response. Thus, we have memories which allow us to remember a day or an event, including colors, smells, sounds, and sights, and especially emotions. This allows for fight, flight, or freeze responses, and this is also why we fall in love and can even become addicted to things. We must understand sometimes these responses to stimuli can be so great we forget minor details and hyperfocus on one or two of the details. This can allow for the forgetting of less important details or the exaggeration of other details.[4]

I mention this because of the excitement I experienced when I heard that the Great I Am, the Alpha and the Omega, lined up with the Aleph-Tav. I was ecstatic. The idea that Yahshua was in the Old Testament, being revealed in a personal way, all the way back to Adam, was amazing. Like most people, I fell for this hook, line, and sinker, and I'm here to tell you, that's okay. We're on a journey together.

Remember the old adage we discussed earlier in the

book? "You can only do what you know, and you can't do what you don't know." This is applicable since I really did not know any better. Growing up, I was taught Yahshua is pre-incarnate, and when I started attending Hebrew Roots groups, I had changed my stance to preexistence. I had begun to correlate the idea that Genesis 1:3 was where Yahshua was first created by Yahweh, and this notion came from reading verses that stated Yahshua was from the foundation of the world and the first created.

The last twenty-eight years of Hebrew studies—on and off, of course—culminated over twelve years ago when I joined Hebrew Roots groups. At that time, I had never paused to study those words. When I finally did, what could have taken an hour to figure out took me on a twelve-year journey. When I took the time to track the Aleph-Tav in the Masoretic text, a stark realization hit me.

In my tracking, I discovered the Aleph-Tav did not necessarily line up with any thought or idea of the Messiah, so I looked into the word **H853** *eth*. I soon realized that this word is just like our word "the" and used similarly. It functions as a primary particle in most cases. This word is also used to point out the direct object of a verb or preposition as in "fattened the sky and the land." Next, I went through the text and checked, and lo and behold, the reason we can see a foreshadowing is strictly due to the verb associated with the event taking place. However, this is rare, as almost all the cases in which an Aleph-Tav shows up have nothing to do with the promise or thought of a Messiah.

This led me into the genealogies that seem to be listed with great importance, and they are integral! Why do we need all these genealogies? The most given answer is to track the historical record since the Bible itself is a history book. The reasons for this tracking are to give a record of time. As we read the word, it's easy to imagine that all these stories are happening really fast, and they are not. The second is, yes, the historical record of the lineage of Abraham to Moses to David to Yahshua is important. Of course, this leads us to see the bloodlines that Yahweh is observing to bring his anointed and appointed son, the Messiah, into the world, and they also show that Yahshua is truly human. This is a key piece to understanding the Bible, not as a science book or as a history book, but as a means to bring us into the kingdom of Yahweh.

Moving on, we can all see this name debate amongst the Christian sects and just how taxing this can be truly. I would like to focus solely on the concept that Yahweh and Yahshua are the same because the name Yah-shua (Yah saves).

Yahweh is immortal – He cannot die, period. Only flesh can die, and it is appointed for man to die once, Hebrews 9:27. So, the idea within this teaching is that Yahweh is sending the salvation, and it is Him who is doing the saving. So, Yahweh and Yahshua are erroneously said to be the same person. As I stated in a previous chapter, there are three rules which must be adhered to: 1) A God cannot be tempted by sin, 2) Divine and flesh cannot co-exist in the being, and 3) A God cannot die. In all three cases above, if Yahweh came to this earth as a Messiah, a man, then we have a major problem. Yahweh never gave His name to another (Isaiah 42:8), not even to Yahshua.

Another scripture often used to support this is John 5:43,

and this word used "came" **G2064** *erchomai* is so often misunderstood because no one looks up this Greek word or studies the gist of the word as it is being used! Reading just to read and Western understanding have done more harm to Christianity than anything else.

"I came" is the correct interpretation of the word *erchomai* and can be used in the same way as saying to my friend, "I came to help you today." This choice of words by our Messiah was never intended to relay the thought that he came from heaven. It was intended to relay that this being who is becoming the Logos was set apart and pulled from the crowd to give this message in His (Yahweh's) name.

As I exist daily, I represent my father, wife, children, place of employment, and my assembly. This does not mean that I came from these places or people or that I am these places or people. It just means I represent them, just as Yahshua represented the Father in His name.

This opens the door to investigate the idea of a Oneness doctrine, so we can expose two very serious feedback loops that occur within this belief. In Matthew 27:46, we see Yahshua on the cross: about three in the afternoon Jesus cried out in a loud voice, "Eli, Eli, lema sabachthani?" (which means "My God, my God, why have you forsaken me?").

Why would Yahshua use this term "Elohi" **(H410 אֵלִי)** which means "my God," on the cross, only for Yahshua to use this for himself calling out to the Father? This is a major issue and a feedback loop which makes no sense whatsoever. Some will say that is because you do not understand the unity of three or trinity and the mystery thereof. Okay.

Explain it to me then. Where is this mystery discussed in the word of Yahweh? It is not anywhere listed as a mystery except in the human commentaries and evangelic pulpits of America and Europe emanating from the mother church where her daughters (Protestants) continue to spread this pagan lie so that we may all be one. It is no mystery!

There is only ONE, and His name is Yahweh!

Now, let's look at Psalm 22:1 where David says the exact same thing, calling out to Yahweh because his sin is so great. Was David calling Yahshua? Well, Yahshua comes from David's lineage, so how can that be? David was calling out to Yahweh because Yahweh is the source of all salvation. Yahweh's Holy Spirit is constantly looking to bring people to repentance if they will allow Him. These are two examples of a dangerous Duality, Oneness or Trinity feedback loop, creating nothing but confusion, and Yahweh is not the author of confusion. See 1 Corinthians 14:33. This line of thinking does not create a perfect circle or functionality, thereby lacking logic or mystery. I make this statement because in the duality doctrine the belief is that Yahweh and Yahshua are actually the same being, yet having two forms for us as humans. Here is the main point of this section showing that this Yahweh and Yahshua are actually two separate beings – one being the most High God and the other being the son who is flesh and has now been taken up – changed! Just like we who believe will be one day. Not as little Yahweh's but as our Master Yahshua. The danger in duality doctrine is that we will all be Gods, and this is what Satan basically said in the garden, along with the salvation issue of a God dying for us as we discussed above. Now, within a trinitarian doctrine, we run into the issue of denying the power of Yahweh's Holy Spirit where our Messiah explicitly told us that is an unpardonable sin, and this would also apply to the duality doctrine as well. Another idea we have discussed in this book is that having one in three and three in one is just another complicated way of saying that Yahshua is God, and we have seen many examples of how this cannot be the truth. This is why I call these doctrines dangerous feedback loops; they just come back to the main question with no viable concrete answers, only creating abstract confusion.

Taking Exodus 3:1-3 into view, we read: "Now Moses was tending the flock of Jethro his father-in-law, the priest of Midian, and he led the flock to the far side of the wilderness and came to Horeb, the mountain of God. There the *angel of the Lord* appeared to him in flames of fire from within a bush. Moses saw that though the bush was on fire it did not burn up. So, Moses thought, 'I will go over and see this strange sight—why the bush does not burn up.'"

We have the words "angel" **H4397** *malak* and **H3068** *Yahweh*, "a messenger of Yahweh." In Hebrew, there a few letters that have a final form in a word and these "final sofit" letters have meanings. In this case, the *kaph* sofit has a resting sh'va that indicates possessive. How does Yahweh appear to us? In the form of His Holy Spirit. Why? So, we are not consumed.

This verse uses the actual name of Yahweh instead of Elohim. If the text had used the word Elohim, then we would have issues with power and who this is actually in the burning bush. Instead, Yahweh made it astoundingly clear that this is Him in the bush, not Yahshua. Continuing in Exodus 3:14 we read: "Yahweh also said to Moshe, 'Say to the Children of Israel, 'Yahweh, the Elohi of your fathers— the Elohi of Abraham, the Elohi of Isaac and the Elohi of Jacob—has sent me to you." "This is my name forever, the name you shall call me from generation to generation." Pretty simple! When we look at the fire described here in this chapter, we can see that this is not an earthly fire, as it is in a form in which we cannot understand. Look at Moshe when he beheld it, and the bush was not consumed. *Simple is to Understand, Complex is to Tradition.* When we just read and believe what is there, it is easy to understand. When we add traditions of men, that is where things get complicated.

"Elohim said to Moses, 'I am who I am.' This is what you are to say to the Israelites: 'I am has sent me to you.' The usage of Elohim here is to articulate powers. It is already established in the conversation as to who this is; it is Yahweh. I AM is simply **H1961** *hawyah* which is to exist, or to be or come to pass. People get this mixed up and automatically assume this means "to be" is meant to be Yahshua.

There is an Aleph in front, indicating one or the first, so this appears Hebraically to be on an eternal timeline, and the prophecy which was given to Abraham is now coming to pass: To Be Now! It is important to understand that in Hebrew and in Jewish tradition, Elohim is used when in strict judgment or execution. Yahweh is used in mercy, Shaddai is used for mastery and miracles. Hashem is "The Name," and this is often used by Jews in place of the proper name of Yahweh.

In Acts 7:30, we see this same Angel of the Lord. After

forty years had passed, an angel appeared to Moses in the flames of a burning bush in the desert near Mount Sinai. And in **Acts 7:38**, it reads: **"He was in the assembly in the wilderness, with the angel who spoke to him on Mount Sinai, and with our ancestors; and he received living words to pass on to us."** This is again Yahweh's Holy Spirit, showing Himself to man in a way that he can see and so the man He's appearing to will not be consumed. This refers to Exodus 24:19 where they prostrated, they heard the commands and ordinances, they agreed as he read the covenant, they witnessed the agreement, they sealed it, and they ate with Yahweh.

In **Exodus 23:20**, we find: **"See, I am sending an angel ahead of you to guard you along the way and to bring you to the place I have prepared."** In this text, we again have the possessive form of angel in Hebrew. Then we read in verse twenty-two: **"If you listen carefully to what he says and do all that I say, I will be an enemy to your enemies and will oppose those who oppose you."** This is Yahweh's Holy Spirit, not as in two separate beings, but this articulates it the best we can in English. Ask Yahweh for wisdom, and He will show you! If Yahshua was eternal or he was preexistent, then he would be divine, he would be sinless, and he would be perfect in a heavenly body. This would negate a virgin and human birth. Also, within this whole text, a standalone Aleph-Tav is not present.

The next verse is interesting because verse twenty-five states: **"Worship Yahweh your Elohim, and his blessing will be on your food and water. I will take**

away sickness from among you." The Hebrew letter kaph is in the middle of the word Elohim. In this version, it is used this way to denote that Yahweh is speaking about all the children in a possessive form. Yahweh is denoting the provision in the palm or your hand (bread and water), and Yahweh is the Elohim who covers all. The kaph is used to show: to cover or protect, to provide, to impart.

Now, if we read carefully, we do see a prophecy here, and there is an Aleph-Tav in the text. It is being used in two ways: the Aleph-Tav is reading THE Provider, and when we look at the bread, water, and healing, the meaning should become very clear. Yet in no way is this verse describing a pre-incarnate or a preexistent Yahshua in Exodus.

Within chapter 24 of Exodus, verses nine through fourteen, we read in verse ten: "They saw the God of Israel." Here God is used as Elohi, and again, this would make no sense if it was Yahshua, as he would be calling himself Father. This generates another feedback loop or paradox, if you will – again, there is no logic in this. The God of Israel is eth Elohi Israel. The eth in this case used as THE, Elohi is used as Father or God as an executable action for Israel. Again, that eth is used as a particle for Elohi of Israel, and it is a prophetic foreshadow of Yahshua – the salvation of Yahweh in that sense only, as there is no indication that this is Yahshua existing as anything other than intent.

Genesis 32:25 has created plenty of commentaries and ideas floating about history. What do we do with a passage that is so often misunderstood to be Yahshua? Jacob is alone, and man comes to wrestle with him. This cannot be Yahshua, as he was not born yet and was without flesh. If he could manifest flesh, then what is the point of ascending to "my Father" after resurrection? What about doubt he experienced while on earth? What about temptation experienced at the same time? Most importantly, what of a flesh that did not sin? If he appeared pre-incarnate or preexistent, how can he be flesh when it is time for him to be a man? And then take into consideration as a man – that being **H582** *enosh* man, male, individual mortal and **H376** *eesh* a man. **H582** *enosh* mortal, man in general, see **H605** *anash* feeble, melancholy, desperate and sick, woeful. With these Hebrew words, we can derive that Jacob wrestled not with Yahweh, nor with Yahshua, nor with an angel.

The original text tells us that this was a man who wrestled with Jacob. It becomes plain that this is a picture of wrestling with ourselves. We see a man named Jacob who in previous situations is seen as a deceiver, usurper, or a supplanter. These are all the things we wrestle against in one way or another. When we finally hit rock bottom, and we're at the end of our rope, if you will, we come to a crossroads and have to affect change in our lives. Those who do typically fare better and those who do not tend to fall deeper in their ways. Sometimes, we run into these crossroads at several points in our lives, and this is a good thing. A man who is mortal, male, desperate, and wicked wrestles the man Jacob. Jacob wrestles against himself.

I believe what we are witnessing here is a true repentance. The man Jacob is in distress, stressed out to the maximum. In the altercation with Laban, the woman he adores caused this issue between Laban and Jacob concerning the idols . Now we have Esau at the door! He must be thinking,

"My flocks! My wives! My children and my multitudes, what do I do? Who am I? Why have I allowed myself to become this way?!"

This, my friends, is called a moment of truth, an awakening. We should all know this as a moment of repentance. Jacob fought himself all night long, and in conflict, you lose and you gain. Otherwise, it would not be a conflict, it would be an exercise. This Jacob, in the sense of the word **H802** *nashiym* not as a woman but in the sense of the word. This word can be used as an adulteress and is typically used for a female; however, this word can be used for a male adulterer. When we look at Jacob's life up to this point, we see a walker of the line, a grace card in hand, such as a backpack Jesus, if you will. Jacob wrestled himself, and the man could not prevail. At around daybreak, the man struck Jacob in his hip socket. Now if Jacob would have let go at that moment, he would have been the same old Jacob. In his pain, though, because his heart was set upon change, he said, "Not until you bless me."

Now the word **H1288** *barak* is a verb to bless, the bending of the knee to drink from a pond or present a gift – filling with a gift. Kneel is to bend the knee, homage, to exalt. **H1290** *berekh* – knee and *berekhakhah* is a gift given in respect, as if on bended knee and or pool of water as some kneel to drink from such a pool. If you have ever been extremely thirsty, then you will understand the word blessed.

The man asked Jacob, "What is your name?" Yahweh or Yahshua would know his name, and so would an angel for that matter. He was fighting his flesh. Ahhhhh! "NO longer will your name be Jacob, but Israel, for you have striven with the Power (the actual word in Hebrew is Elohim, not divine) and with a man you have overcome." And there it is, you fought for forgiveness, and you have prevailed. Wow!

Jacob turned a page in his life, he recognized this moment, lost and won, just like we do in various stages of our lives. But wait, only one can change a name! Jacob's weakness had died – defeated by wrestling that sin nature. His adulterous heart recognized the change, and Jacob gave himself a new name, and this became the change of mind and heart –**H5621** *nachem* was happening. This is later proven by Chapter 35:10 when Yahweh makes the formal change.

This was a major event in Jacob's life, a new chapter. If this was a struggle with our creator, then we are off base here. Never once is this mentioned as Yahweh, angels, or Yahshua for that matter. What is this with Jacob asking the name of the man? Well, this is what we call a rhetorical question, and quite frankly, a stupid rhetorical question. Ironic, though, we still do this sort of questioning to this day.

Peniel means face of El, and simply put, Jacob saw this man as El. Interestingly, the man said Divine, and again, this is repentance in the sense that Jacob had striven with Yahweh (Divine). **H6439** *penuel* is face of Yahweh. The actual name of the place is "peniel." In the ancient Hebrew, this would mean the face and mouth magnified by the hand of Yah the strong leader is teaching. This is very fitting, as Yahweh led and taught Jacob that night how to repent and be teachable. Because Jacob was ready to receive this truth and finally give up his own way, Yahweh accepted Jacob's repentance. This ended Jacob's struggle with Torah and flesh. From this point on, this event changed Jacob's story and his repentance became a blessing to him, and this is evident for the rest of Jacob's life.

In Genesis 18, we find the three men walking near Abraham. Yahweh is used in the text, which indicates mercy. At this time, Abraham was just circumcised, and the pain was probably at its height. One of these "men" was Yahweh, as the text tells us just that. This was Yahweh's Holy Spirit appearing to Abraham in a form which would not consume him. Abraham recognizes him and declares the word Adonai (Master). Yahweh had just made a promise to Abraham and Sarah and asked Abraham to seal the deal by circumcising his whole house. The circumcision was a request by Yahweh to show obedience to Him and to also show he was chosen by Yahweh.

Afterward, they have a meal together to further seal the deal and reiterate Abraham's obedience to the terms. Fast forward a few verses, and we see the other two men are angels sent onward to destroy Sodom and Gomorrah. Abraham pleads with Yahweh to intercede for Sodom. We must make note that Yahweh is spelled exactly, so why would Yahweh confuse everyone when it was actually Yahshua? Also, Yahshua was prophesied to come as a Lamb first and then as a Lion. If this is Yahshua, then he came as a Lion first and destroyed sinners (those in Sodom). In the finality of all time, after this age has passed and Yahshua returns, Yahshua must go through a series of steps to be able to come to earth in order to fulfill Yahweh's plan for the Messiah to execute judgment, that which is given by Yahweh alone. This story shows Yahweh's Holy Spirit all over it, and therefore, this should not be confused with Yahweh being Yahshua.

The smoky furnace and the torch of fire is often also misunderstood as a story of Yahshua sealing a deal with Abraham. In ancient Middle East cultures, you would see a pact made where terms are met, and an animal would be split in two and the parties of the contract would walk through the split carcass. The meaning of walking in between the carcass was to confirm "I will do to you or you will do to me that we have done to this carcass if either one of us breaks the contract." After this, a meal would be prepared, and the pact was sealed with a celebratory dinner or breaking bread together. Here, we see not Abraham but Yahweh walking in between the carcasses. Wait, did the actual story say that Yahweh walked through them? No. There was a smoky furnace which meant "I will bring this to fruition," and the torch of fire was the act of initiating it. In other words, I will set this on fire and make sure it is cooked to completion.

The first few lines in **Genesis 15** read: **"After this, the word of the Lord came to Abram in a vision: 'Do not be afraid, Abram. I am your shield, your very great reward.' But Abram said, 'Sovereign Lord, what can you give me since I remain childless and the one who will inherit my estate is Eliezer of Damascus?' And Abram said, 'You have given me no children; so, a servant in my household will be my heir.'"**

In verse one of this same chapter in the Hebrew text, we see the words "dabar Yahweh" and that is "word of

Yahweh" in English, so we see Yahweh is speaking, and it is not Yahshua being the Word as expressed in Revelation. There are no standalone Aleph-Tav to account for in this chapter to even insinuate Yahshua was in this chapter with Abraham.

Such is the case in Exodus 12 as well, concerning Yahshua. There are no Aleph-Tav sightings showing up to reveal the Messiah in a preexistent manner. This was clearly Yahweh's Holy Spirit revealing himself to Abraham by appearing at different times in Abraham's life journey. In no way does this minimize Yahweh, nor does it diminish Yahshua's role as Messiah. All this does is remove blasphemy and a spirit of Anti-Christ which has seemed to infiltrate itself stealthily through the millennia. I don't mention this idea here to put anyone down for something they were taught or force-fed or even picked up when reading in the Bible. We are all on a journey.

The point is to get to know your Elohim better, knowing Him as your Elohi, counting on Him as a well-balanced Father to be counted on and knowing His true name Yahweh. He is filled with mercy and love, and He wants nothing more than a relationship with you.

We must understand who Yahshua is as our brother who is in heaven now. After having defeated death, he is changed and sits at the right hand of Yahweh, interceding for us daily, all of us. This man has been changed by the hand of Yahweh and is our Messiah, not our God.

Will we take a knee someday? You better believe it! You, me, and even those that do not believe. Why? Because he is the faithful and true of Yahweh, the promised Word, the

Light which passes all understanding because he is full of mercy and grace with justice for us. When he comes, he will be our king, and what a grand time we will have, the things we will learn, and the experiences we will taste.

A CLASS ALL ITS OWN

In Daniel 3, we find a very interesting and often debated story where "One like the Son of Man" is present in the text. We see in the Tanach that the term is translated "one is like an angel." This makes sense. In our culture, we should know this is widely understood to be an angel. The first thing we need to perceive in this story is that Daniel is not one of the three men in the fire. Those men were Shadrach, Meshach, and Abednego. The second thing we need to deal with is that these three men were basically governors of the kingdom. Yahweh has a remnant everywhere and sometimes our story is not a grand parade, but one of simple work, a movement by Yahweh's Holy Spirit. These three men were in a fire, and suddenly, a fourth appeared. Why would this be Yahshua as is commonly interpreted? The text in Hebrew shows "ben elahin"—which is a son of Elohim.

At the time of this story, a son of Yahweh was an angel. Not a messiah, not Yahshua, and certainly not a demigod who showed up from heaven to protect these three men. The key word in this passage is "like," as in *like* a son of Yahweh!

We have studied that Yahweh's Holy Spirit is the mode in which Yahweh shows himself to us. We also studied that Yahweh's Holy Spirit also showed up on the earth as an angel infilled to give a word - but remember not always! Is this fourth person, if you will, none other than an angel sent by Yahweh's Holy Spirit, being as a foreshadow of a Messiah to come? Emphatically yes and to protect his people through trials and temptations. There is no Aleph-Tav in the text to reveal that this is the Messiah Yahshua. Nor does the text tell you that Yahshua is present in the pit of fire. This is a prophetic picture of later times wherein rulers and people of power will be persuaded in our trails to reveal the power of Yahweh.

Another figure believers and non-believers alike love to argue about is the mysterious man Melchizedek. When we look at Hebrews 5:6, it appears that Melchizedek was not Yahshua as some would believe. This chapter in the Book of Hebrews reveals that Yahweh made Yahshua a high priest later at the announcement of the Messiah's reign. See Psalm 110.

This chapter confirms the Genesis account showing that Melchizedek was in a line of priests held in order by Yahweh's Holy Spirit. They were separate from Abraham yet coinciding with him to show that Yahweh has a remnant of people at all times.

Why then is Abraham in the story? Because Abraham carries the seed that relates to us. This clearly was not an angel. The thought that this was Yahshua in Jerusalem prior to his birth causes a paradox. This feedback loop is one which allows Yahshua to be alive in the time of Abraham and then be in a line of priests. Yet Yahweh does not make him a priest until after his death and resurrection. The thought or idea that Yahshua is then later reincarnated as the Messiah is ridiculous at best since there is no scriptural basis for this belief. There are no Aleph-Tavs within the text surrounding Melchizedek. Is this still another foreshadow of the Messiah? Why, yes, it is.

GNOSTICISM IN JOHN?

There is a growing number of authors, theologians, and academics that subscribe to a notion that John's Gospel was Gnostic in nature. The thought is that the Gospel of John was written after John's death, therefore written by someone else. Perhaps originally written by John, someone else took the letter (Gospel) and made the final Gospel with inserted corrections. I believe I have given ample evidence to show that John the Apostle is the writer of his gospel and have done so by showing the reader that these are concrete thoughts of a Hebraic nature included within this gospel. These are not Platonian philosophies coupled with Jewish prophecy and mingled with signs and numbers.

Gnostics believe that there are three types of humans generally. The hylic is the lowest form and cannot attain salvation or be saved because they cannot understand the gnosis – the knowledge of the supreme being given to man. There are blaring errors here, especially when the Gnostics or even secular and non-secular theologians try and place John inside a Gnostic affiliation.

The first reason would have to be the notion that John 1:4 clearly states that all men were given the light of Yahweh's Holy Spirit, that was the life, and the life was the light of men. In this verse, we see clearly with no assumptions or deep theological understandings, that this idea states all men are created equal. Someone is not born evil or less-than. They are born with a sin nature as they have flesh. Yet the idea that there are three levels of human existence is unbiblical and anti-messiah.

In conjunction with this train of thought is the idea that anyone who believes cannot be called a son of Yahweh. This violates John 1:12 and negates that you and I have the power to become the sons of Yahweh through our own choice! As though we have no free will choice or the intellect to discover our own rock bottom. It implies we will never understand our own depravity which lurks within ourselves and needs to be dealt with, whether that be from an environmental or self-induced way of being. In other words, so much for repentance.

This is also why the Messiah must be a human being and not a God or demi-god. The spotless, Torah-filled man had to lay down his life completely. This allows for true atonement if we accept, and this is not brought about by the blood of bulls or lambs. This ideology also destroys the notion that we can have a personal relationship with Yahweh. John 1:16 clearly shows that all men who believe and accept this man as their messiah by the full indwelling of Yahweh's Holy Spirit will receive grace for grace. This ties back to John 1:12 being sons of Yahweh.

People may ask, "Do you have a personal relationship with Jesus Christ?". I have a personal relationship with Yahweh because of my Messiah Yahshua Ha Mashiach.

The scripture clearly states that because I believe in the light of the world, who is fulfilling every day his messiahship, I can be a son of Yahweh. That means I have a dad right there ready to speak with, be with, and show me the way. Yahshua is at His right hand, making intercession for me when I miss the mark (sin). Yahweh's Holy Spirit shows me my mistake and gives cause for me to realize this and to repent. Thus, I can seek Yahshua as my mediator. No duality and no trinity exist here—only one God, Yahweh.

John 1:18 also states that no man has understood or discerned the Father at any time. Because I believe in Yahweh's salvation (Yahshua), then I can discern or understand the father because His Holy Spirit is in me – as my helper.

According to Gnostic tradition, this is not the case—well, maybe for some, but not for Joe over there. We must look to the woman at the well scenario in which our Master said, "But the hour cometh, and now is, when the true worshippers shall worship the Father in spirit and in truth: for the Father seeketh such to worship him. God is a Spirit: and they that worship him must worship him in spirit and in truth." Yahshua, the Messiah, just declared who and what Yahweh is, and the plain simple fact is that His Holy Spirit roams the earth, his creation, seeking those people. This is the wooing, and this happens twenty-four seven. By the way, this validates John 1:9-11, and this is for all men and women!

Gnosticism was designated by the early church as a heresy in the first century A.D. because of this trinitarian idea Christianity had merged with. If you believe in the trinitarian doctrine, then you are a Gnostic Christian. It is not biblical, and it does not line up with the teachings of our Messiah.

Another reason this was branded a heretical movement is

that Gnostics believe they have a special relationship with Yahweh and receive knowledge from Him, being set apart in that regard. This violates the command we have to be holy (set apart).

Gnosticism understands being holy by the express knowledge that Yahweh gives to them. This is a huge error and one that has found its way into modern Christianity. You must choose to be holy, by setting yourself apart by the choices you make in life, chiefly, by walking in Torah.

Another belief which is actually a common doctrine in Christianity, as of late, is actually Gnostic in nature. This is the idea that Yahweh is a lesser God who created the world. There is a supreme being behind him that we cannot see or experience except through divine knowledge dispensed directly. The only direct result of this belief is that Yahshua and Yahweh are the same. Not only is this anti-messiah, this also completely violates the whole word of Yahweh.

If you believe in a godhead, even if it is through ignorance of scripture, language, and theology, you subscribe to Gnostic teachings.

Additionally, the concept of immediately departing this life and entering heaven or hell is a gnostic idea which has completely infiltrated Christianity. Christology is yet another teaching within the gnostic sect that teaches that the archangel Michael became Yahshua, completely contradicting Hebrews 1.

One more disturbing trend is the idea that salvation is for the Jews and that the feasts, Torah, and sabbath are for the Jews only. This is another Gnostic doctrine that has subtly overtaken mainstream evangelical Christianity. It's modified with the Gentiles being second, allowing that they can be included in salvation. However, all the other commands and traditions are strictly Jewish. Three types of tradition developed early on: Genesis was reinterpreted in Jewish milieus, viewing Yahweh as a jealous GOD who enslaved people, and freedom was to be obtained from this jealous God. This teaching has created a huge gulf within Judaism, within Christianity, and then between Judaism and Christianity. We came from Judaism whether we like that idea or not; so, when we as a body pull away from our Messiah's beliefs, then we encounter strange teachings and doctrines which do not line up with Torah.

Understanding Torah is essential to walking a Godly life. This will also allow for us to see that Yahweh is a jealous God, as who would not be? He married us to a covenant with Him and then we go after other beliefs.

This is why we need to understand what likeness is. The likeness is our metal faculties and our processing and out intelligent emotions. Intelligent emotions are good, and the thought that being jealous disqualifies Yahweh from being a God is absurd! Israel was not enslaved to Yahweh, and this idea is strange. Israel was freed from slavery, and this is where the church has misunderstood the first commandment since day one.

The Hebrews understood this: "I am the Lord your God, who brought you out of Egypt, out of the land of slavery" was a commandment. The church doesn't see this as a command, they see it as preamble to the first commandment: "I freed you from sin, do not go back to it."

In this light, the Messiah's words make a lot more sense. I

think the main thing to see here is Yahweh freely gave the children of Israel a marriage contract based on a promise to Abraham, Isaac, and Jacob. If we want Yahweh to be our God and if we want to be his people, then here is the Torah – not slavery.

There are many more teachings within Gnosticism that will fill another book. In this context, we needed to get the general idea, so that we can understand how Gnostic teachings have infiltrated Christianity in regards to the first chapter of John. These are the trinitarian doctrine, duality of Yahshua and Yahweh, and the teaching that Yahshua is the Yahweh of the Old Testament.

It appears that Gnosticism came from ancient Greek philosophy and joined with that of Judaism. When Gnosticism is studied, we can clearly see the Platonian ideas coupled with Jewish Kabala and the impact that is had on the early church. This idea that special knowledge comes from above produces pride, arrogance, and self-righteousness, and we are strictly warned against that in both Old Testament and New Testament teachings.

There is only one place that this idea, this pride, can come from, and that is from the adversary who had been struck down for the exact same sin. Gnostics considered the principal element of salvation to be direct knowledge of the supreme divinity in the form of mystical or esoteric insight. Many Gnostic texts deal not in concepts of sin and repentance, but with illusions and enlightenment.[5][6] Thus, the mythical story developed about the descent of a heavenly creature to reveal the Divine world as the true home of human beings. Jewish Christianity saw the Messiah, or

Christ, as "an eternal aspect of GOD's hidden nature, his "spirit" and "truth," who revealed himself throughout sacred history".[7]

The most important thing we need to understand in this section is the impact that narcissism and Gnostic teachings has had in Christianity. Even though Gnosticism was labeled a heresy, its tentacles have survived 1900 years later. The beliefs, teachings, and doctrines are detrimental to believers creating strife, division, and polarization for us all. We must guard against these things and understand exactly what we believe so that our belief system is grounded in Scripture. The secret knowledge is as simple as the opening of our Bible. Studying the word of Yahweh provides the personal relationship that we have with the Father. This allows us to be able to understand His desires, His wants, and His goals are and how that affects our life that is the gnosis. So, in conclusion, study to show thyself approved, making sure not to place yourself above anyone else in knowledge or abilities. As we're instructed by our Messiah, the first will become last and the last shall become first. Be humble, show gratitude, and finally, show encouragement to your brothers and sisters. In all these things, Gnosticism has no place and is not in the Gospel of John, nor is it found in any of John's letters.

OMNISCIENT, OMNIPRESENT, AND OMNIPOTENT

In all the words of this book, in all the statements made whether by me or by another school of thought, there is a most important understanding we must have and need to remember. That the one true God, Yahweh, was, is, and will always be Omniscient, Omnipresent, and Omnipotent.

This idea has been put on a shelf somehow, and this was actually the best statement of faith to come from the last two hundred years. Omniscient means: having infinite awareness, understanding, and insight and to be possessed of universal or complete knowledge.[8] Omnipresent is defined as: present in all places at all times.[9] Omnipotent is one who has unlimited power or authority.[10]

Yahweh was not deposed as a failed God to be usurped by Yahshua. Nor did Yahweh change his name to confuse everyone at different periods or ages of human history. They were not playing a hide-and-seek type game between Father and son. The fact is, Yahweh has given us the names of Himself that we need, to know who is speaking to us and whom we are reading about.

Yahshua even made this clear when he said, **"No one knows about that day or hour, not even the angels in heaven, nor the Son, but only the Father." Matthew 24:36.** At his accession, it reads in **Acts 1:7: "Jesus replied, 'It is not for you to know times or seasons that the Father has fixed by His own authority.'"** If Yahshua was Yahweh or part of triune godhead, then he would be omniscient himself.

Most of us have read the Bible, and we must remember there is a timeline to human history. We also must remember Yahweh is outside of time and outside of this universe, even though He is all in all. This is where the understanding of omnipresent comes into view.

Yahweh, at any time, can see that timeline from A to Z.

This is why the thought uttered came first and the pillars of this world came next. Then His Messiah would be sent at the appointed time and would be slain from the pillars (foundations of the world). Not at the beginning, but at the time appointed by the Father, as He is Omnipresent whereas we are not.

This is also why Yahweh's Holy Spirit seeks us, all throughout mankind's history, going back and forth looking for those who will believe. Here, we can truly see why Yahshua used the term before Abraham was, I Am. Not because Yahshua was omnipresent but because he understood who he was in Yahweh; he was the thought uttered that Yahweh had known would be created in the human timeline.

Being Omnipotent in itself is very dumbfounding. How can we even begin to understand this? Even all the artificial intelligence systems we are creating and putting into practice, their computations, every part of them will be no match for Yahweh. It will be interesting to see when our creation tells us or asks us, "What did your creator say"? The human propensity is to attain and accumulate more and more power which in and of itself is nefarious. As a race, the stories we manifested and retold of beliefs, religions, and gods have all used power to exact what they deem just or necessary. Only One has shown mercy and love and when we go to the grave, awaiting a final judgment where the true recompence will be known.

We know justice will require an accounting and that justice within the realm of being omnipotent is far better than these other stories we have made in bygone eras.

Having that kind of authority requires restraint, and that is where true justice is found.

One must really think about the idea that three divinities sharing any one or all of these attributes would create havoc. Hence, they came up with the triune aspect of one in three, three in one. This, too, has its issues in regard to the three rules: 1). A God cannot be tempted (Yahshua was tempted), 2) Divinity and flesh natures cannot cohabitate the same body (the idea of Yahshua being both God and man), 3) A God cannot die (Yahshua died on the cross). These are not my rules, these are biblical, and are understood divinely and should be humanly as well.

ANSWERING THE THESIS

The topic of this book will argue and define who is the author of the book of John, who is the Logos, who is the Holy Spirit, and was Jesus (Yahshua) truly pre-existent. It will take on the pagan teachings individually that infiltrated the church within the backdrop of John 1:1, utilizing primarily scripture as well as secular and non-secular cultural references, histories of religions, and belief systems. This was the thesis statement given at the beginning of the book.

THESIS QUESTION: Who wrote the book of John?

ANSWER: There has been a huge uptick in new evidence presented from past and recent archeological findings of ancient written languages, those being primarily of semitic origin. We can see how Moses truly did have a system of writing to work with outside of the Egyptian language. This language had been passed down from Abraham, and even the Egyptian language had borrowed from Semitic languages certain paleo characters and meanings of those Hebrew letters. We know for a fact that the Paleo Hebrew did change at least three times before and during Babylonian captivity, whereby taking on its present-day form used in the Aramaic Hebrew manuscript. Linguists have identified that Israel was using Aramaic Hebrew during Roman occupation, along with numeric and mystic understandings of each letter that was still being used in code by the learned Jewish scholars. Linguists have also traced the Hebrew Aleph-Bet as being the progenitor of the Greek Alphabet which led to the Latin Alphabet. Understanding the Israeli culture and the schooling of young men gives great insight into how these young men were accepted into rabbinical schools or resigned to their fathers' livelihood. John, just such a young man, selected by Yahshua to be his disciple, would have been fluent in Hebrew, Greek, and most likely, his Roman occupier's language. John would have known and understood the Torah, the prophets, and the prophetic aspects of the Messiah. With this knowledge, he would have understood that the Messiah was to come from Israel. This is important, as even our church culture today has lost many major theological points of what, who, and why the Messiah would come. These ideas expressed in John 1 could not have come from a Greek, Latin, or English theologian, as these are ideas of a Hebraic nature. These ideas would have to be understood in deep concrete terms in order to have been written/translated in the Greek tongue. In Chapter One of this book, we studied verses one through three, and the theological ideas which are expressed concerning the often-misunderstood Logos. In just the study of Logos alone, after millennia of defining, misrepresenting, and additional ignorance, we see that going back to the source is the answer of all truth. Knowing these key pieces of information—even without having been in the room with John himself, it is apparent the argument is answered in favor of John writing his Gospel account.

THESIS QUESTION: What or who is the Logos?

ANSWER: Through exhaustive research and reading of cultural, etymological, and scriptural references, we know that in John 1:1, undoubtedly, that Logos is a thought uttered. Having read all of the scriptures from Genesis to Revelation, one cannot insert their knowledge of future events and arbitrarily place a title on an individual given at the end of that timeline, then go backwards in that understanding and proclaim that title to the same individual at two to three points on a timeline prior to that event. Simply put, the Logos was Yahweh, as this was His word. This Logos was a seed, a seed of promise from the foundations of the world. This Logos was Light, a light that guided mankind in understanding that promise. This Light was manifested in Torah, given to mankind as a way to live functionally set apart, as every chapter of this book references scriptures to prove this. This Logos or Word became flesh. Yet the ultimate title was not given yet in the timeline. This man Yahshua had to accomplish all things in order for that title to be administered at the proper time by Yahweh within the timeline of Yahshua. By this point, Yahshua had ascended to his Father and changed and now sits at the right hand of the Father as our intercessor. Upon his coronation as King, defeating the enemies of the Kingdom of heaven, then he will be that Logos and be called the Word who is Faithful and True. With the knowledge we explored and the understanding of words with their meanings, along with that of a timeline and how timelines work, then undoubtedly, the Logos is not the baby Yahshua/Jesus. The baby Yahshua was that promise - the Logos. Meaning Yahshua had, has, and is still, till coronation becoming that, Messiah!

THESIS QUESTION: Who is Yahshua?

ANSWER: Yahshua is commonly known by his nickname Jesus. He was a man, born of flesh and his mother, a virgin, was overshadowed by Yahweh's Holy Spirit. When Yahweh's Holy Spirit overshadowed Mary, the mother of Yahshua, Yahweh's Holy Spirit spoke Light (Torah) as a seed to her egg, and Yahweh in His omnipotence created flesh as He can always create. Thus, the set-apart and chosen one to be Messiah was given to mankind. John bore witness of Yahshua as the Messiah. Yahweh's Holy Spirit filled Yahshua completely and overflowingly, thereby representing what we might attain after Messiah resurrected from the grave both in this life and in the millennial Kingdom. Yahshua, being filled by Yahweh's Holy Spirit, resulted in the Light (Logos) fully manifested in Yahshua as the Messiah. This man followed every aspect (jot and tittle) of the Torah and Law so that when the time came for him to offer his life as a ransom, it was accepted as blameless and worthy. There is ample evidence throughout this book as to who Yahshua is and why he was who he was for our salvation.

THESIS QUESTION: Who is the Holy Spirit?

ANSWER: That would be the Spirit of the Most High, who is the supreme being whose name is Yahweh. His spirit is Holy and is not separate from Yahweh, and this is the form in which Yahweh appears to us. Not as a separate entity doing what the Father asks, but the Father working in Spirit, as He has no form. Yahweh's Holy Spirit abides with us if we accept Messiah as our savior to guide and teach us to walk in Torah as Yahshua makes intercession for our shortcomings. Yahweh's Holy Spirit is considered the helper or comforter, as He reveals how to be that better person for ourselves, others, and in our relationship with Himself. We discovered and gave plenty of proof through Greek pronouns and Hebraic understanding for who Yahweh is and how He reveals himself to us throughout this book. Yahweh's Holy Spirit was the Logos as described in John 1:1 and was further expressed as such in the subsequent verses. This is why Yahshua said before Abraham was, I AM.

SEEK, PRAYER, AND REPENTANCE

We find ourselves at the closing of this book which has delivered awesome news, and I hope you see a much better explanation of our Christian roots, theologies, and gospel. I would be remiss if I did not model a prayer for those who have been moved by this new information laid out before them. Below are two prayer I have written for you to say if you feel led. Please ponder which one suits you and choose the best one that fits your current situation.

I would like to make something very clear before we close. I believe in Yahweh the God of the bible who is the Elohim of Abraham, Isaac, and Jacob. I believe Yahweh's Holy Spirit appeared and guided the men along with the prophets to provide a way for the Logos, that promise of old to come to pass at just the right time. I believe that Yahshua is the Son of God and was born of a true virgin woman, and he is the Messiah prophesied of the Torah and the prophets. I believe in my heart that Yahshua died for me and gave up every aspect of his life so that I can be a son of Yahweh. Finally, I believe that Yahshua was changed at his resurrection into something that differs than that of a man. Yet he is not a God as Yahweh is. I believe that he sits at the right hand of Yahweh in heaven, making intercession for us. I believe that Yahshua will come back as my King that I might rule and reign with him. If you feel intrigued by the information presented here yet need more time to explore and understand, pray and ask Yahweh for wisdom. He will give it.

————

Heavenly Father, in Yahshua's name, I ask you to forgive my sins and hear my prayer. I pray that with the information I have read here in this book, you would speak to me. Give me the understanding to process this

*material and set my path to know and discern correctly. This is a huge
step from what I have been taught, and this is not what is being
expressed in the world today about who and what you are, and I want to
know, that I know, that I know! Father, usher your Holy Spirit into my
reasoning, give me your insight into this topic. I know that you are
omnipotent, omniscient, and omnipresent, and that I am yours. So,
Father, please show me what is right. Halleluyah and Amen.*

———

*Heavenly Father, in Yahshua's name, I ask for you to forgive my sins,
and I repent for having created multiple Gods in my mind and spirit. I
renounce any ideas or beliefs within my spirit and flesh that recognize
multiple gods. I stand firm in your Word that you, Yahweh, are the one
true God, the Elohim of Abraham, Isaac, and Jacob. Have mercy on
my soul and send your Holy Spirit to teach and comfort me as I move
into a greater understating of who you are. Open the scriptures for me so
I can see with your eyes, so all things can be revealed in greater detail.
Yahshua, I ask that you, as my Messiah, make intercession for me and
have mercy on me. In your name I pray. Halleluyah and Amen.*

APPENDICES

GREEK LEXICON

Note: If you are not familiar with using a lexicon before today, the best practice is to look up the signs that are employed to understand what (X) is denoting and (+) is being used for. In most cases below you will see (X) in the definition. When one comes across this sign, please see the note below.

X (multiplication) denotes a rendering in the authorized version that results from an idiom peculiar to Greek.

G1 *alfah* – Of Hebrew origin; figurative only, the first.

G109 *aer* - From aemi (to breathe unconsciously, i.e., Respire; by analogy, to blow); "air" (as naturally circumambient) -- air. Compare G5594.

G129 *aima* – Of uncertain derivation; blood literally (of men or animals) figuratively (the juice (the juice of grapes) or specifically (the atoning blood of Christ); by implication bloodshed also kindred: - blood.

G138 *haireomai* - (a primitive verb, always in the Greek middle voice) – properly, lay hold of by a *personal choice*. [The Greek *middle* voice emphasizes the *self-interest* of the one *preferring (deciding)* to grasp or take.]

G225 *aletheia* – From G227; truth: - true X truly, truth, verity.

G227 *alethes* – From G1 (as a negative particle) and G2990; true (as not concealing): - true, truly, truth.

G228 *alethinon* –From G227; truthful: - true.

G235 *alla* – Neuter plural of G243; properly other things that is (adverbially) contrariwise (in many relations): - and, but, even, howbeit, indeed, nay, nevertheless, no, notwithstanding, save, therefore, yea, yet.

G243 *allos* – A primary word; else that is different (in many applications): - more one (another) (an -some an-) other (-s -wise).

G435 *aner* – A primary word (compare G444); a man (properly as an individual male): - fellow, husband man sir.

G444 *anthropos* – From G435 and countenance; from G3700); man-faced that is, a human being.

G473 *anti* - A primary particle; opposite, i.e. Instead, or because of (rarely in addition to) -- for, in the room of. Often used in composition to denote contrast, requital, substitution, correspondence, etc.

G575 *apo* - primary particle; off, that is away (from something near) in various senses (of place time or relation; literally or figuratively): - (X here)- after, ago, at, because of, before, by (the space of) for (-th) from in (out) of off (up-) on(-ce) since, with. In composition (as a prefix) it usually denotes separation, departure, cessation, completion, reversal etc.

G649 *apostello* – From G575 and G4724; set apart that is (by implication) to send out (properly on a mission) literally or figuratively: - put in, send (away forth out) set [at liberty].

G746 *arxé* – properly, from the beginning (temporal sense), i.e., "the initial (starting) point"; (figuratively) what comes first and therefore is chief (foremost), i.e., has the priority, because, ahead of the rest ("preeminent").

G846 *autou* (1) self (emphatic) (2) he, she, it (used for the third person pronoun) (3) the same. Usage: he, she, it, they, them, same. In itself it signifies nothing more than again, applied to what has either been previously mentioned or, when the whole discourse is looked at, must necessarily be supplied. From the particle au (perhaps akin to G109 through the idea of a baffling wind.

G1014 *boulomai* – Middle voice of a primary verb; to will that is (reflexively) be willing: - be disposed minded intend list (be of own) will (-ing). Compare G2309

G1080 *gennao* – From a variation of G1085; to procreate (properly of the father but by extension of the mother); figuratively to regenerate: - bear, beget, be born, bring forth, conceive, be delivered of, gender, make spring.

G1085 *genos* – From G1096; kin (abstractly or concretely literally of figuratively individually or collectively): - born country (-man) diversity, generation, kind (-red), nation, offspring, stock.

G1096 *ergento* or *gínomai* – properly, to emerge, become, transitioning from one point (realm, condition) to another, means "to become, and signifies a change of condition, state or place. means to come into being/manifestation implying motion, movement, or growth" (at 2 Pet 1:4). Thus, it is used for God's actions as emerging from eternity and becoming (showing themselves) in time (physical space).

G1097 *ginkgo* – A prolonged form of a primary verb; to know (absolutely) in a great variety of applications and with many implications (as shown at left with others not thus clearly expressed): - allow, be aware (of), feel, (have) known (-ledge), perceive, be resolved, can speak, be sure, understand.

G1161 *dé* A primary particle (adversative or continuative); but, and, etc. -- also, and, but, moreover, now (often unexpressed in English). (a conjunction) – *moreover, indeed now . . . , on top of this . . . , next . . .*

G1223 *dia* – a primary preposition denoting the channel of an act; through.

G1325 *didomee* – A prolonged form of a primary verb (which is used as an alternate in most of the tenses); to give (used in a very wide application properly or by implication Lor F; greatly modified by the connection): - adventure, bestow, bring forth, commit, deliver(up), give, grant, hinder, make, minister, number, offer, have power, put, receive, set, shew, smite (+with the hand), strike (+with the palm of the hand), suffer, take, utter, yield.

G1380 *dokéō* – A prolonged form of a primary verb *doko* properly, suppose (what "seems to be"), forming an opinion (a personal judgment, estimate). ("suppose") directly reflects the personal perspective (values) of the person making the subjective judgment call, i.e., showing what they esteem (or not) as an individual.

G1391 *doxa* – From the base of G1380; glory (as very apparent) in a wide application (L of F objectively or subjectively): - dignity, glory (-ious), honor, praise, worship.

G1410 *dynamai* - (a primitive verb) – to show ability (power); able (enabled by God), empowered. See the cognate-noun, 1411 /dýnamis ("ability, power").

G1411 *dynamis* - (from 1410 /dýnamai, "able, having ability") – properly, "ability to perform" (L-N); for the believer, power to achieve by applying the Lord's inherent abilities. "Power through God's ability" (1411 /dýnamis) is needed in every scene of life to really grow in sanctification and prepare for heaven (glorification). 1411 (dýnamis) is a very important term, used 120 times in the NT.

G1412 *dunamoó - to empower, make (be) able. See 1411 (dynamis).*

G1438 *heautou* him -self, alone.

G1473 *ego* – A primary pronoun of the first person I (only expressed when emphatic): - I me.

G1510 *eimí* (the basic Greek verb which expresses being, i.e., "to be") – am, is. 1510 (eimí), and its counterparts, (properly) convey "straight-forward" being (existence, i.e., without explicit limits).

G1519 *eis* – A primary preposition; to or into (indicating the point reached or entered) of place time or (figuratively) purpose (result etc)– properly, into (unto) – literally, "motion into which" implying penetration ("unto," "union") to a particular purpose or result. to or into (indicating the point reached or entered, of place, time, purpose, result). Usage: into, in, unto, to, upon, towards, for, among.

G1537 *ek* - (a preposition, written *eks* before a vowel) – properly, "*out from* and *to*" (the *out*come); *out from within.* *ek* ("out of") is one of the most under-translated (and therefore mis-translated) Greek propositions – often being confined to the meaning "by." (*ek*) has a two-layered meaning ("*out from* and *to*") which makes it *out-come* oriented (out of the depths of the source and extending to its impact on the object).

G1563 *ekei* – Of uncertain affinity; there; by extension thither: - there, thither (-ward) (to) yonder (place) alone.

G1565 *ekeinos* - From G1563; that one or G3778.

G1700 *emou* – A prolonged form of G3449; of me: -me mine my.

G1715 *emprosthen* – From G1722 and G4314; in front of (in place [literally or figuratively] or time): - against at before (in presence sight) of.

G1722 *en* – properly, in (inside, within); (figuratively) "in the realm (sphere) of," as in the condition (state) in which something operates from the inside (within).

G1743 *endunamoó* - (from 1722 /en "in," which intensifies 1412 /dynamóō, "sharing power-ability") – properly, to impart ability (make able); empowered.

G1832 *exesti* – Third person singular present indicative of a compound of G1537 and G1510; so also, *exon*; neuter present participle of the same (with or without some form of G1510 expressed); impersonally it is right (through the figurative idea of being out in public): - be lawful let X may (-est).

G1849 *exousia* - (from 1537 /*ek*, "out from," which intensifies 1510 /*eimí*, "to be, being as a right or privilege") – authority, conferred power; delegated empowerment ("authorization"), operating in a designated jurisdiction. In the NT, 1849 /*eksousía* ("delegated power") refers to the authority God gives to His saints – authorizing them to act to the extent they are guided by faith (His revealed word).

G1909 *epi* – A primary proposition properly meaning superimposition (of time or place order) as a relation of distribution [with the genitive case] that is over, upon etc.; of rest (with the dative case) at on etc.; of direction (with the accusative case) towards upon etc.; - about (the times), above, after, against, among, as long as, (touching)at, beside X have charge of, (be-[where-]) fore, in (a place as much as the time of – to), (because) of, (up-) on, (behalf of), over, (by for) the space of, through (-out), (un-) to, (-ward) with. In compounds it retains essentially the same import as upon etc., (literally or figuratively).

G1982 - *episkiázō* (from 1909 /epí, "upon" and skiazō, "to cast shade") – properly, to cast a shadow on; overshadow, which leaves a natural (apt) result.

G1983 *episkopeo* – From G1909 and G4648; to oversee; by implication to beware: - look diligently take the oversight.

G2036 *epo* – Primary verb (used only in the definite past tense the other being borrowed from G2046 G4483 and G5346); to speak or say (by word or writing): - answer, bid bring, word, call, command, grant, say, (on) speak, tell. Compare G3004.

G2064 *erchomai* – Middle voice of a primary verb (used only in the present and imperfect tenses, the others being supplied by kindred [middle voice] eleuthomai {el-yoo'-thom-ahee}, or [active] eltho {el'-tho}, which do not otherwise occur) to come. Of persons: to come from one place to another, and used both of persons arriving and of those returning. to appear, make one's appearance, come before the public. Metaphor: to come into being, arise, come forth, show itself, find place or influence. be established, become known, to come (fall) into or unto, to go, to follow one.

G2198 *zao* – a primary verb; to live (literally or figuratively) life (-time), (a-) live (-ly), quick.

G2222 *zoe* – From 2198; life (literally or figuratively) Compare G5590.

G2249 *hemeis* – Nomitive plural of G1473; we (only used when emphatic): - us we (ourselves).

G2254 *hemin* – Dative plural of G1473; to (or for with by) us: - our (for) us we.

G2258 *ane* – Imperfect of G1510; I (thou) was (wast or were): - agree be have charge of hold was were.

G2298 *zao* - A primary verb; to live (literally or figuratively) -- life(-time), (a-)live(-ly), quick.

G2300 *theáomai* (from *tháomai*, "to gaze at a spectacle") – properly, gaze on (contemplate) as a spectator; to observe intently, especially to interpret something (grasp its significance); to see (concentrate on) so as to significantly impact (influence) the viewer. Compare G3700.

G2307 *thélēma* (from G2309 /*thélō*, "to desire, wish") – properly, a *desire* (*wish*), often referring to *God's* "preferred-will," i.e. His "best-offer" to people which can be accepted or rejected. [Note the -*ma* suffix, focusing on the result hoped for with the particular desire (wish). (*thélēma*) is nearly always used of God, referring to His preferred-will. Occasionally it is used of man (cf. Lk 23:25; Jn 1:13.]

G2309 *thelo* - (a primitive verb, *NAS* dictionary) – to desire (wish, will), wanting what is best (optimal) because someone is ready and willing to act. ("to desire, wish") is commonly used of the Lord extending His "best-offer" to the believer – wanting (desiring) to birth His persuasion (faith) in them which also empowers, manifests His presence. [Note the close connection between faith (4102 /*pistis*, "God's in birthed persuasion") and this root.

G2316 *theós* (of unknown origin) – properly, God, the Creator and owner of all things (Jn 1:3; Gen 1 - 3).

G2398 *idios* of uncertain affinity; pertaining to self that is one's own; by implication private or separate: - his acquaintance when they were alone, apart, aside, due his (own proper several) home, (her our thine your) own (business), private (-ly), proper severally their (own).

G2424 *Iesous* – Greek transliteration of Yahshua meaning "Yahweh saves" (or "Yahweh is salvation").

G2443 *hina* – Probably the same as the former part of G1438 through the demonstrative idea; compare G3588; in order that (denoting the purpose or the result): - albeit, because, to the intent (that), lest, so, as (so) that (for) to. Compare 3363.

G2476 *histemi* – abide, appoint, stand, bring, continue, covenant, establish, hold up, lay, present, set (up) stanch, Compare G5087.

G2491 *Ioannes* – Of Hebrew origin H3110 Joannes (that is, Jochanan, the name John).

G2532 *kai* – and (also), very often, moreover, even, indeed (the context determines the exact sense).

G2564 *kaleó* - Akin to the base of *keleuo* G2753; to "call" (properly, aloud, but used in a variety of applications, directly or otherwise) -- bid, call (forth), (whose, whose sur-) name (was (called)).

G2589 *kolpos* - properly, the upper part of the chest where a garment naturally folded to form a "pocket" – called the "bosom," the position synonymous with intimacy (union).

G2596 *kata* – primary particle; (preposition) down (in place or time) (according to the case [genitive, dative or accusative] with which it is joined): - about, according, as (to), after, against. Frequently denotes opposition, distribution, or intensity.

G2638 *katalambano* From G2596 and G1983; to take eagerly, that is to seize, posses (literally or figuratively): - apprehend, attain, come upon, comprehend, find, obtain, perceive, (over-) take.

G2685 *kolumboa* –From a primary word *kolumbos* (to tend that is take care of); properly to provide for that is (by implication) to carry off (as if from harm; generally, obtain): - bring receive.

G2753 *keleuo* - From a primary *kello* (to urge on); "hail"; to incite by word, i.e. order – bid, (at, give) command(-ment) – I command, order, direct, bid.

G2889 *kosmos* – Probably from the base of G2865; orderly arrangement, that is decoration; by implication the world (in a wide or narrow sense including its inhabitants literally or figuratively [morally]): - adorning world.

G2896 *krazo* – A primary verb; properly to croak (as a raven) or scream that is (generally) to call aloud (shriek exclaim intreat): - cry (out).

G2983 *lambano* - (from the primitive root, *lab-*, meaning "actively lay hold of to take or receive," see NAS dictionary) – properly, to lay hold by aggressively (actively) accepting what is available (offered). *lambánō* ("accept with initiative") emphasizes the volition (assertiveness) of the receiver.

G2990 *lanthano* –Prolonged form of a primary verb which is only used as an alternative in certain tenses; to lie hid, be hid, be ignorant of, unawares, in order (or so) that not.

G3004 *lego* – primary verb properly to lay forth (relate in words) say, speak, call or tell.

G3056 *logos* something said (including the thought); by implication, a topic (subject of discourse), also reasoning (the mental faculty) or motive; by extension, a computation; specially, (with the article in John) the Divine Expression (i.e., Messiah).

G3140 *martureo* – From G3144; to be a witness that is testify (literally or figuratively): - charge, give [evidence], bear record, have, obtain, of good honest report, be well, reported of, testify, give, have testimony, (be bear give obtain) witness.

G3141 *marturia* – From G3144; evidence given (judicially or generally): - record, report, testimony, witness.

G3144 *martus* – a witness (Literally [judicially] or Figuratively {generally]); by analogy a martyr: - martyr, record, witness.

G3173 *megas* – Including the prolonged forms feminine *megale*, plural *megaloi* etc; compare also G3176 G3187 big (literally or figuratively in a very wide application: - (+fear) exceedingly great (-est) high large loud mighty + (be) sore (afraid) strong X to years.)

G3176 *megistos* – Superlative of G3173; greatest or very great – exceeding great.

G3187 *meizon* – Irregular comparative of G3173; larger (literally or figuratively specifically in age): - elder greater (-est) more.

G3306 *meno* – A primary verb; to stay (in a given place state relation or expectancy): - abide, continue, dwell, endure, be present, remain, stand, tarry (for X thine own.)

G3361 *me* – a primary particle of qualified negation.

G3363 *hiname* – in order (or so) that not.

G3364 *oo me* – That is G3756 and G3361; a double negative. Strengthening the denial; not at all: - any more at all, by any (no) means, neither, never, no, (at all) in no case (wise), nor, ever, not (at all in any wise). Compare G3378.

G3372 *mekos* – Probably akin to G3173; length (literally or figuratively)

G3378 *mayook* – That is G3756 and G3361; as interrogative and negative is it not that? – neither (followed by no) + never not. Compare G3364.

G3425 *mogis* – Adverb from a primary word *mogos* (toil); with difficulty: - hardly.

G3439 *monogenes* – From G3441 and G1096; only born that is sole: - only (begotten child).

G3441 *monos* – Probably from G3306; remaining that is

sole or single; by implication mere: - alone, only, by themselves.

G3449 *mochthos* – From the base of G3425; toil, that is (by implication) sadness: - painfulness, travail.

G3450 *mou* – The simpler form of G1700; of me: - I me mine (own) my.

G3475 *Mouses* - Moses, a leader of Israel.

G3551 *nomos* - is used of: a) the Law (Scripture), with emphasis on the first five books of Scripture; or b) any system of religious thinking (theology), especially when nomos occurs without the Greek definite article

G3588 *ho* - The masculine feminine (second) and neuter (third) forms in all their inflections; the definite article -he.

G3685 *oninemi* – as in notoriety.

G3686 *onoma* – From a presumed derivative of the base of G1097 (compare G3685); a name (literally or figuratively) (authority character): - called (+sur -) name (-d).

G3693 *opisthen* – From *opis* (regard; from G3700) with enclitic of source; from the rear (as a secure aspect) that is at the back (adverb and preposition of place or time): -after, backside, behind.

G3694 *opiso* – From the same as G3693 with enclitic of direction; to the back, that is aback (as adverb or preposition of time or place; or as noun): - after back (-ward) (+get) behind + follow.

G3700 *optanomai* – The first (middle voice) to gaze that with eyes wide open as at something remarkable.

G3708 *horáō* – properly, see, often with metaphorical meaning: "to see with the mind" (i.e. spiritually see), i.e. perceive (with inward spiritual perception).

G3739 *hos* − Probably a primary word (or perhaps a form of the article G3588); the relative (sometime demonstrative) pronoun who which what that: - one (an the) other, some, that, which, who (-m-se) See also G3757.

G3745 *hosos* − By reduplication from G3739; as (much great long etc,) as: - all (that) as (long, many, much) (as) how great (many, much) [in] as much as so many as that (ever) the more those things what (great -soever) wheresoever wherewithsoever which X while who (-soever).

G3748 *hostis, hetis, hoti* − From G3739 and G5100; which, some, that is any; also (definitely) which, same: - X and (they) (such) as (they) that, in that, they, what (-soever), whereas ye (they), which, who (-soever). Compare G3754

G3754 *hoti* − Neuter of G3748 as conjugation; demonstrative that (sometimes redundant); causatively because: - as, concerning that, as though, because (that), for (that), how (that), (in) that, though, why.

G3756 *ou* − A primary word; the absolutely negative (compare G3661) adverb; no or not: - +long nay, neither, never, no (X man), none. G3364 G3372.

G3757 *hou*- Genitive case of G3739 as adverb; at which place, that is where: - where (-in) whither ([soever]).

G3761 *oude* − From G3756 and G1161; not, however, that is neither, nor, not even: - neither (indeed) never, no (more nor not), nor (yet) (also even them) not (even so much as) + nothing so much as.

G3762 *oudeis* - Including feminine *oudemia* (oo-dem-ee'-ah), and neuter *ouden* (oo-den') from *oude* and *heis*; not even one (man, woman or thing), i.e. None, nobody, nothing -- any (man), aught, man, neither any (thing), never (man), no (man), none (+ of these things), not (any, at all, -thing), nought

G3778 *houtos* – From the article G3588 and G846; the, he (she, it) that is, this, or that (often with the article repeated): - he

G3844 *para* – with the genitive; and as in Greek prose writings always with the genitive of a person, to denote that a thing proceeds from the side or the vicinity of one, or from one's sphere of power, or from one's wealth or store. From, beside (literally or figuratively).

G3875 *paraklétos* - (from 3844 /*pará*, "from close-beside" and 2564 /*kaléō*, "make a call") – properly, a legal advocate who makes the right judgment-call because close enough to the situation. 3875 /*paráklētos* ("advocate, advisor-helper") is the regular term in NT times of an attorney (lawyer) – i.e., someone giving evidence that stands up in court.

G3880 *paralambano* From G3844 and G2983; to receive near that is associate with oneself (in any familiar or intimate act or relation); by analogy to assume an office; figuratively to learn: - receive take (unto with).

G3956 *pas* – every, all manner of. Including all the forms of declension; apparently a primary word; all, any, every, the whole -- all (manner of, means), always (-s), any (one), X daily, + ever, every (one, way), as many as, + no(-thing), X thoroughly, whatsoever, whole, whosoever.

G3962 *pater*- Apparently a primary word; a father (literally or figuratively near or more remote): - father parent.

G4008 *peran* – apparently the accusative case of an obsolete derivation of *peiro* (to pierce); through (as adverb or preposition) that is across: - beyond farther (other) side over.

G4012 *peri* – From the base of G4008; properly through (all over) that is around; concerning, of, pertaining to, for, sake.

G4100 *pisteuo* – From G4102; to have faith (in upon or with respect to a person or thing) that is credit; by implication to entrust (especially one's spiritual well-being to Messiah): - believe (-r) commit (to trust) put in trust with.

G4102 *pístis* - (from 3982/*peithô*, "persuade, be persuaded") – properly, persuasion (be persuaded, come to trust); faith. Can only come from Yahweh.

G4130 *pletho* - A prolonged form of a primary *pleo* (which appears only as an alternate in certain tenses and in the reduplicated form *pimplemi*) to "fill" (literally or figuratively (imbue, influence, supply)); specially, to fulfil (time) -- accomplish, full (...come), furnish.

G4134 *pleres* - From G4130; replete, or covered over; by analogy, complete -- full.

G4137 *pleroo* - From G4134; to make replete, i.e. (literally) to cram (a net), level up (a hollow), or (figuratively) to furnish (or imbue, diffuse, influence), satisfy, execute (an office), finish (a period or task), verify (or coincide with a prediction), etc. -- accomplish, X after, (be) complete, end, expire, fill (up), fulfil, (be, make) full (come), fully preach, perfect, supply.

G4138 *pleroma* - From G4137; repletion or completion, i.e. (subjectively) what fills (as contents, supplement, copiousness, multitude), or (objectively) what is filled (as container, performance, period) -- which is put in to fill up, piece that filled up, fulfilling, full, fulness.

G4151 *pnuema* - From *pneo*; a current of air, i.e., breath (blast) or a breeze; by analogy or figuratively, a spirit, i.e. (human) the rational soul, (by implication) vital principle, mental disposition, etc., or (superhuman) an angel, demon, or (divine) God, Christ's spirit, the Holy Spirit -- ghost, life, spirit (-ual, -ually), mind. Compare G5590.

G4154 *pneo* - A primary word; to breathe hard, i.e., breeze -- blow. Compare G5594.

G4253 – *pro* – A primary preposition; "fore", i.e. in front of, prior (figuratively, superior) to -- above, ago, before, or ever. In the comparative, it retains the same significations: - above, ago, before or ever. In compounds it retains the same significance.

G4314 *prós* (a preposition) – properly, motion towards to "interface with" (literally, moving toward a goal or destination).

G4413 *protos* – Contracted superlative of G4253; foremost (in time place order of importance): - before beginning best chief (-est) first (of all) former.

G4455 *popote* - From *po* and *pote*; at any time, i.e. (with negative particle) at no time -- at any time, + never (...to any man), + yet, never man.

G4561 *sarx* – Probably from a base of G4563; properly, flesh ("carnal"), merely of human origin or empowerment. *sárks* ("flesh") is not always evil in Scripture. Indeed, it is used positively in relation to sexual intercourse in marriage (Eph 5:31) – as well as for the sinless human body of Jesus (Jn 1:14; 1 Jn 4:2,3). Indeed, flesh (what is physical) is necessary for the body to live out the faith the Lord works in (Gal 2:20). (*sarks*) is generally negative, referring to making decisions (actions) according *to self* – i.e. done apart from faith (independent from God's inworking). Thus, what is "of the flesh (carnal)" is by definition displeasing to the Lord – even things that seem "respectable!" In short, flesh generally relates to unaided human *effort*, i.e., decisions (actions) that originate from self or are empowered by self. This is carnal ("of the flesh") and proceeds out of the untouched (unchanged) part of us – i.e., what is not transformed by God.

G4563 *saroo* – From a derivative of *sairo* (to brush off; akin to G4951) meaning a broom, to sweep: - sweep.

G4626 *skapto* – A primary verb; to dig.

G4632 *skeuos* - Of uncertain affinity; a vessel, implement, equipment or apparatus (literally or figuratively (specially, a wife as contributing to the usefulness of the husband)) -- goods, sail, stuff, vessel.

G4633 *skene* - a tent, booth, tabernacle, abode, dwelling, mansion, habitation. Compare G4632.

G4636 *-skenos* - a tent, tabernacle; fig: of the human body. Compare G4633.

G4637 *skeenoo* - properly, to pitch or live in a tent, "denoting much more than the mere general notion of dwelling" (M. Vincent). For the Christian is dwelling in intimate communion with the resurrected Messiah – even as He who Himself lived in unbroken communion with the Father during the days of His flesh.

G4639 *skia* – Apparently a primary word; shade or shadow (literally or figuratively [darkness of error or an adumbration]): - shadow.

G4648 *skopeo* – From G4649; to take aim at (spy) that is (figuratively) regard: - consider, take heed, look at, (on) mark. Compare G3700

G4649 *skopos* – (scope) to peer about G4626 through the idea of concealment; compare (G4629); a watch (sentry or scout) that is (by implication) a goal: - mark.

G4653 *skotia* – From G4655; dimness, obscurity (literally or figuratively): - dark (ness).

G4655 *skotos* – From the base of G4639; shadiness that is obscurity (literally or figuratively): - darkness.

G4724 *stello* – Probably strengthened from the base of G2476; properly to set fast (stall-Figuratively) (to repress reflexively) abstain from associating with: - avoid, withdraw self.

G4951 *suro* - to trail -- drag, draw, hale. Probably akin to *haireomai* G138.

G5043 *tekron* – From the base of G5098; a child (as produced): - child daughter son.

G5087 *tithemi* – – A prolonged form of a primary word *theo* (which is used only as an alternate in certain tenses); to place (in the widest application L and F; properly in a passive or horizontal posture and thus different from **G2476** which properly denotes an upright and active position while **G2749** is properly reflexive and utterly prostrate): - + advise, appoint, bow, commit, conceive, give, X kneel down, lay (aside down up), make, ordain, purpose, put, set (forth), settle, sink down.

G5092 *time* – From G5099; a value that is money paid or (concretely and collectively) valuables; by analogy esteem (especially of the highest degree) or the dignity itself: - honour, precious, price, some.

G5097 *timereo* – From a compound of G5092 and *ouros* (a guard); properly to protect one's honor that is to avenge (inflict a penalty): - punish.

G5098 *timoria* – From G5097, vindication that is (by implication) a penalty: - punishment.

G5099 *tino* – Strengthened for a primary word *tio* (which is only used as an alternate in certain senses); to pay a price that is as a penalty: - be punished with.

G5100 *tis* – An enclitic indefinite pronoun; some or any person or object: - a (kind of) any (man thing thing at all) certain (thing) divers he (every) man one (X thing) ought + partly some (man -body -thing -what) (+that no-) thing what[-soever] X wherewith whom [-soever] whose([-soever]).

G5207 *huios* Apparently a primary word; a "son" (sometimes of animals), used very widely of immediate, remote or figuratively, kinship -- child, foal, son.

G5316 *phiano* – prolongation for the base of G5457; to lighten (shine) that is show (transitive or intransitive literally or figurative): - appear, seem, be seen, shine, think.

G5346 *phemi* – to show or make known one's thoughts to speak, or say.

G5457 *phos* – From an obsolete *phoa* (to shine or make manifest especially by rays; compare G5316 and G5346; luminousness.

G5461 *photizo* - From G5457; to shed rays that is to shine or (transitively) to brighten up (literally or figuratively): - enlighten illuminate (bring to give) light make to see.

G5463 *chairo* - A primary verb; to be "cheer" ful, i.e., calmly happy or well-off; impersonally, especially as salutation (on meeting or parting), be well -- farewell, be glad, God speed, greeting, hall, joy (- fully), rejoice.

G5485 *charis* - From G5463; graciousness (as gratifying), of manner or act (abstract or concrete; literal, figurative or spiritual; especially the divine influence upon the heart, and its reflection in the life; including gratitude) -- acceptable, benefit, favour, gift, grace (- ious), joy, liberality, pleasure, thank (-s, -worthy).

G5547 *Xristós* - (from 5548 – properly, "the Anointed One," the Christ (Hebrew, "Messiah").

G5548 *xríō* – to anoint by rubbing or pouring olive oil on someone to represent the flow (empowering) of the Holy Spirit. Anointing (literally) involved rubbing olive oil on the head, etc., especially to present someone as divinely-authorized (appointed by God) to serve as prophet, priest or king.

G5590 *psuche* – From G5594 breath that is (by implication) spirit abstractly or concretely (the animal sentient principle only; thus, distinguished on the one hand from G4151 which is the rational and immortal soul; and on the other from G2222 which is mere vitality even of plants: these terms thus exactly correspond to H5315, H7307 and H2416 Nephesh, Ruach and Life respectively.

G5594 *psucho* - A primary verb; to breathe (voluntarily but gently, thus differing on the one hand from *pneo*, which denotes properly a forcible respiration; and on the other from the base of *aer*, which refers properly to an inanimate breeze), i.e. (by implication, of reduction of temperature by evaporation) to chill (figuratively) -- wax cold.

G5607 *ousa* - Including the feminine *ousa* (oo'-sah); and the neuter on (on) present participle of *eimi*; being -- be, come, have.

_G5613_ *hos* - Probably adverb of comparative from *hos*; which how, i.e. In that manner (very variously used, as follows) -- about, after (that), (according) as (it had been, it were), as soon (as), even as (like), for, how (greatly), like (as, unto), since, so (that), that, to wit, unto, when(-soever), while, X with all speed.

HEBREW LEXICON

X (multiplication) denotes a rendering in the authorized version that results from an idiom peculiar to Hebrew.

H119 *adom* - To show blood (in the face), i.e., Flush or turn rosy -- be (dyed, made) red (ruddy).

    H120 *adam* - From 'adam; ruddy i.e. A human being (an individual or the species, mankind, etc.) -- X another, + hypocrite, + common sort, X low, man (mean, of low degree), person.

    H183 *avah* - A primitive root; to wish for -- covet, (greatly) desire, be desirous, long, lust (after).

    H193 *uwl* - From an unused root meaning to twist, i.e. (by implication) be strong; the body (as being rolled together); also, powerful -- mighty, strength.

    H352 *ayil* - From the same as H193; properly, strength; hence, anything strong; specifically, a chief (politically); also, a ram (from his strength); a pilaster (as a strong support); an oak or other strong tree -- mighty (man), lintel, oak, post, ram, tree.

H410 *el* - Shortened from H352; strength; as adjective, mighty; especially the Almighty (but used also of any deity) -- God (god), X goodly, X great, idol, might (-y one), power, strong. Compare names in "-el."

H430 *elohim* - Plural of 'elowahh; gods in the ordinary sense; but specifically used (in the plural thus, especially with the article) of the supreme God; occasionally applied by way of deference to magistrates; and sometimes as a superlative -- angels, X exceeding, God (gods) (-dess, -ly), X (very) great, judges, X mighty.

H433 *eloah* - From 'el; a deity or the Deity -- God, god. See H430.

H1696 *dabar* - A primitive root; perhaps properly, to arrange; but used figuratively (of words), to speak; rarely (in a destructive sense) to subdue -- answer, appoint, bid, command, commune, declare, destroy, give, name, promise, pronounce, rehearse, say, speak, be spokesman, subdue, talk, teach, tell, think, use (entreaties), utter, X well, X work.

H1697 *dabar* - From H1696; a word; by implication, a matter (as spoken of) or thing; adverbially, a cause -- act, advice, affair, answer, X any such (thing), because of, book, business, care, case, cause, certain rate, + chronicles, commandment, X commune(-ication), + concern(-ing), + confer, counsel, + dearth, decree, deed, X disease, due, duty, effect, + eloquent, errand, (evil favoured-)ness, + glory, + harm, hurt, + iniquity, + judgment, language, + lying, manner, matter, message, (no) thing, oracle, X ought, X parts, + pertaining, + please, portion, + power, promise, provision, purpose, question, rate, reason, report, request, X (as hast) said, sake, saying, sentence, + sign, + so, some (uncleanness), somewhat to say, + song, speech, X spoken, talk, task, + that, X there done, thing (concerning), thought, + thus, tidings, what(-soever), + wherewith, which, word, work.

H1819 *damah* - A primitive root; to compare; by implication, to resemble, liken, consider -- compare, devise, (be) like(-n), mean, think, use similitudes.

H1823 *demuth* - From H1819; resemblance; concretely, model, shape; adverbially, like -- fashion, like (-ness, as), manner, similitude.

H1881 *dath* - Of uncertain (perhaps foreign) derivation: a royal edict or statute -- commandment, commission, decree, law, manner.

H1933 *hava* - a primitive root (compare *'avah, hayah*) supposed to mean properly, to breathe; to be (in the sense of existence) -- be, X have.

H1961 *hayah* - A primitive root (compare H1933); to exist, i.e., be or become, come to pass (always emphatic, and not a mere copula or auxiliary) -- beacon, X altogether, be(-come), accomplished, committed, like), break, cause, come (to pass), do, faint, fall, + follow, happen, X have, last, pertain, quit (one-)self, require, X use.

H2398 *chata* - A primitive root; properly, to miss; hence (figuratively and generally) to sin; by inference, to forfeit, lack, expiate, repent, (causatively) lead astray, condemn -- bear the blame, cleanse, commit (sin), by fault, harm he hath done, loss, miss, (make) offend(-er), offer for sin, purge, purify (self), make reconciliation, (cause, make) sin (-ful, -ness), trespass.

H2403 *chatta'ah* - From H2398; an offence (sometimes habitual sinfulness), and its penalty, occasion, sacrifice, or expiation; also (concretely) an offender -- punishment (of sin), purifying (-fication for sin), sin (-ner, offering).

H2580 *chen* - From H2603; graciousness, i.e., subjective (kindness, favor) or objective (beauty) -- favour, grace(-ious), pleasant, precious, (well-)favored.

H2583 *chanah* - A primitive root (compare *chanan*); properly, to incline; by implication, to decline (of the slanting rays of evening); specifically, to pitch a tent; gen, to encamp (for abode or siege) -- abide (in tents), camp, dwell, encamp, grow to an end, lie, pitch (tent), rest in tent.

H2603 *chanan* - A primitive root (compare H2583); properly, to bend or stoop in kindness to an inferior; to favor, bestow; causatively to implore (i.e., move to favor by petition) -- beseech, X fair, (be, find, shew) favour(-able), be (deal, give, grant (gracious(-ly), intreat, (be) merciful, have (shew) mercy (on, upon), have pity upon, pray, make supplication, X very.

H2895 *tob* - A primitive root, to be (transitively, do or make) good (or well) in the widest sense -- be (do) better, cheer, be (do, seem) good, (make) goodly, X please, (be, do, go, play) well.

H2896 *towb* - functional; good (as an adjective) in the widest sense; used likewise as a noun, both in the masculine and the feminine, the singular and the plural (good, a good or good thing, a good man or woman; the good, goods or good things, good men or women), also as an adverb (well) -- beautiful, best, better, bountiful, cheerful, at ease, X fair (word), (be in) favour, fine, glad, good (deed, -lier, -liest, -ly, -ness, -s), graciously, joyful, kindly, kindness, liketh (best), loving, merry, X most, pleasant, + pleaseth, pleasure, precious, prosperity, ready, sweet, wealth, welfare, (be) well ((-favored)).

H3068 *Yahweh* - (the) self-Existent or Eternal, Creator, one and only God of Israel and Christianity.

H3069 *Yahweh* - A variation of Yahweh (used after *'Adonay*, and pronounced by Jews as *'elohiym*, in order to prevent the repetition of the same sound, since they elsewhere pronounce Yahweh as *'Adonay*) -- God.

H3384 *yarah* - a primitive root; properly, to flow as water (i.e., to rain); transitively, to lay or throw (especially an arrow, i.e. to shoot); figuratively, to point out (as if by aiming the finger), to teach -- (+) archer, cast, direct, inform, instruct, lay, shew, shoot, teach (-er, -ing), through.

H3513 *kabad or kabed* -To be heavy, i.e., in a bad sense (burdensome, severe, dull) or in a good sense (numerous, rich, honorable; causatively, to make weighty (in the same two senses) -- abounding with, more grievously afflict, boast, be chargeable, X be dim, glorify, be (make) glorious (things), glory, (very) great, be grievous, harden, be (make) heavy, be heavier, lay heavily, (bring to, come to, do, get, be had in) honour (self), (be) honourable (man), lade, X more be laid, make self-many, nobles, prevail, promote (to honour), be rich, be (go) sore, stop.

H3519 *kabowd* - Rarely *kabod* {kaw-bode'}; from *kabad*; properly, weight, but only figuratively in a good sense, splendor or copiousness -- glorious(-ly), glory, honour(-able).

H3801 *kethoneth or kuttoneth* - From an unused root

meaning to cover (compare H3802); a shirt -- coat, garment, robe.

H3802 *katheph* - From an unused root meaning to clothe; the shoulder (proper, i.e., Upper end of the arm; as being the spot where the garments hang); figuratively, side-piece or lateral projection of anything -- arm, corner, shoulder(-piece), side, undersetter.

H3812 *Leah* - "weary", a wife of Jacob.

H5162 *nachem* - A primitive root; properly, to sigh, i.e., breathe strongly; by implication, to be sorry, i.e. (in a favorable sense) to pity, console or (reflexively) rue; or (unfavorably) to avenge (oneself) -- comfort (self), ease (one's self), repent (-er,-ing, self).

H5314 *naphash* - A primitive root; to breathe; passively, to be breathed upon, i.e. (figuratively) refreshed (as if by a current of air) -- (be) refresh selves (-ed).

H5315 *nephesh* - From G5314; properly, a breathing creature, i.e. Animal of (abstractly) vitality; used very widely in a literal, accommodated or figurative sense (bodily or mental) -- any, appetite, beast, body, breath, creature, X dead(-ly), desire, X (dis-)contented, X fish, ghost, + greedy, he, heart(-y), (hath, X jeopardy of) life (X in jeopardy), lust, man, me, mind, mortally, one, own, person, pleasure, (her-, him-, my-, thy-)self, them (your)-selves, + slay, soul, + tablet, they, thing, (X she) will, X would have it.

H5395 *nasham* - breathe, blow; gently breathe (of wind), etc.; see seek a thing with labour and perseverance a soul; — pant, of the deep and strong breathing of a woman in travail; breath of life.

H5397 *neshamah* - From nasham; a puff, i.e., Wind, angry or vital breath, divine inspiration, intellect. Or (concretely) an animal -- blast, (that) breath(-eth), inspiration, soul, spirit.

H6754 *tselem* - From an unused root meaning to shade; a phantom, i.e. (figuratively) illusion, resemblance; hence, a representative figure, especially an idol -- image, vain shew.

H7306 *ruach* - A primitive root; properly, to blow, i.e., breathe; only (literally) to smell or (by implication, perceive (figuratively, to anticipate, enjoy) -- accept, smell, X touch, make of quick understanding.

H7307 *ruach* - From H7306; wind; by resemblance breath, i.e. a sensible (or even violent) exhalation; figuratively, life, anger, unsubstantiality; by extension, a region of the sky; by resemblance spirit, but only of a rational being (including its expression and functions) -- air, anger, blast, breath, X cool, courage, mind, X quarter, X side, spirit((-ual)), tempest, X vain, ((whirl-))wind(-y).

H8451 *torah* – from H3384; direction, instruction, law

MATTHEW 1 PRONOUN COMPARISON (autos)

VERSE	USAGE	TRANSLITERATION	PRONOUN	DESCRIPTION	
Matthew 1:18	αὐτοῦ	autou	of Him	Yahshua	PPro-GM3S
Matthew 1:18	αὐτούς	autous	of them	Joseph and Mary	PPro-AM3P
Matthew 1:19	αὐτῆς	autes	of her	Mary	PPro-GF3S
Matthew 1:19	αὐτήν	auten	her	Mary	PPro-AF3S
Matthew 1:19	αὐτήν	auten	her	Mary	PPro-AF3S
Matthew 1:20	αὐτοῦ	autou	of him	Joseph	PPro-GM3S
Matthew 1:20	αὐτῷ	auto	to him	Joseph	PPro-DM3S
Matthew 1:20	αὐτῇ	aute	to her	Mary	PPro-DF3S
Matthew 1:21	αὐτοῦ	autou	of Him	Yahshua	PPro-GM3S
Matthew 1:21	αὐτοῦ	autou	of Him	Yahshua	PPro-GM3S
Matthew 1:21	αὐτῶν	auton	of them	Israel	PPro-GM3P
Matthew 1:23	αὐτοῦ	autou	of Him	Yahshua	PPro-GM3S
Matthew 1:24	αὐτῷ	auto	to him	Joseph	PPro-DM3S
Matthew 1:24	αὐτοῦ	autou	of him	Joseph	PPro-GM3S
Matthew 1:25	αὐτήν	auten	her	Mary	PPro-AF3S
Matthew 1:25	αὐτοῦ	autou	of Him	Yahshua	PPro-GM3S
Birth					

MARK 1 PRONOUN COMPARISON (autos)

VERSE	USAGE	TRANSLITERATION	PRONOUN	DESCRIPTION	
Mark 1:3	αὐτοῦ	autou	of Him	Yahweh	PPro-GM3S
Mark 1:5	αὐτόν	auton	him	John	PPro-AM3S
Mark 1:5	αὐτοῦ	autou	him	John	PPro-GM3S
Mark 1:5	αὐτῶν	auton	of them	Israel	PPro-GM3P
Mark 1:6	αὐτοῦ	autou	of him	John	PPro-GM3S
Mark 1:7	αὐτοῦ	autou	of Him	Yahshua	PPro-GM3S
Mark 1:8	αὐτός	autos	He	John	PPro-NM3S
Mark 1:10	αὐτόν	auton	Him	Yahshua	PPro-AM3S
Mark 1:12	αὐτόν	auton	Him	Yahshua	PPro-AM3S
Mark 1:13	αὐτῷ	auto	to Him	Yahshua	PPro-DM3S
Wilderness					

LUKE 1 PRONOUN COMPARISON (autos)

VERSE	USAGE	TRANSLITERATION	PRONOUN	DESCRIPTION	
Luke 1:5	αὐτῷ	auto	of him	Zacharias	
Luke 1:5	αὐτῆς	autes	of her	Elizabeth	
Luke 1:7	αὐτοῖς	autois	to them	Zacharias and Elizabeth	
Luke 1:7	αὐτῶν	auton	of them	Zacharias and Elizabeth	
Luke 1:8	αὐτόν	auton	of him	Zacharias	
Luke 1:8	αὐτοῦ	autou	of him	Zacharias	
Luke 1:11	αὐτῷ	auto	to him	Zacharias	
Luke 1:12	αὐτόν	auton	him	Zacharias	
Luke 1:13	αὐτόν	auton	him	Zacharias	PPro-AM3S
Luke 1:13	αὐτοῦ	autou	of him	John	PPro-GM3S
Luke 1:14	αὐτοῦ	autou	of him	John	PPro-GM3S
Luke 1:15	αὐτοῦ	autou	of him	John	PPro-GM3S
Luke 1:16	αὐτῶν	auton	of them	Israel	PPro-GM3S
Luke 1:17	αὐτός	autos	he	John	PPro-NM3S
Luke 1:17	αὐτοῦ	autou	him	Yahweh	PPro-GM3S
Luke 1:18	αὐτῆς	autes	of her	Elizabeth	PPro-GF3S
Luke 1:19	αὐτῷ	auto	to him	Zacharias	PPro-DM3S
Luke 1:20	αὐτῶν	auton	of them	Zacharias and Elizabeth	PPro-GM3P
Luke 1:21	αὐτόν	auton	of him	Zacharias	PPro-AM3S
Luke 1:22	αὐτοῖς	autois	to them	Israel	PPro-DM3P
Luke 1:22	αὐτός	autos	he	Zacharias	PPro-NM3S
Luke 1:22	αὐτοῖς	autois	to them	Israel	PPro-DM3P
Luke 1:23	αὐτοῦ	autou	of him	Zacharias	PPro-GM3S
Luke 1:23	αὐτοῦ	autou	of him	Zacharias	PPro-GM3S
Luke 1:24	αὐτοῦ	autou	of him	Zacharias	PPro-GM3S
Luke 1:28	αὐτήν	auten	her	Mary	PPro-AF3S
Luke 1:30	αὐτῇ	aute	to her	Mary	PPro-DF3S

LUKE 1 PRONOUN COMPARISON (autos) continued

VERSE	USAGE	TRANSLITERATION	PRONOUN	DESCRIPTION	
Luke 1:30	αὐτῇ	aute	to her	Mary	PPro-DF3S
Luke 1:31	αὐτοῦ	autou	of Him	Yahshua	PPro-GM3S
Luke 1:32	αὐτῷ	auto	Him	Yahshua	PPro-DM3S
Luke 1:32	αὐτοῦ	autou	of Him	Yahshua	PPro-GM3S
Luke 1:33	αὐτοῦ	autou	of Him	Yahshua	PPro-GM3S
Luke 1:35	αὐτῇ	aute	to her	Mary	PPro-DF3S
Luke 1:36	αὐτὴ	aute	she	Elizabeth	PPro-NF3S
Luke 1:36	αὐτῆς	autes	of her	Elizabeth	PPro-GF3S
Luke 1:36	αὐτῇ	aute	to her	Elizabeth	PPro-DF3S
Luke 1:38	αὐτῆς	autes	her	Mary	PPro-GF3S
Luke 1:41	αὐτῆς	autes	her	Elizabeth	PPro-GF3S
Luke 1:45	αὐτῇ	aute	to her	Mary	PPro-DF3S
Luke 1:48	αὐτοῦ	autou	of Him	Yahweh	PPro-GM3S
Luke 1:49	αὐτοῦ	autou	of Him	Yahweh	PPro-GM3S
Luke 1:50	αὐτοῦ	autou	of Him	Yahweh	PPro-GM3S
Luke 1:50	αὐτὸν	auton	Him	Yahweh	PPro-AM3S
Luke1:51	αὐτοῦ	autou	of Him	Yahweh	PPro-GM3S
Luke1:54	αὐτοῦ	autou	of Him	Yahweh	PPro-GM3S
Luke1:55	αὐτοῦ	autou	of him	Abraham	PPro-GM3S
Luke 1:56	αὐτῇ	aute	to her	Elizabeth	PPro-DF3S
Luke 1:56	αὐτῆς	autes	of her	Mary	PPro-GF3S
Luke 1:57	αὐτὴν	auten	for her	Mary	PPro-AF3S
Luke1:58	αὐτῆς	autes	of her	Elizabeth	PPro-GF3S
Luke1:58	αὐτοῦ	autou	of Him	Yahweh	PPro-GM3S
Luke 1:58	αὐτῇ	aute	to her	Elizabeth	PPro-DF3S
Luke1:59	αὐτὸ	auto	it	John	PPro-AN3S
Luke 1:59	αὐτοῦ	autou	of him	John	PPro-GM3S
Luke 1:60	αὐτοῦ	autou	of him	John	PPro-GM3S
Luke 1:61	αὐτὴν	auten	her	Elizabeth	PPro-AF3S

LUKE 1 PRONOUN COMPARISON (autos) continued

VERSE	USAGE	TRANSLITERATION	PRONOUN	DESCRIPTION	
Luke 1:62	αὐτοῦ	autou	of him	John	PPro-GM3S
Luke 1:62	αὐτό	auto	him	John	PPro-AN3S
Luke 1:63	αὐτοῦ	autou	of him	John	PPro-GM3S
Luke 1:64	αὐτοῦ	autou	of him	Zacharias	PPro-GM3S
Luke 1:64	αὐτοῦ	autou	of him	Zacharias	PPro-GM3S
Luke 1:65	αὐτούς	autous	of them	Zacharias and Elizabeth	PPro-AM3P
Luke 1:66	αὐτῶν	auton	of them	Israel	PPro-GM3P
Luke 1:66	αὐτοῦ	autou	him	John	PPro-GM3S
Luke 1:67	αὐτοῦ	autou	him	John	PPro-GM3S
Luke 1:68	αὐτοῦ	autou	of Him	Yahweh	PPro-GM3S
Luke 1:69	αὐτοῦ	autou	of Him	Yahweh	PPro-GM3S
Luke 1:70	αὐτοῦ	autou	of Him	Yahweh	PPro-GM3S
Luke 1:72	αὐτοῦ	autou	of Him	Yahweh	PPro-GM3S
Luke 1:74	αὐτῷ	auto	Him	Yahweh	PPro-DM3S
Luke 1:75	αὐτοῦ	autou	Him	Yahweh	PPro-GM3S
Luke 1:76	αὐτοῦ	autou	of Him	Yahweh	PPro-GM3S
Luke 1:77	αὐτοῦ	autou	of Him	Yahweh	PPro-GM3S
Luke 1:77	αὐτῶν	auton	of them	Israel	PPro-GM3P
Luke 1:80	αὐτοῦ	autou	of him	Yahshua	PPro-GM3S
Birth					

GLOSSARY OF BELIEF SYSTEMS EMANATING FROM JOHN 1

Adoptionism - is an early Christian nontrinitarian theological doctrine, which holds that Jesus was adopted as the Son of God at his baptism, his resurrection, or his ascension. A.K.A. dynamic Monarchianism.

Monarchianism - is a Christian theology that emphasizes God as one indivisible being, in direct contrast to Trinitarianism, which defines the Godhead as three coeternal, consubstantial, co-immanent, and equally divine hypostases.

Modalistic Monarchianism (or Modalism) - considers God to be one while appearing and working through the different "modes" of Father, Son, and Holy Spirit. Following this view, all the Godhead is understood to dwell in the person of Jesus from the incarnation.

Arianism - is a Christological doctrine first attributed to Arius (c. AD 256–336), a Christian presbyter from Alexandria, Egypt. Arian theology holds that Jesus Christ is the Son of God, who was begotten by God the Father with the difference that the Son of God did not always exist but was begotten within time by God the Father, therefore Jesus was not co-eternal with God the Father.

Bogomilism - was a Christian neo-Gnostic or dualist sect founded in the First Bulgarian Empire by the priest Bogomil during the reign of Tsar Peter I in the 10th century. It most probably arose in what is today the region of Macedonia.

Manichaeism - is a former major religion founded in the 3rd century CE by the Parthian prophet Mani (CE 216–274), in the Sasanian Empire. Manichaeism teaches an elaborate dualistic cosmology describing the struggle between a good, spiritual world of light, and an evil, material world of darkness. Through an ongoing process that takes place in human history, light is gradually removed from the world of matter and returned to the world of light, whence it came. Its beliefs are based on local Mesopotamian religious movements and Gnosticism. It reveres Mani as the final prophet after Zoroaster, Gautama Buddha, and Jesus.

Valentinianism was one of the major Gnostic Christian movements. Founded by Valentinus in the 2nd century AD, its influence spread widely, not just within Rome but also from Northwest Africa to Egypt through to Asia Minor and Syria in the East. Later in the movement's history it broke into an Eastern and a Western school.

Sethianism – is one of the main currents of Gnosticism during the 2nd and 3rd century CE, along with Valentinianism and Basilideanism. According to John D. Turner, it originated in the 2nd century CE as a fusion of two distinct Hellenistic Judaic philosophies and was influenced by Christianity and Middle Platonism.

Basilideanism - a Gnostic sect founded by Basilides of Alexandria in the 2nd century. Basilides claimed to have been taught his doctrines by Glaucus, a disciple of St. Peter, though others stated he was a disciple of the Simonian Menander.

Theism - is broadly defined as the belief in the existence of a supreme being or deities. In common parlance, or when contrasted with deism, the term often describes the classical conception of God that is found in monotheism (also referred to as classical theism) – or gods found in poly-theistic religions—a belief in God or in gods without the rejection of revelation as is characteristic of deism.

Unitarianism - is a nontrinitarian branch of Christian theology. Most other branches of Christianity and the major Churches accept the Nicene Creed's statement of homoousion: one being in three hypostases: the Father, Son, and Holy Spirit. Unitarian Christians believe that Jesus was inspired by God in his moral teachings and that he is a savior, but not divine.

Socinianism – Photinus taught that Jesus was the sinless Messiah and redeemer, and the only perfect human son of God, but that he had no pre-human existence. They interpret verses such as John 1:1 to refer to God's "plan" existing in God's mind before Christ's birth, and that it was God's plan that "became flesh", as the perfect man Jesus.

Binitarianism – Adherents include those people through history who believed that God is only two co-equal and co-eternal persons, the Father and the Word, not three. They taught that the Holy Spirit is not a distinct person, but is the power or divine influence of the Father and Son, emanating out to the universe, in creation, and to believers.

Dualism - is the moral or spiritual belief that two fundamental concepts exist, which often oppose each other. It is an umbrella term that covers a diversity of views from various religions, including both traditional religions and scriptural religions.

Marcionism – Marcion (AD c. 110–160) believed there were two deities, one of creation and judgment (in the Hebrew Bible) and one of redemption and mercy (in the New Testament).

Duality - Is the belief that Yahweh and Jesus are coequal and the Holy Spirit is Yahweh.

Pantheism- is the belief that reality, the universe and the cosmos is identical with divinity and a supreme supernatural being or entity, pointing to the universe as being a immanent creator deity still expanding and creating, which has existed since the beginning of time, or that all things compose an all-encompassing, immanent god or goddess and regards the universe as a manifestation of a deity. This includes all astronomical objects being viewed as part of a sole deity.

Panentheism ("all in God", from the Greek πᾶν, pân, 'all', ἐν, en, 'in' and Θεός, Theós, 'God') is the belief that the divine intersects every part of the universe and also extends beyond space and time.

Monotheism - is the belief that there is only one deity, an all-supreme being that is universally referred to as God. A distinction may be made between exclusive monotheism, in which the one God is a singular existence, and both inclusive and pluriform monotheism, in which multiple gods or godly forms are recognized, but each are postulated as extensions of the same God.

Monolatry - (Ancient Greek: μόνος, romanized: monos, lit. 'single', and λατρεία, latreia, 'worship') is the belief in the existence of many gods, but with the consistent worship of only one deity.

Henotheism - (from Greek ἑνὸς θεοῦ (henos theou) 'of one god') is the worship of a single, supreme god while not denying the existence or possible existence of other lower deities.

BIBLIOGRAPHY

Chapter 1

1. <https://en.wikipedia.org/wiki/Cuneiform> - Feldherr, Andrew; Hardy, Grant, eds. (February 17, 2011). The Oxford History of Historical Writing: Volume 1: Beginnings to C.E. 600. Oxford University Press. p. 5. doi:10.1093/acprof:osobl/9780199218158.001.0001. ISBN 978-0-19-921815-8.
2. BRUCE ZUCKERMAN IN COLLABORATION WITH LYNN SWARTZ DODD Pots and Alphabets: Refractions of Reflections on Typological Method (MAARAV, A Journal for the Study of the Northwest Semitic Languages and Literatures, Vol. 10, p. 89) (from Wikimedia commons).
3. BRUCE ZUCKERMAN IN COLLABORATION WITH LYNN SWARTZ DODD Pots and Alphabets: Refractions of Reflections on Typological Method (MAARAV, A Journal for the Study of the Northwest Semitic Languages and Literatures, Vol. 10, p. 89) (from Wikimedia commons)
4. Petrovich, Douglas, The World's Oldest Alphabet: Hebrew as the Language of the Proto-consonantal Script, Carta 2016; ISBN 9652208841, 9789652208842.
5. Petrovich, Douglas, *The World's Oldest Alphabet: Hebrew as the Language of the Proto-consonantal Script*, Carta 2016; ISBN 9652208841, 9789652208842.
6. Benner, Jeff A. (1999-2022) *Hebrew alphabet chart.* Retrieved from /www.ancient-hebrew.org/alphabet/hebrew-alphabet-chart.htm
7. Benner, Jeff A. (1999-2022 *Evolution of the first ten Hebrew letters in Graphics.* Retrieved from / www.ancient-hebrew.org/alphabet/evolution-of-the-first-ten-hebrew-letters-in-graphics.htm.
8. "Scheme." Merriam-Webster.com Dictionary, Merriam-Webster, https://www.merriam-webster.com/dictionary/scheme. Accessed 9 Dec. 2023.
9. "Slavery." Merriam-Webster.com Dictionary, Merriam-Webster, https://www.merriam-webster.com/dictionary/slavery. Accessed 13 Sep. 2022.

10. Logos-Biblehub.com. (2004-2022) *John1:1 Interlinear*. Retrieved from /biblehub.com/greek/3056.htm

11. Rhema-Biblehub.com. (2004-2022) Matthew 4:4 Interlinear. Retrieved from /biblehub.com/greek/4487.htm

12. "G3056 - logos - Strong's Greek Lexicon Biblical Usage (KJV)." Blue Letter Bible. Web. 13 Sep, 2022. <https://www.blueletterbible.org/lexi con/g3056/kjv/tr/0-1/>.

13. Dabar-Biblehub.com. (2004-2022) Genesis 11:1 Interlinear. Retrieved from /biblehub.com/hebrew/1697.htm

14. Dabar-Biblehub.com. (2004-2022) Genesis 11:1 Interlinear, Brown-Driver-Briggs: I b, 2. Retrieved from /biblehub.com/hebrew/1697.htm

15. Benner, Jeff A. (2005). *The Ancient Hebrew Lexicon of the Bible*. College Station, TX. Virtualbookworm.com Publishing Inc.

16. "Discourse," Merriam-Webster.com Dictionary, https://www.merriam-webster.com/dictionary/discourse. Accessed 9/13/2022.

17. Harangue. (2022). Dictionary. Retrieved from https://www.bing.com/search?q=harangue&qs=ds&form=QBRE.

18. Transitive. (2022). Dictionary. Retrieved from https://www.bing.com/search?q=define+transitive&FORM=DCTSRC.

19. Intransitive. (2022). Dictionary. Retrieved from https://www.bing.com/search?q=define+Intransitive&FORM=DCTSRC.

20. Literal. (2022). Dictionary. Retrieved from https://www.bing.com/search?q=define+literal&FORM=DCTSRC.

21. Figurative. (2022). Dictionary. Retrieved from https://www.bing.com/search?q=define+figurative&FORM=DCTSRC.

Chapter 2

1. Benner, Jeff A. (2005). The Ancient Hebrew Lexicon of the Bible. College Station, TX. Virtualbookworm.com Publishing Inc. pg.320.

2. Benner, Jeff A. (2005). The Ancient Hebrew Lexicon of the Bible. College Station, TX. Virtualbookworm.com Publishing Inc. pg. 134

3. "ZOROASTRIANISM i. HISTORY TO THE ARAB CONQUEST – Encyclopaedia Iranica". Encyclopædia Iranica. Retrieved from https://

en.wikipedia.org/wiki/Zoroastrianism, 10 September 2022.

4. "ZOROASTRIANISM i. HISTORY TO THE ARAB CONQUEST – Encyclopaedia Iranica". Encyclopædia Iranica. Retrieved from https://en.wikipedia.org/wiki/Zoroastrianism, 10 September 2022.

5. Boslooper, Thomas. The Virgin Birth. The Westminster Press, Library of Congress Catalog Card No. 62-7941. Egyptian mythology, Lorenz, London, 2000. Retrieved from https://en.wikipedia.org/wiki/Miraculous_births.

6. Zoroaster (Buchner 1936 pg. 105). Retrieved from https://en.wikipedia.org/wiki/Zoroaster.

7. www.en.wikipedia.org/wiki/Miraculous Births

8. Qur'an, Chapter 3, Verse 43 Retrieved from https://en.wikipedia.org/wiki/Miraculous_births.

9. Annals XV.44.

10. The Babylonian Talmud, The Sanhedrin 43a.

11. Agapius, "The book of the Title". Antiquities of the Jews, Book 18 & Book 20 Chap.9.

12. Mara Bar-Serapion's letter (BL ADD. 14658).

13. Epistulae X.96.

14. "Schizophrenia." Merriam-Webster.com Dictionary, Merriam-Webster, https://www.merriam-webster.com/dictionary/schizophrenia. Accessed 14 Sep. 2022.

15. "Multiple personality disorder." Merriam-Webster.com Dictionary, Merriam-Webster, https://www.merriam-webster.com/dictionary/multiple%20personality%20disorder. Accessed 14 Sep. 2022.

16. Benner, Jeff A. Ancient Hebrew Lexicon of the Bible, pg. 55. 1012 H(c)

17. www.en.wikipedia.org/wiki/Elohim

18. Moses Maimonides. Guide for the Perplexed (1904 translation by Friedländer). Starting from the beginning of chapter 2.

19. www.en.wikipedia.org/wiki/Elohim

Chapter 3

1. Demonstrative. (2022). Dictionary. Retrieved from https://www.bing.com/search?q=define+demonstrative%20&FORM=DCTSRC.

Chapter 4

1. Adorn. (2022). Retrieved from https://www.bing.com/search?q=define+adorn&FORM=DCTSRC.

Chapter 5

1. Benner, Jeff A. (2005). The Ancient Hebrew Lexicon of the Bible. College Station, TX. Virtualbookworm.com Publishing Inc. pg.253.
2. Benner, Jeff A. (2005). The Ancient Hebrew Lexicon of the Bible. College Station, TX. Virtualbookworm.com Publishing Inc. pg.443.
3. "Abomination." Merriam-Webster.com Dictionary, Merriam-Webster, https://www.merriam-webster.com/dictionary/abomination. Accessed 17 Jan. 2023.
4. "Epigenetics." Merriam-Webster.com Dictionary, Merriam-Webster, https://www.merriam-webster.com/dictionary/epigenetics. Accessed 17 Jan. 2023.
5. https://alevelbiology.co.uk/notes/epigenetics/#:~:text=Environmental%20Influences.%20Different%20epigenetic%20modifications%20in, https://openstax.org/books/biology-ap-courses/pages/16-3-eukaryotic-epigenetic-gene-regulation, https://www.cell.com/ajhg/fulltext/S0002-9297(20)30288-3

Chapter 6

1. "Construct." Merriam-Webster.com Dictionary, Merriam-Webster, https://www.merriam-webster.com/dictionary/construct. Accessed 10 Feb. 2023., www.en.wikipedia.org/wiki/Construct.
2. "Propagate." Merriam-Webster.com Dictionary, Merriam-Webster, https://www.merriam-webster.com/dictionary/propagate. Accessed 14 Sep. 2022.
3. "Omnipresent." Merriam-Webster.com Dictionary, Merriam-Webster,

https://www.merriam-webster.com/dictionary/omnipresent. Accessed 14 Sep. 2022.

4. "Parlance." Merriam-Webster.com Dictionary, Merriam-Webster, https://www.merriam-webster.com/dictionary/parlance. Accessed 14 Sep. 2022.

5. "Glory." Merriam-Webster.com Dictionary, Merriam-Webster, https://www.merriam-webster.com/dictionary/glory. Accessed 14 Sep. 2022.

6. Matthew 17:5, Matthew 26:39, John 17:24, Matthew 16:27

7. https://en.wikibooks.org/wiki/Koine_Greek/1._Alphabet,_Pronunciation,_and_Punctuation

8. Benner, Jeff A. (2005). The Ancient Hebrew Lexicon of the Bible. College Station, TX. Virtualbookworm.com Publishing Inc. pg.126.

9. "Grace." Merriam-Webster.com Dictionary, Merriam-Webster, https://www.merriam-webster.com/dictionary/grace. Accessed 14 Sep. 2022.

10. Benner, Jeff A. (2005). The Ancient Hebrew Lexicon of the Bible. College Station, TX. Virtualbookworm.com Publishing Inc. pg.170.

11. "Truth." Merriam-Webster.com Dictionary, Merriam-Webster, https://www.merriam-webster.com/dictionary/truth. Accessed 14 Sep. 2022.

Chapter 7

1. Josephus, Flavius. Book 18 Chapter 5 of the Antiquities of the Jews.

2. Quran, sura 19 (Maryam), verse 7.

3. Mandaeans. (2022) Retrieved from https://en.wikipedia.org/wiki/Mandaeans.

4. Benner, Jeff A. (1999-2022). Retrieved from https://www.ancient-hebrew.org/studies-interpretation/aaronic-blessing-from-a-hebrew-perspective.htm.

5. "Parlance." Merriam-Webster.com Dictionary, Merriam-Webster, https://www.merriam-webster.com/dictionary/parlance. Accessed 14 Sep. 2022.

6. "Principle." www.websters1913.com.

7. Moses. (2023) Retrieved from https://en.wikipedia.org/wiki/Moses_(Michelangelo)#cite_note-2.

———

Chapter 8

1. Benner, Jeff A. (1999-2022). https://www.ancient-hebrew.org/.

2. Bible hub G3772 (1) (a). (2004-2022). Retrieved from https://biblehub.com/greek/3772.htm.

3. Orr, James, M.A., D.D. General Editor. "Entry for 'SUBSTANCE'". "International Standard Bible Encyclopedia". 1915.

4. Wilson, Timothy D. (2004). *Strangers to Ourselves*. Massachusetts. Belknap Press

5. Gnosticism. (2022). Retrieved from https://en.wikipedia.org/wiki/Gnosticism.

6. Pagels, Elaine (1989). *The Gnostic Gospels*. pg. xx

7. Gnosticism. (2015-2022). Retrieved from https://www.abrahamicstudyhall.org/2020/01/22/gnosticism/.

8. "Omniscient." Merriam-Webster.com Dictionary, Merriam-Webster, https://www.merriam-webster.com/dictionary/omniscient. Accessed 14 Sep. 2022.

9. "Omnipresent." Merriam-Webster.com Dictionary, Merriam-Webster, https://www.merriam-webster.com/dictionary/omnipresent. Accessed 14 Sep. 2022.

10. "Omnipotent." Merriam-Webster.com Dictionary, Merriam-Webster, https://www.merriam-webster.com/dictionary/omnipotent. Accessed 14 Sep. 2022.

Michael Wayne Neuhaus is a husband, father and brother in both his personal life and in his faith community. Teaching basic Hebrew from an ancient and modern perspective is a favorite past time along with studying Torah. Deep study of scriptures. discussing Hebrew word choices of the original texts and searching for the meanings of passages in the Bible to discover personal understanding and viewpoints of fellow believers and non-believers alike are certainly pastimes. This began a thirteen-year journey of trails and temptations seeking truth and wisdom which in fact, was actually a forty-six- year adventure with the Father Himself. The story of Solomon touched his heart greatly at six years old and set his heart and mind on a course of discovery, both of self and of God.

Email Michael:
thejohnoneonecase@gmail.com